D0806198

SLAVISTIC PRINTINGS AND REPRINTINGS

edited by

C. H. VAN SCHOONEVELD

Indiana University

302

DONALD RAYMOND HITCHCOCK

THE APPEAL OF ADAM TO LAZARUS IN HELL

ANNEXE DE LA BIBLIOTHÈQUE
Universitas
BIBLIOTHECA
Ottaviensis
U.Otta
LIBRARY ANNEX

MOUTON PUBLISHERS
THE HAGUE · PARIS · NEW YORK

549723

PG
705
.S46 Z69
1979

ISBN 90 279 7856 5
© Copyright 1979 by Mouton Publishers, The Hague. All rights reserved,
including those of translation into foreign languages. No part of this book may be
reproduced in any form – by photoprint, microfilm, or any other means – nor
transmitted nor translated into a machine language without written permission
from the publisher. – Printing: Karl Gerike, Berlin. – Binding: Lüderitz & Bauer
Buchgewerbe GmbH, Berlin.
Printed in Germany

TABLE OF CONTENTS

I

THE COPIES OF THE TEXT

The seven copies of the text of the apocryphal tale,
The Appeal of Adam in Hell to Lazarus, have been preserved in six manuscripts. Three of the copies have
previously been published. See chapter 2 of this work
for information concerning these editions. Copy "S",
according to I. Porfir'ev, was edited by him from manuscript no. 848 of the Soloveckij collection.[1] A description of the Soloveckij collection is found in I.
Porfir'ev, et al. (eds.), Opisanie rukopisej Soloved-
kogo Monastyrja, naxodjaščixsja v biblioteke Kazanskoj
Duxovnoj Akademii, pts. 1-3 (Kazan', 1891-98). The
manuscript collection of the Soloveckij Monastery,
transferred in 1855 to the Ecclesiastical Academy in
Kazan', was incorporated in 1928 with the Leningrad
Public Library holdings, where it forms coll. no.717.[2]
Copy "K", according to I. Franko, was edited by him
from manuscript no. 27 of the collection of the Kievan
Ecclesiastical Academy.[3] The collection of the Kievan
Ecclesiastical Academy is described in Petrov, N.P.,
"Opisanie rukopisej Cerkovno-Arxeologičeskogo Muzeja
pri Kievskoj Duxovnoj Akademii," Trudy Kievskoj Duxov-

noj Akademii (Kiev, 1874-78), and is now found in the
Central Library of the Academy of Sciences of the
Ukrainian SSR in Kiev.[4] Copy "P" was edited by A.
Pypin, who does not give the location of the manuscript
from which his edition was made. Immediately preceding
the text of his edition, he states that his edition of
the apocrypha is based on a Zlatoust, without stating
which Zlatoust.[5] In the forward to the volume in which
the edition of the copy "P" is found, Pypin says that
the works edited in this volume come from the manuscript
collection of the Public Library, the Rumjancov Museum,
the Nevskaja Lavra, the Troickaja Lavra, etc.[6] The present location of the manuscript from which this copy was
made has not been established, despite the efforts of
the Manuscript Division of the Lenin Library. Copy "V"
is from the collection of the Iosifo-Volokolamskij Monastery, now located in the Lenin Library, coll, no. 113,
no. 521, where it forms pp. 31-34 rev. of a manuscript
without title.[7] Copy "U" is from the Undol'skij Collection, now in the Lenin Library, coll. 310, no. 1109,
where it forms pp. 137 rev. -139 of a manuscript enti-
tled Zlatoust i Sobornik.[8] Copies "Z" and "Z2" are from
the Uvarov Collection, no. III/316, 179/-1 of the State
Historical Museum holdings, the title of the manuscript
being Ioanna Zlatousta i drugix poučenija.[9] The first
three mentioned copies have been examined by me only in

the printed editions; the last four have been examined
in manuscript form. This investigation will concern
primarily those copies examined by me in manuscript.
One printed copy, "P", is included in the edition of the
copies, chap. 8, and discussed for its phonological and
morphological features in chaps. 4 and 5 respectively.
The other published copies "S" and "K", representing
simply variants of the two prototypes, are discussed in
Appendix 2, where a full list of all words not found in
the other copies is given.

4

NOTES

1. I. Porfir'ev, Apokrifičeskie skazanija o novozavetnyx licax i sobytijax, SORJS, 52, 4 (St.Petersburg, 1890), p. 228.

2. Cf. N. Bel'čikov, et al. (comps.), Spravočnik-ukaza-tel' pečatnyx opisanij slavjano-russkix rukopisej (Moscow-Leningrad, 1963), p. 103.

3. I. Franko, Apokryfy i legendy z ukrajins'kyx ruko-pysiv, vol. 2, Pamjatky ukrajins'ko-rus'koji movy i literatury (L'vov, 1899), p. 315.

4. Cf. N. Bel'čikov, et al. (comps.), op. cit., p. 228.

5. G. Kušelev-Bezborodko (ed.), Pamjatniki starinnoj russkoj literatury, vol. 3 (St. Petersburg, 1862), p. 11.

6. Ibid., last page of the foreword, which is not paginated.

7. Cf. N. Bel'čikov, et al. (comps.), op. cit., p. 147.

8. Ibid., p. 142.

9. Ibid., p. 158.

II

SCHOLARSHIP

No true studies have thus been accorded to the apocrypha,
The Appeal of Adam to Lazarus in Hell, the only treatments
consisting of summary comments by I. Franko, M. Hruševs'-
kyj, and D. Čiževs'kyj.[1] Franko has devoted more scholar-
ship to this apocrypha than the others. His work is contained in the Zapysky naukovoho tovarystva im. Ševčenka v
L'vovi, vols. 35, 36 (L'vov, 1900), pp. 1-56. He recon-
structs the text according to his own metrical theories
into regular four-line stanzas, with varying numbers of
syllables. He believes that the Zlatoust copy of the apocrypha was wtitten in either Novgorod or Belo-Russia.[2]
Much of what this author offers is very original, even
eccentric. The views of Hruševs'kyj are contained in his
great work, Istorija ukrajins'koji literatury, part 1
(Kiev-L'vov, 1923), pp.232-50. His approach is primarily
literary. He rejects Franko's attempt to divide the apocrypha into regular four-line stanzas with a varying number of syllables per line, but does hold that this apocrypha has a definite rhythmic structure, one similar to
that of the Igor' Tale.[3] In complete contrast to Franko,
Hruševs'kyj believes that this work does not represent a
decline in družina poetry, but rather that družina
poetry and religious poetry maintained a parallel development, employing similar poetic tools, this apocrypha

6

being one of the earliest monuments of this religious poetry, if not the earliest. Čiževs'kyj's treatment is much more cursory, being contained in his Geschichte der altrussischen Literatur im 11., 12. und 13. Jahrhundert, Kiever Epoche (Frankfurt/Main, 1948), pp. 381-84. The same material is contained in his History of Russian Literature (Hague, 1960), pp. 135-37. His remarks are suggestive and stimulating, but remain possibilities to be further investigated, rather than positive or definite information.[4] He indicates the similarity of the introduction of the apocrypha to the Molenie Daniila Zatočnika,[5] a parallel to a sermon of Cyril of Turov,[6] and a number of similarities to the Igor' Tale, suggesting that the apocrypha is in some relation to the epic tradition. Only a summary has been outlined of the works of these scholars, further details being found in later chapters.[7] Other material may be found concerning this apocrypha in scattered places among various authors. I. Porfir'ev in his Istorija russkoj slovesnosti (Kazan', 1909), part 1, pp. 271-72, gives sparse comments, most of the space in his book allocated to a translation of the work.

Copies of three texts of this apocrypha have previously been published. A Zlatoust copy was published by A. Pypin in the compilation edited by G. Kušelev-Bezborodko, Pamjatniki starinnoj russkoj literatury, vol. 3, Ložnye i otrečennye knigi russkoj stariny (St. Petersburg, 1862), pp. 11-12. The Soloveckij copy was published by Porfir'ev in his Apokrifičeskie skazanija o novozavetnych licax i sobytijax, SORJS, vol. 52, 4 (St. Petersburg, 1890), pp.228-31. Franko published the Kievan Ecclesiastical Academy copy in Apokryfy i legendy z ukrajins'kyx rukopysiv, vol. 2, Pamjatky ukrajins'ko-rus'koji movy i literatury (L'vov, 1899), pp. 315-17. It is believed by Pypin that his Zlatoust copy dates no later than the sixteenth century,[8] by Porfir'ev that the Soloveckij copy dates from the sixteenth-seventeenth centuries,[9] and by Franko that the Kievan Ecclesiastical Academy copy dates from the sixteenth century.[10]

NOTES

1. Of these three, the most scholarly treatment is given by Hruševs'kyj, the most eccentric by Franko. Čizevš'kyj's is extremely brief. Other material may be found in scattered places among various authors, notably I. Porfir'ev, mentioned later in this chapter.

2. I. Franko in his study in the Zapysky naukovoho tovarystva im. Ševčenka v L'vovi, vols. 35, 36 (L'vov, 1900), pp. 1-56, states that the Zlatoust version of Pypin dates from sixteenth century and originates in either Belo-Russia or Novgorod. Pypin himself in Kuŝelev-Bezborodko, G. (ed.), Pamjatniki starinnoj russkoj literatury, vol. 3 (St. Petersburg, 1862), pp. 11-12, agrees with this dating, but says nothing about the place of origin of the copy.

3. Hrusevš'kyj, M., Istorija ukrajins'koji literatury, part 1 (Kiev-L'vov, 1923), p. 233.

4. Here Čiževs'kyj only indicates the relationship very briefly.

5. Cf. Zarubin, N. (ed.), Molenie Daniila Zatočnika, Pamjatniki drevnerusskoj literatury, vol. 3 (Leningrad, 1932).

6. For this work of Cyril of Turov, see Kalajdovič, K., Pamjatniki rossijskoj slovesnosti 12 veka

(Moscow, 1821), p. 35.

7. Cf. chapter 12 of this work, pp. 194-207.

8. Op. cit., pp. 11-12.

9. I. Porfir'ev, Apokrifičeskie skazanija o novozavetnyx licax i sobytijax, SORJS, 52, 4 (St. Petersburg, 1890), pp. 228-31.

10. I. Franko, Apokryfy i legendy z ukrajins'kyx ruko-
    pysiv, vol. 2, Pamjatky ukrajins'ko-rus'koji movy
    i literatury (L'vov, 1899), pp. 315-17.

III

THE MANUSCRIPTS

A. THE SCRIPTS

The apocrypha The Appeal of Adam to Lazarus in Hell is
examined, in varying portions, in three separate manuscripts. In each, the script may safely be identified as semi-uncial, although in Old Russian documents,
the uncial, semi-uncial, and the cursive scripts are
not sharply contained within strict chronological limits. Yet one merges into another imperceptibly, the
time of the disappearance of one style and the introduction of another style being also contingent upon the
additional factor of geography. In general, the oldest
Russian script known is the uncial, which was super-
ceded by the semi-uncial, which was in its turn super-
ceded by the semi-uncial, which was in its turn super-
ceded by the cursive.

In the fifteenth century, Russian semi-uncial
script may be conveniently divided into two distinct
types, each of which betrays strong influence of a Balkan or South Slavic style of writing. One type of Rus-

sian semi-uncial is written with the Rumanian hand,
sometimes also termed the Moldavo-Wallachian hand;
the other type of Russian semi-uncial is of the Macedonian hand. Shortly stated, the salient features
of the Rumanian hand are a verticality and broadness
of the letters, as well as a certain mannerism in the
curved strokes, together with a sharp differentiation
between the narrow and broad strokes. The distinguishing characteristics of the Macedonian hand are an
inclination of the letters toward the end of the
line, or less often toward the beginning of the line,
an irregularity in both the inclination and the
height of the letters, and finally a general impression of great simplicity, verging upon rudeness. Both
these varieties of the Russian semi-uncial script
were quite extensively employed in the Russian West
and South-west, as well as in Great Russia in the
fifteenth century.[1] However, in addition to these two
major types of semi-uncial script, also extant were
hands revealing an Eastern Bulgarian origin.[2] The Eastern Bulgarian scripts were quite probably the best of
the time in the Balkan peninsula. One such Eastern
Balkan script served as a prototype for the previously
mentioned Rumanian hand. Another Eastern Bulgarian
script, characterized by letters inclining forward,
letters sharply outlined and rather delicate, is first

encountered somewhat rarely in the fifteenth century,
its extensive expansion occuring in the sixteenth century within the Moscow state. The Russian South and
South-west, on the other hand, witnessed the predomi-
nance of the Rumanian hand in the sixteenth century and
the initial decades of the seventeenth century. The general excellence and wide extension of these Eastern
Bulgarian scripts, also termed Trnovo scripts, very log-
ically corresponds to the superior cultural level of
the Eastern Bulgarian state under the rulers of the Second Bulgarian Empire.[3] The problem of this so-called
"second South Slavic influence" is very complex, and not
limited to questions of paleography, but extends to
other sides of Russian medieval culture, including the
stylistics and content of this medieval literature.[4]

Throughout the fifteenth and the first half of the
sixteenth century, numerous South Slavic orthographic
peculiarities dominated Russian manuscripts. Such are
the use of the "big jus", r" instead of or, and l"
instead of ol. However, subsequent to the middle of the
sixteenth century, these phenomena of South Slavic orthography are no longer apparent in the Moscow state,
though they are retained in the Russian West and
South-west into the opening years of the seventeenth
century.[5]

In manuscript "V", the following South Slavic orthographic characteristics exist:

1. the employment of <u>a</u> after a vowel, instead of **ꙗ**.
For example, lines 6, 7 тих*і*а, line 73 жел**ѣ**н*і*а.
These are the only examples.

2. the occasional observation of the rule that preceding vowels, **і** must be written, not и. For example,
lines 6, 7 тих*і*а, lines 15, 12 скот*і*ихъ, line 18 пр*і*иде-
те, line 56 **і**ерусалимѣ, line 73 жел**ѣ**н*і*а, line 96 воп*і*еть.
In manuscripts "V", the following South Slavic orthographic characteristics do <u>not</u> exist:

1. the employment of <u>ъ</u> and <u>ь</u> after liquids, instead
of the Eastern Slavic <u>o</u> and <u>e</u> before liquids. For example, line 26, первозданныи, line 86, прискорбна.

2. the employment of **ѫ** for <u>у</u>. For example, line 26
руками, line 57 будеть.
In manuscript "V", the following South Slavic features
in graphics exist:

1. the employment of **m** instead of <u>т</u>. For example,
line 4 с**m**ежавшаго, line 46 **m**вои, line 86 ес**m**ь.

2. the employment of the omega with a high middle
stroke. For example, line 14 **ѡ** , line 20 **ѡ**твѣ*ѣ*щаста,
line 56 **ѡ**рла.

3. the employment of the <u>ы</u> instead of the **ꙑ**. For
example, line 1 слыши, line 27 живыи, line 101 славы.

4. the employment of the asymmetric <u>ч</u> instead of
the symmetric **ҁ** . For example, lines 6, 7

многоѡчиṃака, line 58 час, line 106 оучаще.

5. the appearance of the ѣ and the ъ with elongated left-hand serifs. For example, line 10 перскыхѣ ,
line 14 восхотѣ, line 22 замъцѣ .

In manuscript "V", the following South Slavic features in graphics do not exist:

1. the employment of the rounded or square в. For
example, line 1 внꙋши, line 51 вои, line 85 ваю.

2. the employment of the ε instead of the e. For
example, line 1 ꙃемле, line 56 се, line 91 е͡смь.

3. the employment of the non-geometric з, similar
to the cipher 3, instead of the geometric ꙃ. For
example, line 1 землe, line 23a ꙃı , line 27 изнеси.

4. the employment of the e of great width in place
of the jotized e. For example, lines 6, 7 емꙋ , line
10 емꙋ , lines 29, 30 еси.

5. the employment of the e in the shape of an
anchor, thus ℓ. For example, line 1 ꙃемле, line 13
пеленами, line 16 скрежьṃаша.

Witnessed in the preceding investigation of manuscript
"V" are numerous South Slavic features, in the domains
of both graphics and ortography. However, a very significant number of Balkan Slavic features are non-ex-
tant in the manuscript. Nonetheless, it can be stated
that a considerable South Slavic influence is present

in this copy of the apocrypha. The letters throughout
the manuscript exhibit a forward inclination, an irregularity in this inclination and in the height of the
letters, and a certain aspect of carelessness, even
crudity. From this evidence, the conclusion is that
the script most nearly approximates the Russian
semi-uncial of the Macedonian hand, which can also be
termed the Russian semi-uncial transitional to the
cursive. As certain very important Balkan Slavic
orthographic phenomena are not encountered in this
manuscript, features which disappeared from manuscripts of Russian origin by the middle of the sixteenth century, the manuscript may be assumed to have
originated during the middle or later sixteenth century. Such orthographic peculiarities which are not
encountered are the use of the combinations ръ, лъ,
and Ӿ. The manuscript is of Great-Russian origin, of
semi-uncial script of the Macedonian hand, dating from
the sixteenth century.

In manuscript "U", the following South Slavic orthographic features exist:

  1. the employment of a post-vocalically, instead
of ꙗ. For example, line 7 живыа, line 42 земнаа, line
63 въпиаше.

  2. the general rule that preceding vowels, ι

must be written, not и. For example, line 12 подножіе,
line 18 прıидетъ, line 76 бл(а)говернıи.

In manuscript "U", the following South Slavic orthographic features do not exist:

    1. the employment of ъ and ь after liquids, instead
of the Eastern Slavic o and e before liquids. For
example, line 26 первозданныи, line 28 первозданныи.An
exception however is line 74 долготрьпеливъ.

    2. the employment of ѫ instead of у. For example,
line 26 рукама.

In manuscript "U", the following South Slavic features
in graphics exist:

    1. the employment of the ε post-vocalically or ini-
tially instead of the e. For example, line 1 Въспоεм,
line 11 εсмѧ , line 15 εси.

    2. the employment occasionally of the non-geometric
з, resembling the cipher 3, beside the normal geometric ꙁ. For example, line 7 възложи, line 10 земли,
line 27 Лазорю.

    3. the employment of the omega with a high middle
stroke, instead of the omega with a low middle stroke.
For example, line 6 ѡ̄ложимъ, line 14 ѡ , line 32 ѡ .

    4. the employment of the т instead of the т. For
example, line 6 ѡ̄ложимъ, line 33 тꙋгою, line 76 тебѣ.

5. the employment of the asymmetric ч instead of the symmetric ү. For example, line 6 пла^ч, line 26 члкъ, line 62 чmо.

6. the employment of the ы instead of the ъ. For example, line 7 живыа, line 9 слышю, line 30 быmи.

7. the employment of a new type of ѣ, one with a serif pointed downward from the left side of the cross-bar, e.g., ѣ. For example, line 7 адѣ, line 20 силѣ, line 65 пр^орцѣ.

8. the employment of a new type of ъ, one with a serif pointed downward from the left side of the cross-bar, e.g., ъ. For example, line 6 Въ спо є м, line 15 въ схотелъ, line 66 въ спита.

In manuscript "U", the following South Slavic features in graphics do not exist:

1. the employment of the rounded or square в. For example, line 6 Въ спо є м, line 19 весть, line 38 всех.

2. the employment of и, н, and ю with slanted cross-bars in the middle of the letter. For example, line 6 пѣми, line 8 сп^сниѧ , line 10 но^г.

A wide Balkan Slavic influence exists in this manuscript, as attested by various features of orthography and graphics. Although certain South Slavic features are absent, the total impression remains one of pro-

found influence from the Balkan Slavic written tradition, more penetrating than in manuscript "V". The
letters in this manuscript bear a forward inclination
in the height of the letters, and an appearance of
an unrefined technique. This script may be termed the
Russian semi-uncial script of the Macedonian hand, a
semi-uncial in the transition stage to the cursive.
As varieties of this Macedonian hand predominated in
the Russian scribal tradition in the Russian West and
South-west, although for the most part in business
documents and in the fifteenth century, it is reasonable to assume that the manuscript was written either
in one of these two areas in the sixteenth century,
considering the numerous South Slavic features (more
than in "V") found in the copy, South Slavic influence
declining only at the start of the seventeenth century in the Russian West and South-west,[6] or in Great
Russia prior to the sixteenth century, since the Rumanian hand predominated there in the sixteenth century. The Macedonian uncial disappeared by the seventeenth century, so if of South Russian origin, the
manuscript must date from the sixteenth century.
In manuscript "Z", the following South Slavic orthographic characteristics exist:
    1. the general rule requiring ι to be written pre-
ceding a vowel, instead of и. For example, line 8

спсенıа, line 14 великıи, line 32 възлюбленнıи.

In manuscript "Z", the following South Slavic orthographic characteristics do <u>not</u> exist:

1. the employment of <u>ъ</u> and <u>ь</u> after liquids, instead
of the Eastern Slavic <u>o</u> and <u>e</u> before liquids. For
example, line 26 первозданныи, line 30 первозданныи.
But note line 95 of the second copy in the manuscript
"Z2", пръвозданныи.

In manuscript "Z", the following South Slavic features
in graphics exist:

1. the employment of the square <u>в</u>, instead of the <u>в</u>.
For example, line 7 възложи, line 9 сварꙗютъ   line
19 жи в ыи.

2. the employment of <u>m</u> instead of the <u>т</u>. For example,
line 9 пасmыри, line 13 mого, line 76 mобѣ.

3. the employment of the non-geometric <u>з</u>, similar
to the cipher 3, instead of the former geometric <u>ꙃ</u>. For
example, line 7 възложи, line 10 земли, line 14 землю.

4. the employment of the <u>ы</u> instead of the <u>ꙑ</u>. For
example, line 7 персты, line 9 слышꙗ, line 10 дары.

5. the employment of the asymmetric <u>ч</u> instead of the
symmetric <u>ꙗ</u>. For example, line 7 рече, line 24
чеmвероднєвныи, line 34 часъ.

6. the employment of the <u>ѣ</u> and the <u>ъ</u> with elongated
serifs. For example, line 6 пѣ сньми, line 38 всѣ хъ,
line 75 скорѣ.

7. the employment of the omega with a high middle
stroke instead of the omega with a low middle stroke,
although the latter does appear rarely. For example,
line 65 ₁ш̆а, line 67 ш̆ , line 76 ₿ ц̂а.

8. the employment of и, н, and ю with slanted cross-
bars in the middle of the letter. For example, line 6
Въспоимъ, line 10 кон̂ь, line 13 мт̂и.
In manuscript "Z", the following South Slavic features
in graphics do <u>not</u> exist:

1. the employment of є instead of е post-vocalically
or for initial е. For example, line 10 емоꙋ, line 20
їеремїа, line 28 въпїетъ.
In copies "Z" and "Z2", both contained in the same
manuscript, numerous South Slavic traits are encountered,especially in the graphics. The script of the
manuscript is semi-uncial, however of a different type
from the other two manuscripts. It is characterized
by a forward inclination of the letters, a rather
sharp , clear-cut appearance, and a general aspect of
refinement in contradistinction to the Macedonian
hand. The script of this manuscript derives from one
of the Trnovo hands, discussed at the beginning of the
chapter. Seldom encountered in the fifteenth century,
it became in the sixteenth century the favorite Great
Russian type.[7] Therefore, the employment of this style
of writing derived from one of the Trnovo hands argues

for the origin of the manuscript within the limits of
the Moscow state. Considering the South Slavic influence, it is reasonable to conclude that the manuscript
was written in the first half of the sixteenth century, for South Slavic influence in Great Russian
orthography had vanished by the middle of the sixteenth century. From the evidence, the script is Russian semi-uncial, a variant of one of the Trnovo hands
of Great Russian origin, dating from the earlier part
of the sixteenth century.

NOTES

1. Ščepkin, V. Učebnik russkoj paleografii
   (Moscow, 1920), p. 121

2. Ibid., p. 122

3. Cf. Deržavin, N., Istorija Bolgarii, vol. 2
   (Moscow-Leningrad, 1946), pp. 135-53; Jireček, K.,
   Geschichte der Bulgaren (Prague, 1876), pp. 252-
   58; Pypin, A., and Spasovič, N., Histoire des littératures slaves (Paris, 1881), tr. by Denis, E.,
   p. 125; Trogrančić, F., Letteratura medioevale
   degli Slavi meridionali (Rome, 1950), pp. 159-62,
   199-200, 202-03; Zlatarski, V., Istorija na
   b"lgarskata d"ržava prez srědnitě věkove, vol. 3
   (Sofia, 1940), passim.

4. Cf. Lixačev, D., Nekotorye zadači izučenija vtorogo južnoslavjanskogo vlijanija v Rossii
   (Moscow, 1958), passim. Cf. also Mošin, V., " O periodizacii russko-južnoslavjanskix literaturnyx
   svjazej X-XV vv.", TODRL, 19 (1963), pp. 28-106.

5. Durnovo, N., Vvedenie v istoriju russkogo jazyka,
   1, Istočniki (Brno, 1927), p. 17.

6. Ščepkin, V., op.cit., p.122.

7. Karskij, E., Slavjanskaja kirillovskaja paleografija (Leningrad, 1928), p. 103; Ščepkin, V., op.
   cit., p. 122.

B. THE DIACRITICS

In the manuscripts, numerous superliteral diacritic
notations exist. These markings may be conveniently
divided into the following types: the acute, the grave,
the circumflex, the apostrophe (furher subdivided into
the so-called spiritus asper and the spiritus lenis),
and the tittle, a symbol denoting abbreviation. The
exact identification and therefore the frequency of
occurrence of each of these various notations is
rather often quite difficult to determine, since in
some cases the marks do not correspond to any of the
typical shapes of our classification.

 The formulation of a logical system for diacritics
in Slavic also poses a complex problem. The employment and distribution of these marks differ in various
manuscripts, meaning different things at different
times. In the Kiev Fragments, a portion of a glagolit-
ic sacramentary of the Western rite displaying dis-
tinctive Czech phonetic features, a valid system has

been ascertained.[1] Superliteral diacritic notations can often constitute a system of musical notations, and not a coherent formula for the indication of vowel quantity, pitch, or stress.[2]

In manuscript "Z", the diacritics are found to be meaningful. The diacritic symbol most frequently encountered is the acute. This mark is found over vowels, in the syllable which is stressed in modern Russian. For example, line 9 slýšu, line 63 části, line 72 vrémeni. It is also used to denote the shift of the accent to the preposition. For example, line 48 íz čreva, line 54 zá mir" (These two lines are from the second copy in the manuscript, "Z2", here given for lack of examples in the first copy).[3]

The grave accent is found also over vowels, usually in the last syllable of a word. The frequency of the grave accent is approximately one-third that of the acute. Apparently the function of the grave is to denote stress in the final syllable. For example, line 11 togò, line 38 segò, line 41 tebè.

The circumflex occurs about one-fifth as often as the grave, about twenty times in the manuscript. It occurs as a diacritic over the letter o, almost every time in conjunction with an o accented in modern Russian. Line 14 contains an exception, v"sxotèlo. L. L. Vasil'ev was the first to study those manu-

scripts which distinguished the o̱ originating from the
old "acute" o̱ from the o̱ of other origin by means of
the circumflex placed over the o̱ arising from the
"acute" o̱. N. N. Durnovo later connected this practice
with Pskov manuscripts.[4] Manuscript "Z" does not always
have the the circumflex over the stressed o̱ however,
without apparent system in the omission. Instances of
the circumflex are line 9 proxõdit, line 16 xõščet",
line 34 mnõga. A sign somewhat resembling the circumflex is found over initial vowels. It is, however,
most probable that these diacritics were meant by the
scribe to represent spiriti leni, rather than circumflex signs. The spiritus lenis is to be found over
vowels, either initially or at the beginning of grammatical endings.[5] (Again this symbol might stand for
the spiritus asper.) Infrequently it occurs in the
place of a dropped jer. In terms of frequency, this
diacritic ranks second to the acute, occurring over
one-half as often as the acute. This diacritic pos-
sesses no value whatsoever, constituting simply a graphic imitation of the spiritus lenis of the older
Grek manuscripts.[6] The spiritus asper appears to be
almost totally absent from the manuscript. In the instances when it does occur, it is written over a vowel,
either initially or within a word. There can be no

logical system deduced from its application. Examples
of the use of the spiritus lenis are line 6 v"spoĭm",
line 7 ắdě, line 9 ꞌǔši. Examples of the spiritus asper
are line 29 lĭ, line 37 ạ, line 75 ị. However, these
marks are very illegible in the copy. A diacritic of
possibly more importance is one quite easily mistaken
for the spiritus asper. This mark is found over the
vowel i, and indicates the jod. Although relatively
rare in the manuscript, so are the instances of the
jod. For example, line 44 Noĭ, line 46 Moiseĭ. Marks
of punctuation exist rather systematically in this
manuscript, those employed being a mark resembling
the comma, one resembling the period, one similar to
a period of larger dimensions, and finally a mark
resembling a large period bisected by a horizontal
line.[7] An exact distinction between the period and the
comma is difficult to define, both signs appearing to
denote some kind of syntactic pause. However, the
period is employed to a far greater extent than the
comma, which appears relatively rarely. The sign resembling a large period indicates divisions between
major portions of the text. The period bisected by the
horizontal line is met with only once, at the conclusion of the text, line 76 A my vsi čl(ově)cy bl(a)go-
věrnii poklanjaemsja tobě X(rist)e, imeni tvoemu
s(vja)tomu, slavjašče s(vja)tuju Tro(i)cu, otca i

s(y)na i s(vja)t(o)go duxa ⚏. With the exception offered
by these punctuation marks, no systematic attempt to
indicate word division is made. Examples of the use of
the comma are line 6 <u>V"spoim družino pěsn'mi dnes', a</u>
<u>plač otložim" i utěšimsja</u>, line 7 <u>...i v"zloži persty</u>
<u>svoja na živyja struny, i inyja nakladaja, a sědja v</u>
<u>preispodnem" adě</u>, line 9 <u>... a glas ix" proxodit adova</u>
<u>vrata, i v moi uši prixodit"</u>. An example of the use of
the large period is at the end of the title, <u>Bl(agos-</u>
<u>lo)vi Otče •</u>.

The use of Cyrillic letters as numerals does not
occur at all in this manuscript.

Dittography does occur in manuscript "Z" with the use
of the letter <u>n</u>. For example, line 28 <u>pervozdannyi</u>, line
41 <u>v"zljublennago</u>, line 76 <u>istinnago</u>.

Haplography is absent in the manuscript.

Ligatures are also not encountered in the course of
the manuscript.

Abbreviations are frequent in "Z", however, moder-
ately so in comparison with other old Russian manuscripts.
The abbreviations may be conveniently divided into two
classes. The first class consist of <u>nomina sacra</u>, which
has words abbreviated by writing the first and last letter of the stem plus the grammatical ending, all this
completed by a superscribed line (◡). This class of
abbreviations accounts for approximately two-thirds of

the total number of abbreviations in this manuscript.
For example, line 12 n̂bo, line 24 x̂v", line 76 d̂xa. The
second class consists of words not linked at all in any
definite category, abbreviated by placing the tittle
over the word. For example, line 9 ĝla, line 10 dn̂e.

   In strong contradistinction to manuscript "Z", manuscript "V" contains no marks of any kind that can be
positively identified as acute accents. In the case of
the grave, once more, difficulties are encountered, due
to lack of clarity in the script. The very existence of
the grave in this manuscript is dubious, for it occurs
in the overwhelming majority of cases as doublet (")
over the character ı. It is often difficult to decide
whether this superscription is a double grave, two
apostrophes, or simply two dots over the letter (manuscript "Z" contained marks which were clearly two dots
over the ı). For example, line 13 prïklanjajuščisja,
line 18 prïidete, line 20 ĝlšči. The circumflex occurs
in the majority of cases over an initial a, but is rarely encountered over other vowels. No significant system
can be deduced from this employment of the circumflex
in manuscript "V". Examples of the use of the circumflex are line 8 bl(a)gopriâtna, lines 15, 12 â, line
83 âšče. Again we have the trouble of legibility here.
The spiritus lenis is the predominant diacritic in this

manuscript. As with the other diacritics, this mark is
sometimes quite difficult to distinguish, the spiritus
lenis often resembling the spiritus asper. When the
spiritus lenis is distinguished, it is written over a
vowel not after a consonant. For example, line 5 moěja,
lines 6, 7 v"spoěm", line 20 ěrěmějǎ. The spiritus
asper, again a symbol hard to distinguish, seems to
occur often in conjunction with the spiritus lenis,
superscribed over the omega. Its function in these
cases seems to be only one of decoration. For example,
line 21 ǒ, line 56 dva ǒrla zlata, line 103 ǒ že sokrušit"sja.

The punctuation employed in this manuscript is modest,
consisting in the majority of cases of a dot placed in
the middle of the line, approximately one-half of the
distance up the letter. For example, line 1 Slyši ñbo
vnuši zemle•, line 14 o vysokyi c͂rju•, etc. At the very
end of the text is another sign (✝), marking a greater
division, the conclusion of the Appeal of Adam to Lazarus in Hell, followed by the opening lines of a new
text.

The employment of Cyrillic characters as numerals is
encountered but once. This is indicated by a line drawn
above the letters plus two dots on either side of the
letters midway in the line. The example is line 23a,•З͂l•,
the sixteen Prophets.

Dittography occurs rather frequently in manuscript "S", generally in past passive participles in the employment of the letter n. Haplography is not encountered in this manuscript.

Abbreviations are present everywhere in manuscript "S". The marking most often used to designate an abbreviation is a diacritic resembling a circumflex. Rather more rarely encountered are two other symbols, the (↪) and the (⌒). Occasionally abbreviations occur without any tittle at all, one letter of the missing portion being superscribed. For example, line 1 n͡bo, line 16 g̑i, line 21 vl̑cě.

In manuscript "U", the second most frequent diacritic mark is the acute accent. As in the other manuscripts, it is a difficult task to distinguish this diacritic. It apparently occurs over a vowel, although it is very hard to decide whether it stands over the vowel or the adjoining consonant. For example, line 7 ínyja, line 10 íže, line 16 írod.

Rather infrequently this acute is doubled over the characters omega and oy. For example, line 6 útešimsja, line 16 úbiti, line 16 óstrit. The vowel over which this acute most often is found is и, in which cases the diacritic seems to be employed indiscriminately, having no real function. The grave is encountered about

one-half as often as the acute, allowing for error due
to lack of clarity in the script. It is found over a
vowel not after a consonant. The grave is also found
doubled over the terminal vowel of a word. For example,
line 16 bezumnẏ', line 9 ä, line 65 velikẏ. This
double grave may also be an attempt at a superscription of the и. Again it is hard to read the text. The
circumflex is the most frequently encountered diacritic
in this manuscript. A circumflex resembling the mark
(⌐) is especially frequent. The circumflex is found
in the majority of cases over vowels. The circumflex is
quite often used in conjunction with abbreviations, but
aside from this employment of the circumflex, no logical system can be formulated from its use. For example,
line 6 plͣa, line 7 živyâ, line 13 m'gloĵu. Both the
spiritus lenis and the spiritus asper, graphically
exceedingly similar to other marks, occur without apparent logical system. For example, line 7 u̇darim", line
19 živyi̇. The task of distinguishing these two diacritics
is very difficult.

Marks of punctuation exist rather systematically, a
single dot being the common sign of punctuation, ser-
ving to denote different types of syntactic pauses. This
mark is located either on or somewhat above the line, no
distinction probably intended. For example, line 13
...ǵlše , line 15 ...ležiši , line 23 ...jasno reče .

At the conclusion of the text is found the following
(: •), line 76 ...prno :•, denoting a major demarca-
tion.

The appearance of letters used as numerals occurs
in line 24 ...d-rodněv"nyi, where the Cyrillic letter
means "four".

Dittography occurs with the letter n in past
passive participles. For example, line 26 pervozdannyi, line 28 pervozdannyi.

Haplography does not occur in manuscript "U".

Ligatures are not encountered in this manuscript.

A number of abbreviations occur in manuscript "U".
They are indicated by the use of either of the two
superliteral marks, (⌣) and (⌢), or by these
same superliteral marks with one of the letters
omitted from the body of the word, or simply by
placing one of the letters omitted from the body
of the word above that word without either of the
superliteral marks. For example, line 8 dn', line
12 prtl", line 23 dvy.

NOTES

1. See the study of Vondrák, V., <u>O původu Kijevských</u>
   <u>listů a Pražských zlomků</u> (Prague, 1904).

2. For a concise discussion of diacritics in the Kiev
   Fragments, see Trubetzkoy, N., <u>Altkirchenslavische</u>
   <u>Grammatik</u> (Vienna, 1954), pp. 43-50

3. For a complete listing, see chapter 9. In the text
   only a few examples of each feature are mentioned.

4. Vasil'ev, L., <u>O značenii kamory v nekotoryx drevne-</u>
   <u>russkix pamjatnikax 16-17 vekov</u> (Leningrad, 1929),
   p. 9, states that in the manuscripts studied by him
   that $\widehat{o}$ indicates an o arising from an old o with
   rising pitch, accented (vȏlja), while o is from an
   old o with falling pitch (góru), accented. Durnovo,
   N., "Manuscripts russes distinguant l'ancien o
   'acuté' et l'o d'une autre origine", <u>Mélanges de</u>
   <u>philologie offerts à M. J. J. Mikkola</u> (Helsinki,
   1931), pp. 7-13, studies four mss. of Pskov with
   the use of the kamora or circumflex, where the
   circumflex occurs over non-stressed o as often as
   over stressed o (p. 10).

5. Vondrák, V., <u>Altkirchenslavische Grammatik</u>, 2nd ed.
   (Berlin, 1912), p. 71. However, the meaning of the
   diacritics is different at different times.

6. Trubetzkoy, N., <u>op. cit.</u>, p. 42. Karskij, E.,
   <u>Slavjanskaja kirillovskaja paleografija</u> (Leningrad,

1928), p. 147, states that the signs in general have
no significance.

7. Concerning punctuation, see Karskij, E., <u>op. cit.</u>,
pp. 138-41, and Čerepnin, L., <u>Russkaja paleografija</u>
(Moscow, 1956), pp. 374-76.

IV

PHONOLOGY

The Appeal of Adam to Lazarus in Hell is for the most
part an ecclesiastical work, and its language therefore
is preponderantly Church Slavonic with few Russianisms.
The following section deals with the system of reduced
vowels, pleophony, and the jat' in the examined texts,
etc.

In manuscript "V", we have the replacement of the
strong reduced vowels - the strong front reduced vowel
being replaced by e, the strong back reduced vowel being
replaced by o. For example, line 4 osel", line 96
vopiet', line 101 silen". The weak reduced vowels dis-
appear. For example, line 14 čto, line 18 pravednici.
However, the jer at the end of nouns is correctly
retained in almost all instances. For example, line 10
ropot", line 22a věst', etc. The lone word in which the
end-jer is missing is in line 98 Rasuil. A confusion of
jers is met in the 3rd person present/future, where the
endings -t", -t', and -t alternate.[1] For example, line
99 vnidet', line 105 izvodit", line 24 xoščet. The jers
hace been correctly retained within the word occasionally, and when this occurs, it is for the most part in
verbal prefixes. For example, line 5 l'sti, lines 6, 7

v"spoem", line 48 v"znes".

The same conditions hold in manuscript "Z" as in manuscript "V". We have the expected change of strong jers
to e̲ and o̲, the disappearance of weak jers, except at
the end of nouns, adjectives, and pronouns, the same
confusion in 3rd person present/future endings in the
verb. However, again the spelling system of the jers is
sometimes maintained, for the most part in verbal prefixes. For example, line 7 v"zolo̱ži, line 10 per'skix",
line 14 v"sxotě̲lo.

In manuscripts "U", the same conditions hold as for
the preceding manuscripts, with the exception that the
third person/future verbal endings drop the jer entirely
in the majority of cases, fifteen times in all. For example, line 9 svirjajut, line 10 nesut, line 16 ostrit.
Otherwise the spelling system of jers is infrequently
maintained, and then for the most part in verbal prefixes.[2] For example, line 10 per'skix", line 14 v"sxo-
tě̲lo, line 44 v"zdy̌set.

In our three manuscripts, we have only six cases of
pleophony. In manuscript "V". the lone case occurs in
lines 29, 30 korotko; in "Ž", line 29 korotkii, line 35
polonjanik"; in "Z2", line 29 korotkii; and in "U", line
29 k(o)rotkii, line 35 polonjanik". These forms occur
in Adam's address to the Lord, bitterly complaining of

his fate, indicating a colloquial element by the non-Church Slavonic forms.[3]

In all our manuscripts, there is confusion in the writing of the jat'. The confusion for the most part is between ě and e.

In manuscript "V", some examples of the errors are line 18 pridete, line 22 kamene, and line 95 pr^{o}rcě. The last example has ě in place of i. This may be a North Russian dialectal feature, where final unstressed ě in general changed to i, thus explaining this error.[4]

In manuscript "Z", some examples of the errors are line 32 sedjat", line 47 sedit".

In manuscript "U", some examples of the errors are line 6 utešimsja, line 7 sedja, line 33 tešat.

In manuscript "P" we have one interesting error in line 34 vidixo^m, where we have i for the correct ě. This again is very likely a North Russian dialectal feature, where in some dialects after the stress and before a hard consonant ě became i.[5]

The Church Slavonic šč is used exclusively in all the manuscripts and copies, never the colloquial č. For example, S20 ově^{t}ščasta, Z2-21 xoščet, Z72 xóščeši, U16 xoščet, P19 xoščet'.

The Church Slavonic žd and the colloquial East Slavic ž are both used in the copies. E.g., Z37 vižu, U37 vižju, P37 vižju, S10 rož^{d}ešusja, Z2-10 róšusja,

Z10 rŏšu, U10 rož^d'šusja, P10 rož^d'šusja.

Only one instance is found in the copies of initial vowel going back to Proto-Slavic *ju-. In each instance, the Church Slavonic form is not used but the form found in Old East Slavic and occasionally in the Old Russian standard language; i.e., u- is found, not ju-. For example, Z66 ŭnosti, K66 ŭnosti, P66 ŭnosti.

The Church Slavonic form (j)e- is used consistently for the initial vowel going back to Proto-Slavic *(j)e-, never o-. Some examples are Z72 edin", K72 edĭ, P72 edin".

The Church Slavonic forms are exclusively used to express the Proto-Slavic *ort-, the norm in the Old Russian standard language being the same as in Church Slavonic. E.g., Z2-93 razrĕšite, S97 rašt'e, the only two examples. The colloquial Old East Slavic form, expressed by the formula rot-, is not found.

The last point to be noted is the akan'e found in copy "S". E.g., line 8 blgopriatna (ntr. n. sg.), line 51 tĕla (a. sg.), line 51 porozi^vyi, line 56 serofĕmu, line 82 podosta, line 95 potriarx".

NOTES

1. This may be a confusion of the South Slavic jers or, more probably, a confusion due to the North Russian hardening of the ending in the third person.

2. The verbal prefixes are v"z- and s"-.

3. Paschen, A., _Die semasiologische und stylistische Funktion der trat/torot Alternationen in der alt-russischen Literatursprache_ (Heidelberg, 1933), p. 56, contrasts the _trat_ and _torot_ words, the former having a religious-affective connotation, the latter being characteristic of the profane style.

4. Durnovo, N., _Očerk istorii russkogo jazyka_, _SPR_, 22 (Hague, 1959) (reprint of Moscow-Leningrad, 1924 ed.), pp. 199-200.

5. _Ibid._, p. 199.

V

MORPHOLOGY

The following pages examine the dual number, the particle sja, and the vocative case in the examined manuscripts.

In manuscript "V", the dual is used, although not always with the correct endings. For example, line 57 orla si, line 58 Orla že nosiv"ša po c(e)rkvi, v"neso-stasja na n(e)b(e)sa, line 81 sestrě lazorevě.

In manuscript "Z", the dual is used, but not correctly. For example, line 20 A Isaia i Eremia rugajuščesja Adovi i nemošč'nei ego silě, i rekosta, line 71 Il'ja i Enox ugodiša tobě.

In manuscript "U", the dual is used, but not always correctly. For example, line 20 A Isaa i Ereměa rugaju-ščisja Adovi i nemoščnoi silě eg(o), i r(e)kosta, line 26 nača biti rukama, line 71 ugod(i)ša (where Elijah and Enoch are the subject, no dual but a plural is used).

The monosyllabic accusative and dative forms of the personal pronouns in Slavic are enclitic, and in Old Russian were immediately after the first stressed word in a clause,[1] later becoming a simple affix to the verb.[2] The traces which we have in the manuscripts of the reflexive pronoun after the first stressed word of a clause very probably goes back to the protograph,

these archaisms being one of the best proofs of the age
of the text. The reflexive pronoun in most of the cases,
however, follows the verb.

In manuscript "V", the particle follows the verb in
every instance but one. For example, line 3 otvergoša-
šasja (sic!), line 14 na čto ti sja vosxotě, lines 39,
40 posmixaet'sja, the second example being an archaism.

In manuscript "Z", the particle follows the verb,
with but one exception. In the second copy in this
manuscript, "Z2", there are only two exceptions, line 3
Těm že sja mene otvergoša,[3] line 14 čto sja ti v"sxotě,
the latter example placing the enclitics before the verb,
but incorrectly so.[4] Examples in the first copy, "Z"
are line 6 utěšimsja, line 14 čto ti sja v"sxotělo, line
39 rugaet mi sja, the last example being the only case
where the accusative enclitic is separated from the verb
when following the verb, in this case by the dative
enclitic of the personal pronoun.

In manuscript "U", only once does the particle precede
the verb, in all other instances coming immediately after
the verb, with one exception, where mi intervenes. For
example, line 10 rožd'šusja, line 14 čto ti sja v"sxotělo, line 39 rugaet" mi sja. The second example is
archaic.

Thus, in the texts examined, there are cases of the enclitic reflexive pronoun after the first word of the clause, these exceptions reflecting the usage very probably of the protograph.

In our manuscripts, the vocative exists, being omitted only in one manuscript in one speech.

In manuscript "V", there are eight omissions of the vocative, in a speech which does not occur in the other copies of the apocrypha. In all other instances, the vocative is used. For example, line 14 c(ěsa)rju, line 15, 12 g(o)s(pod)i - the examples of this vocative are very numerous, line 23a Isaija, Irěměja, Avvakum", Aron", Izěkel", Solomon", Adam", Avraame, Isače, Ijako-ve, Samoile, Danil". where we have the eight omissions.

In manuscript "Z", the vocative is not once omitted. For example, line 6 družino, line 27 druže, Lazore, line 42 Avraame.

In manuscript "U", the vocative is never omitted. For example, line 11 družino, line 14 c(ěsa)rju, line 32 vl(a)d(y)ko.

Also to be mentioned are the forms of the 1 pl. pr. of byti. We notice the forms Z2-86 esmi, Z11 eśi, Z74 esmi, Z74 esmi, P11 esmi, which are a confusion of the artificial bookish form of the 1 sg. pr. of byti with the 1 pl. pr., which Bulaxovskij has noted as occurring in the seventeenth century.[5] We notice in Z2-73 esmjå, Z34 esmja, U11 esmja, U34 esmja, P34 esme, P74

esme, which are most probably reproductions of the
Bulgarism esme. T he form esmja is attested from the
fourteenth century, the final vowel probably the
phonetic change of final e to a in unstressed position.[6]
We find then South Slavic influence in the morphology
as well as the orthography and graphics of the copies.
In S73 is the form e^s my, which along with the form věmy
in Z2-84, reflects the influence of the personal
pronoun my on the verb ending.[7]

The m.d.sg. endings -ovi/-evi are used with words not
indicating persons apparently to convey a sense of
personification. For example, Z20 Ádovi, U20 Âdovi,
P20 Ádovi. The d.sg. is used with this word eight
times, the other cases using the ending -u; V20 Àdu,
Z2-20 Ádu, Z35 Ádu, U35 Àdu, P35 Ádu. These other
five cases use the word with a sense of personification,
so there is no regularity in the usage of copies, Z, U,
and P. In the word for king or emperor, we note the
following forms: Z10 črvì, U10 črvì, P10 črvì, but V10
črjù, Z2-10 črju. So, once more, the alternate ending
-ju being used by the same copies probably reflects the
usage of the protograph.

In the prepositional singular, the usage is the normal -ě ending, with the exception of copy V, which uses
ad" with the ending -u only three times out of a total
of nine occurrences, V23a, V97, V95. The ending is an

alternative for certain masculine monosyllabics.

In the copies, the 3rd person verbal suffix is
commonly -t', the Old East Slavic form, very rarely
the Church Slavonic form -t".[8] The exceptional forms
are for the most part found in copies "Z" and "Z2",
twice in "P" and three times in "V". E.g., Z64
budet", Z63 v"zdyxaet", Z2-95 v"pijut", Z2-96 v"piet",
Z70 želájut", Z21 možet", Z2-10 nesút", Z16 ostrit",
Z24 poidet", Z10 prinósjat", Z9 prixódit", P9 prixodit", P9 proxo^dit", Z2-80 smerdit", V104 sokrušit",
V103 sokrušit"sja, V103 sotret"sja, Z75 uvĕdjat",
Z2-79 umret", Z16 xoščet", Z19 xoščet".

The dative singular of the personal pronoun ty is
found in both the Church Slavonic and Old East Slavic
forms, except copy "P", which in both cases uses the
Church Slavonic forms. The examples are V15, 12 tobĕ,
V48 tebĕ, Z2-15, 12 tebĕ, Z2-56 tobĕ, Z71 tebĕ, Z76
tobĕ, U71 tobĕ, U76 tebĕ, P71 tobĕ, P76 tobĕ.

The Church Slavonic forms in -ja are used exclusively for the soft feminine genitive singular, nom.
-acc.pl.; m.acc.pl.; fem.gen.sg.pron. The Old East
Slavic -ĕ is never used. Examples are rare, but some
are V5 moeja, U15 sia, P15 sija, V51 Ezĕkĕja, Z2-51
Ezekia, Z37 burja, U37 burja, P37 burja.

NOTES

1. Cf. Berneker, E., Die Wortfolge in den slavischen
   Sprachen (Berlin, 1900), pp. 60-62; Gunnarson, G.,
   Studien über die Stellung des Reflexivs im Russi-
   schen (Uppsala, 1935), pp. 102-03; Margulie's, A.,
   Die Verba reflexiva in den slavischen Sprachen
   (Heidelberg, 1924), pp. 29-31; Havránek, B., Genera
   verbi v slovanských jazycích, vol. 1 (Prague,
   1928), pp. 29-31, 35-36.

2. Jakobson, R., "Les enclitiques slaves", Atti del
   III Congresso internazionale dei linguisti, ed. by
   Migliorini, B., and Pisani, V. (Florence, 1935),
   p. 387.

3. In Old Russian, if a number of enclitics are found
   together, the particles bo, že, and li stand first.
   Cf. Berneker, E., op. cit., p. 64

4. In Old Russian, the dative enclitic often stands
   before the accusative enclitic. Cf. Berneker,E.
   op. cit., p. 64.

5. Bulaxovskij, L., Istoričeskij kommentarij k russkomu literaturnomu jazyku (Kiev, 1958), p. 215

6. Durnovo, N., Očerk istorii russkogo jazyka
   (Hague, 1959), p. 330.

7. Kuznecov, P., Istoričeskaja grammatika russkogo
   jazyka (Moscow, 1953), p. 206.

8. Durnovo, N., op. cit., pp.315-316.

VI

SYNTAX

This section will examine the use of the tenses in the
copies of the apocrypha.

The present tense imperfective aspect signifies
action simultaneous with the utterance or time in the
past or future defined by the context, also actions of
repeated or general validity. Examples in manuscript
"V" are line 10 <u>Uže bo slyšim" ropot"</u> 'For we already
hear the noise', lines 12, 15 <u>Tobě bo G(ospod)i sut'</u>
<u>n(e)b(e)sa pr(ě)st(o)l"</u> 'For to you Lord, the heavens
are a throne', line 24 <u>Se že xoščet</u> 'Lo, (this one)
wants'. Examples in "Z" are line 12 <u>I tomu bo est'</u>
<u>n(e)bo pr(ěs)t(o)l"</u> 'And to this one heaven is a
throne', line 15 <u>v nix že n(y)ně ležiši</u> 'in which you
now lie', line 21 <u>A kto možet" otselě tamo věst'</u>
<u>donesti?</u> 'But who can bear news there from here?'
Examples in manuscript "U" are line 9 <u>glas ix proxo-</u>
<u>djat adova vrata</u> 'their sound passes through the gates
of Hell', line 32 <u>vnucy v" tmě sedjat</u> 'descendants sit
in darkness', line 33 <u>Skorbiju i tugoju s(e)rdce tešat</u>
'With sorrow and woe they comfort their hearts'.

There is no specific form for the future tense, the
most common way, and in the mss. here examined the only

way, of expressing it being the use of the present
tense, especially the perfective present, which
specifies that the end of the action in the future
or any time defined by the context is envisaged.
Examples in manuscript "V" are line 5 <u>A se az" inomu</u>
<u>slavy moeja ne dam"</u> 'And lo, I shall not give my glory
to another', line 5 <u>da sp(a)su ljudi oto l'sti soto-</u>
<u>niny</u> 'so that I shall save the people from the decep-
tion of Satan', line 25 <u>Da tot" izneset" věst'</u>... 'So
that that one will carry news...' Examples in "Z" are
line 24 <u>A se zautra ot nas" poidet" Lazor'</u> 'And lo,
tomorrow Lazarus will go from us', line 25 <u>I toi ot</u>
<u>nas" k nemu doneset' věst'</u> 'And that one will carry
news from us to him'. Examples in "U" are line 24
<u>A se zautra ot nas poidet Lazor'</u> 'And lo, tomorrow
Lazarus will go', line 25 <u>T" ot nas k nemu doneset</u>
<u>věst</u> 'That one will carry news from us to him'.

The imperfect indicates an action occurring prior
to the moment of utterance, concurrent with a fact or
act in the past. It denotes a generalized situation,
repeated action, has a descriptive function. Examples
in "V" are lines 6, 7 <u>Emu ... gl(agola)še D(a)v(y)d"</u>
'To him ...David said ', line 13 <u>Ego že mati...ljubov'ju</u>
<u>gl(agola)še</u> 'His mother... with love said'. Apparent-
ly there is a confusion in the copy between the imperfect and aorist, for the quotations do not fit the

definitions. Examples in "Z" are line 13 ...m(a)ti
...prinikši k nemu, gl(agol)aše '...mother...bending
to him, said', line 26 I se slyšav" Adam'...tjažko
v"piaše ... 'And having heard this, Adam... grievously
cried out...'; Once more the imperfect as used it seems
simply as a variant of the aorist. Examples in "U" are
line 13 ...m(a)ti...prinikši k nemu, gl(agola)še
'...mother...bending to him, said', line 26 I se slyšav" Adam"...gl(agola)še 'And having heard this, Adam
said'. The imperfect is relatively rare, the instances
cited being the majority of occurrences in the manuscripts.

The aorist specifies no concurrence, being a narrative device. The texts contain overwhelmingly more
aorists than imperfects. Examples in "V" are line 8
Uze bo nasta vremja bl(a)gopriatna 'For already a favorable time has drawn near', line 23 Togda reč(e) D(a)-
v(y)d... 'Then said David', line 43 Ili... Avraam" so-
greši 'Or has Abraham sinned'. Examples in "Z" are line
7 ...i v"zloži persty svoja na živyja struny... '...and
lay his fingers on the living strings', line 17 I gl(a-
gol) Adam suščim" v" adě 'And said Adam to those in
Hell', line 35 V malě čas" az c(ěsa)r' byx"... ' For a
short time I was king... ' Examples in "U" are line 8
Se bo vremja veselo nasta 'For a joyous time has drawn
near', line 26 I se slyšav" Adam"...nača biti rukama po

licju svoemu... 'And having heard this, Adam...began to
beat his face with his hands', line 31 <u>Togo li radi na-</u>
<u>polnix zemlju?</u> 'For the sake of this I replenished the
earth?' These are all examples of the aorist denoting a
simple action in the past, not specifying concurrence,
often denoting succeeding actions.

The perfect expresses an action taken place in the
past, the results of which are still meaningful. It is
a retrospective past. Examples in "V" are lines 29,30
<u>Na se li mja esi...narodil"</u>... 'For this have you...
had me born...', line 105 <u>...tja sozdal" ot věka</u> '...
created you for eternity.' Examples in "Z" are line 14
<u>čto ti sja v"sxotělo k nam"</u>...sniti 'why did you want to
descend to us,' line 14 <u>Sia li peščery v"sxotěl" esi</u>
'Did you want this cave', line 62 <u>To čto...toi sogrěšil"</u>?
'Then how...did that one sin?' Examples in "U" are line
11 <u>A togo esmja družino mnozi dni žadali</u> 'And we have
longed for that one many days, družina', line 14 <u>...čto</u>
<u>ti sja v"sxotělo k nam...sniti na zemlju?</u> '...why did
you want to descend to us?', line 15 <u>Sia li peščery</u>
<u>v"sxotěl" esi...</u> 'Did you want this cave...' The per-
fect is used in these cases to present action as ab-
stracted from its development in time, action in contradistinction to the main body of the story, action
anterior to the moment of utterance, belonging already
to objective knowledge. In these texts the auxiliary

is missing in the third person. The ellipse of the
auxiliary is common in Old Russian preverbs, dicta, and
direct speech, often marked by a preceding particle,
such as se.[1] This we note in these texts.

The pluperfect is lacking the texts, but the future
perfect is found, although it is very rare. This tense
denotes an action viewed as completed at a moment after
the moment of utterance. In "V" there are no examples
of the future perfect. Examples in "Z" are line 45
...i to ada li...ne možeši izbaviti, to ašče budet sei
sogrěšil" jako ž(e) az" '...and if you cannot save him
from Hell, then he will have sinned even as I', line 64
Ašče li budet" tako ze sogrěšil" jako i az" 'If he will
have sinned in the same way as I'. Examples in "U" are
line 45 I to ada li ne možeši izbaviti, to ašče budut
sii sogrěšili jako ž(e) i az" 'And if you cannot save
them from Hell, then they will have sinned even as I'
line 64 Ašče li budet tako ž(e) s"grěšil jako i az"
'If he will have sinned in the same way as I'. This future perfect is used only with ašče in special conditions.

NOTES

1. For a brief treatment of the meaning of the tense
   system in Old Church Slavonic, see Lunt, H., _Old
   Church Slavonic Grammar_, _SPR_, 3 (Hague, 1955),
   pp. 98-99, 136-37, for those tenses discussed in
   this chapter. For a full treatment of the past
   tense in Old Russian, see Schooneveld, C. van, _A
   Semantic Analysis of the Old Russian Preterite Sys-
   tem_, _SPR_, 7 (Hague, 1959).

VII

LEXICON

The vocabulary of the apocrypha is Church Slavonic. As
the text is primarily ecclesiastical, the language is
thus to be the expected Church Slavonic with only rare
secular elements. A number of borrowings exist in the
text, but this is also not unusual, for the philosophi-
cal and theological terminology of Church Slavonic was
very heavily based on Greek.[1] The one enigmatic word
in the texts is the word Tartail", line 98, manuscript
"V". This occurs in the list of the heavenly host de-
scending to Hell. It may be that the scribe has con-
fused Tar"tar", Tartarus, with the idea that this is an
angel, prophet, or one of the righteous. The most
striking word, perhaps, in our copies is the word mnogoočitaja, lines 6, 7, manuscript "V". This is a loan-
translation of the Greek polyommatos, and is attested
in other ecclesiastical texts.[2] However, the most interesting question is that of the use of composites.

In manuscript "V" examples are lines 6, 7, mnogoočitaja, line 8 blagopriatna, line 73 světozarnago. The
use of composites is relatively moderate.

In manuscript "Z" examples are line 26 pervozdannyi,

line 37 presvĕtlago, line 43 bl(ago)s(lo)vjatsja.

In manuscript "U" examples are moderate in number,
as they also were in manuscript "Z". Some examples are
line 37 presvĕtlago, line 42 bl(ago)s(lo)vjatsja, line
76 bl(a)govĕrnii.

Thus, the examples in the various manuscripts are
relatively moderate, the quoted examples being about
one-half of the total number found.

NOTES

1. Cf. Schumann, K., Die griechischen Lehnbildungen und Lehnbedeutungen im Altbulgarischen (Berlin, 1958). Also see Miklosich, F., Die christliche Terminologie der slavischen Sprachen (Vienna, 1876).

2. Cf. Sreznevskij, I., Materialy dlja slovarja drevne- russkogo jazyka (St. Petersburg, 1895; reprint, Moscow, 1959), vol. 2, col. 208.

VIII

EDITION OF THE COPIES

Copy "V"

СЛОВО О С(ВЯ)ТЫХ ПРОР(О)ЦѢХ.

Г(О)С(ПОД)И БЛ(А)Г(О)С(ЛО)ВИ О(Т)ЧЕ.

1. Слыши н(е)бо внуши земле, яко

   Г(о)с(под)ь г(лаго)ла:

2. С(ы)ны породихъ и възнесохъѦ .

3. И ты и мене отвергошашасѦ ,[1]

   людие мои не познаша мене.

4. А волъ не позна стежавшаго[2] и,

   и осель ясли[3] Г(о)с(поди)на своего.

5. А се азъ иному славы моеѦ не дамь, но пущу слово

   мое на землю, да сп(а)су люди ото льсти сотонины.

6, 7. Ему же гл(агола)ше Д(а)в(ы)дъ сѣдѦ въ преиспод-

   немѣадѣ, накладая многоочитая персты на живыя

   струпы,[4] а въспоемъ пѣс(ни) тихиа и веселья,

   дружина моѦ , дн(е)сь; положим [5] пла(ч)ь

   и скорбь, утѣшимъсѦ Г(о)с(поде)мь Б(о)гамъ[6] нашимъ.

8. Уже бо наста времѦ бл(а)гоприатна.[7]

10. Уже бо слышимъ ропотъ волхвовъ перьскыхъ конь несутъ

    ему дары, н(е)б(е)сному ц(ѣса)рю на земли рождешусѦ .

56

Copy "Z2"

В С(У)Б(ОТ)У ЦВѢТНУЮ. СЛОВО С(ВЯ)Т(А)ГО ИАКОВА
БРАТА Г(ОСПОДЬ)НЯ НА ВZСКР(ЕСЕ)НИЕ ДРУГА Б(О)ЖИА
ЛАЗОРѦ.

1. Слыши н(е)бо и внуши землѦ, яко Г(оспод)ь гл(агол)а-
ше:

2. С(ы)ны породихъ и възнесохъ.

3. Тѣм же сѦ мене отвергоша и людие мои не познаша мѦ.

4. А оселъ во яслехъ позна Г(оспод)а своего.

5. Се азъ иному славы моеѦ не дамъ, но пущу слово мое
на землю, да спасу люди моѦ от льсти сотонины.

6, 7 И се гл(агол)аше Д(а)в(ы)дъ въ преисподнемъ адѣ
сѣдѦ и, накладаѦ персты на живыѦ струны и гл(агол)а-
ше, въспоемъ дружино пѣсни тихи и веселы дн(е)сь;
отложимъ плачь и скорбъ и утѣшимсѦ Г(о)с(по)демъ
нашимъ.

8. Уже бо наста свѣтлыи д(е)нь и времѦ бл(а)гоприатно.

10. Уже бо слышахомъ топотъ перскихъ конь и несутъ
дары н(е)б(е)сному ц(ѣса)рю на земли рожшусѦ.

Copy "V"

13. Его же м(а)ти пр(ѣ)ч(и)стая д(ѣ)в(и)ца повивающи
    пеленами прикланѧющисѧ к нему, любовью гл(агола)-
    ше:

14. О, высокыи ц(ѣса)рю, на что ти сѧ восхотѣ к намъ
    нищимъ на землю снити?

15, 12. Пещеры восхотѣ или въ яслехъ скотиихъ восхотѣ
    полежати пеленами повиваемъ? А ты Г(о)с(под)и самъ
    н(е)б(е)са облакы одѣвая. Тобѣ бо Г(о)с(под)и сугь
    н(е)б(е)са пр(ѣ)ст(о)лъ, а землѧ подножие его же.

16. Иродъ безумныи скрежьташа зубы своими, Г(о)с(под)и,
    хотѧть убити.

18. Но приидите прор(о)ци, приидете[8] праведници.

20. Исаия и Ерѣмѣя ругающесѧ Аду отвѣщаста, гл(аго-
    лю)щи:

21. О немощныи Дьяволе! Д(а)в(ы)де, гл(агола)и, кто от
    нас на ны[9] изнесеть вѣсть на живыи свѣтъ ко Вл(а)-
    д(ы)цѣ?

22. Се бо Д(а)в(ы)дъ въ замьцѣ[10] камене, а врата мѣд -
    на, а верея желѣзна; о твердо Д(а)в(ы)дъ заключенъ.

22a. Д(а)в(ы)дъ, гл(агола)и, кто от нас на ны[11] изне-
    сеть вѣсть на живыи свѣтъ ко Вл(а)д(ы)цѣ?

58

13. Его же м(а)ти пр(ѣ)ч(ис)та д(ѣ)в(и)ца, повивающи пеленами и приклан/Ающис/А к нему, умилно гл(агол)аше:

14. О, высокии и страшныи бесмертныи ц(ѣса)рю, что с/А ти въсхотѣ к намъ нищимъ снити на землю?

15, 12. Пещеры ли въсхотѣ или въ яслехъ полежати пеленами повиваемъ. А ты Г(оспод)и сам облаки облача/А . Тебѣ Г(оспод)и н(е)бо пр(ѣ)ст(о)лъ а земл/А подножие его же.

16. Иродъ безумныи скрегташе зубы своими, хот/Аше т/А Г(оспод)и убити.

18. Но приидете прор(о)цы и вси праведницы.

19. Да прогл(ас)имъ слово о Г(о)с(по)дѣ[1] нашемъ И(су)се Х(рист)е.

20. Исаиа же прор(о)къ, Иеремѣ ругающес/А Аду и немощнеи его силѣ, рекоша къ Д(а)в(ы)ду:

21. О Д(а)в(ы)де, гл(агола)и, кто от насъ н(ы)нѣ изнесеть вѣсть на живыи онъ свѣтъ къ Вл(а)д(ы)цѣ Х(рист)у? - хощет ли насъ избавити изо ада сего?

Copy "V"

23. Тогда реч(е) Д(а)в(ы)дъ яснымъ гласомъ:

23а. Исаия, Ирѣмѣѧ, [12] Аввакумъ, Аронъ, Изѣкель, Соломонъ, Адамъ, Аврааме, Исаче, Иякове, Сомоиле, Даниилъ, [13]
   и всѧ 31 прор(о)къ, послушаите моего гласа во аду
   семъ:

24. Се же хощет изити от нас на живыи свѣтъ ко Вл(а)д(ы)-
   це - Лазарь другъ г(осподь)нь.

25. Да тотъ изнесетъ вѣсть на живыи свѣтъ ко Вл(а)д(ы-
   цѣ.

26. Тогда услышавъ первозданныи чл(овѣ)къ Адамъ, и воз-
   бисѧ в лице свое руками, гл(агол)ѧ:

27. Лазарю, друже г(о)с(подь)нь, изнеси на мѧ вѣсть на
   живыи свѣтъ ко Вл(а)д(ы)цѣ.

29,30. На се ли мѧ еси Г(о)с(под)и народилъ коротко на
   свѣтѣ семъ жити а многа лѣта въ адѣ мучену быти?

31. Да сего делѧ, Г(о)с(под)и, чл(овѣ)кы на землю наплодихъ?

38. Да мнѣ бо Г(о)с(под)и жаль и не жаль; азъ бо Г(о)с(под)и
   согрѣших в дѣлѣхъ своих, но того ми Г(о)с(под)и жаль.

39,40. О же твоею тварью Адъ посмихаетьсѧ и поругаетьсѧ,
   аще Г(о)с(под)и азъ Адамъ согрѣших.

41. А се твои изволници а мои внуци - Аврамъ съ с(ы)номъ съ
   Исаакамъ [14] и со внукомъ съ Яковомъ въ вратехъ сѣдѧ
   въ преисподнемъ адѣ.

42а. Да сниди, Г(о)с(под)и, Авраама дѣлѧ.

Copy "Z2"

23. Тогда Д(а)в(ы)дъ яснымъ гласомъ рече: послушаите
    гласа моего.

24. А се от нас заутра изыдетъ Лазорь другъ б(о)жии.

26. И тогда слышавъ прьвозданныи Адамъ, въпиаше,
    биющи в перси своѦ, гл(агол)аше:

27. Лазарю, друже г(осподь)нь, изнеси, реч(е), вѣсть
    от мене на живыи онъ свѣтъ къ Вл(а)д(ы)цѣ Х(рист)у.

29. На се ли мѦ еси Г(оспод)и создалъ на короткии онъ
    вѣкъ во свѣте твоемъ пожити?

31. И сего ли ти ради землю наплодихъ человѣки?

38. Но не жалуюсѦ Г(оспод)и; азъ бо согрѣшихъ в дѣлехъ
    своихъ пред тобою, но сего жаль ми, иже по твоему
    образу сотворенъ есмь.

39. И твоимъ созданиемъ Адъ со Диаволомъ поругаетсѦ.

40. Аще азъ, Г(оспод)и, согрѣшилъ, то по дѣломъ моимъ
    въздалъ ми еси муку сию.

41. А се твои изволныи другъ Авраамъ с с(ы)номъ своимъ
    Исаакомъ и со внукомъ Иаковомъ в работѣ седѦ в
    преисподнемъ адѣ.

Copy "V"

43. Или ты Г(о)с(под)и, Авраамъ согрѣши?

46. А се твои прор(о)къ Моисии проведы и жезломъ Черм-
    ное Море и гла(гола)выи с тобою на Синаистѣи Горѣ
    в купинѣ лицемъ к лицю.

47. А тот ти Г(о)с(под)и с нами во адѣ, или ти Г(о)с-
    (под)и Моисѣи согрѣши?

48. А Исаия тебѣ Г(о)с(под)и и что согрѣши? - ис[15]
    чрева м(а)т(е)рнѧ възнесъ на н(е)б(е)са; и ты сни-
    ди[16] с нимъ въ чрево д(ѣ)в(и)че.

49. А тоть ти Г(о)с(под)и с нами во адѣ.

50. Или ти Г(о)с(под)и Исаиѧ что согрѣши?

51. А се твои прор(о)кы[17] великыи Данилъ, с(ы)нъ Езѣ-
    кѣя ц(ѣса)рѧ, и прор(о)ка порози(вы)[18] тѣла златое
    в Вавилонѣ и ввержень ко лвомъ в ровъ.

52. А тот ти Г(о)с(под)и с нами въ адѣ.

53. Или ти Данилъ что согрѣши?

54. А Ерѣмѣ Г(о)с(под)и что согрѣши? Носивыи дре-
    вѧ ныи козелъ на рамѣ прообразова сп(а)с(е)ныя
    твоея страсти.

55. Или ти Г(о)с(под)и тии прор(о)ци что согрѣшиша?

56. А се с(ы)нъ д(а)в(ы)д(о)въ Соломонъ създавы и ти
    с(вя)таа с(вя)тыхъ въ Иерусалимѣ и сковавы два
    орла злата подобна херувиму и серо•ѣму.[19]

62

Copy "Z2"

43. Или Г(оспод)и и тои согрѣши я(ко)же азъ?

46. А се твои прор(о)къ Моисеи иже провелъ жидовъ
    сквозѣ Чермное Море десницею твоею и гл(агол)авъ с
    тобою на Синаистеи Горѣ в купинѣ лицемъ к лицу.

47. То и тои Г(оспод)и с нами въ адѣ мучимъ от Сотоны,
    или и тои согрѣшилъ яко же азъ?

48. А се, Г(оспод)и, твои прор(о)къ Исаиа - из чрева
    м(а)т(е)рнѧ възнесенъ на н(е)б(е)са; и паки сниде
    во чрево м(а)т(е)рнѣ[2] дѣиствомъ и силою С(вя)т(о)-
    го Д(у)ха.

49. То и тои Г(оспод)и с нами въ адѣ.

50. Или Г(оспод)и той согрѣшилъ якож(е) азъ?

51. А се твои великии прор(о)къ Данилъ с(ы)нъ Езекиа
    прор(о)ка, поразивъ тѣло злато в Вавилонѣ и ввер-
    женъ бысть ко львомъ во снѣдь в ровъ.

52, 53. А тои Г(оспод)и что согрѣши, и тои с нами во
    адѣ.

54. Иже носивыи древѧнъ козелъ на рамѣ прообразоваше
    сп(а)с(е)ныѧ твоѧ стр(а)сти и за миръ умертвие.

56. А се Г(оспод)и с(ы)нъ д(а)в(ы)д(о)въ Соломонъ со-
    зда тобѣ храмъ въ Иер(у)с(а)лимѣ и скова два орла
    злата подобна херувимомъ и серафимомъ.

Copy "V"

57. И гл(агола)ше аще будеть Б(ог)ъ на земли, то сни-
    деть Д(у)хъ С(вя)тыи во орла си.

58. Орла же в тои час носивъшаса по ц(е)ркви, възнесос-
    таса на н(е)б(е)са.

73. И уже бо Г(о)с(под)и не видимъ[20] твоего свѣтазарна-
    го[21] с(о)лнца ни бл(а)г(о)д(а)тнаго твоего вѣтра,
    но тугою желѣниа нашего уныли есмы.

77. Слыша Г(о)с(под)ь плачь ихъ въ адѣ.

81. И прииде к сестрѣ лазоревѣ М(а)рье и Марфѣ в Вифа-
    нию.

82. И слышавши же М(а)рья и Марфа, скоро текоста и па-
    доста[22] на нози г(о)с(под)ни, гл(аголю)ще:

64

59. Но и тои с нами въ адѣ поруганъ от Диавола.

71a. А се Г(оспод)и прор(о)къ твои Самуилъ, иже пома-
    завыи рогомъ на ц(ѣсарс)тво и обновль ц(ѣса)рьскии
    венецъ - и тои с нами въ адѣ мучитсѧ ; и се уже
    Г(оспод)и вси праведницы на многа времена въ адѣ
    мучимы от Сотоны и слезами зеницы омываху свои.

73. Уже бо Г(оспод)и на многа лѣта не видимъ свѣтозар-
    наго твоего с(о)лнца ни бл(а)годарнаго твоего вѣт-
    ра, но тугою одержими есмѧ уныли.

74. Но мы Г(оспод)и чл(о)в(ѣ)цы тощави,[3] а ты Г(оспод)и
    долготерпѣливъ, Вл(а)д(ы)ко.

75. Но сп(а)си свое создание и изведи ны Г(оспод)и изо
    ада сего и свѧжи Диавола и услыша Г(оспод)ь м(о)-
    л(и)тву ихъ и въздыхание.

78. И рече Г(оспод)ь уч(е)н(и)къмъ[4] своимъ - другъ нашъ
    Лазарь успе.

79. Они же рекоша к нему: аще умретъ то сп(а)сетсѧ.

80. И(су)съ же рече: но идемъ во Вифанию въздвигнути
    Лазорѧ от мертвыхъ.

81. И прииде в Вифанию и сретоша его сестрѣ лазоревы,
    Мариа и Марфа.

82. Скоро притекши и падши пред ногами ис(ус)овыми и
    власы своими отерши нозѣ его, и гл(агол)ющи:

Copy "V"

83. Аще бы ты былъ,[23] не бы умерлъ братъ наю Лазорь.

85. И гл(агол)а Г(о)с(под)ь к М(а)рье и Марфе - въскре-
    снеть братъ ваю Лазорь.

86. И гл(агол)а Адъ ко Дьяволу: силы моя прискорбна ми
    есть д(у)ша отпустити Лазорѧ, нудимъ бо есмь от-
    рыгнути Адама.

Copy "Z2"

83. Г(оспод)и, аще бы ты здѣ былъ, то не бы ум(е)рлъ
    братъ нашъ Лазорь. И гл(агол)а Г(оспод)ь Марфе и
    Марии; аще имаете вѣру, то въскр(ес)нетъ братъ вашъ
    Лазорь.

84. Они же рекоша ему, вѣмы Г(оспод)и яко въскр(е)с-
    нетъ в послѣднии д(е)нь.

86. И гл(агол)а Адъ къ Диаволу: слышу яко прискорбна
    ми есть д(у)ша отпустити Лазорѧ и нудимъ есми от-
    ригнути Адама, яко сила моѧ в немощъ претворѧ ет-
    сѧ.

87. И рече Г(оспод)ь Марии и Марфѣ: гдѣ положисте его?

88. И идоста на гробъ лазоревъ; и ту предстоѧ ху мно-
    ж(е)ство народа жидовъска.

89. И повелѣ Г(оспод)ь отвалити камень от дверии гроба.

90. И рече⁵ Мариа и Марфа: Г(оспод)и, уже смердитъ че-
    твородневенъ бо есть.

91. И рече Г(оспод)ь: аще вѣруете в мѧ , то узрите
    славу божию, и възрѣвъ на н(е)бо и прослезисѧ , и
    рече: Лазорь, грѧ ди вонъ.

92. И абие въста Лазорь укроемъ обѧ занъ.

93. И рече Г(оспод)ь: разрѣшите его.

Copy "V"

94. Тогда въскр(е)слъ Лазорь изь аду, и реч(е) : Г(о)с-
(под)и:

95. Вопиют ти прор(о)цѣ[24] въ аду, первозданныи чл(о-
вѣ)къ Адамъ, патриархъ[25] Авраамъ со с(ы)номъ Иса-
комъ[26] и со внукомъ Ияковомъ.

96. Д(а)в(ы)дъ же вопиеть о с(ы)ну своемъ Соломонѣ:
изведи Г(о)с(под)и изъ аду!

97. И гл(агол)а Г(о)с(под)ь к Лазорю: аще бы не Д(а)-
в(ы)да делѧ раба моего возлюбленаго, а Соломона
быхъ въ аду искоренилъ, предавысѧ Г(о)с(под)ь волею на распѧтье.

98. И сниде д(у)хомъ на ада и вси полци н(е)б(е)с-
ныхъ, Семиелъ,[27] Расуилъ[28] Измаилъ, Нафанаилъ,[29]
Тартаилъ,[30] Михаилъ, и Гаврилъ,[31] и вси анг(е)ли
идуть со кр(е)стомъ.

99. Възмѣте врата вѣчныя, да внидеть ц(ѣса)рь славы.

100. И гл(агол)а Адъ къ Дьяволу: кто[32] хощеть у нас
быти ц(ѣса)рь славы?

101. И гл(агол)аша анг(е)ли съ прор(о)ки: Г(о)с(под)ь
силенъ и страшенъ въ бранѣхъ, то бо есть ц(ѣса)рь
славы.

102. Тогда реч(е) великыи ц(ѣса)рь Д(а)в(ы)дъ: коли
бѣхъ въ животе в дахъ.

103. О же сокрушитъсѧ врата мѣдѧная и вереѧ железны
сотретъсѧ .

68

94. Егда въскр(е)съ Лазорь изо ада, и гл(агол)а к Г(ос-
    под)у:

95. Г(оспод)и, въпиютъ ти прор(о)цы и вси праведницы в
    адѣ, пръвозданныи Адамъ и патриархъ Авраамъ съ
    с(ы)номъ своимъ Исаакомъ и со внукомъ Яковомъ.

96. Д(а)в(ы)дъ же ти Г(оспод)и въпиетъ о с(ы)ну Соло-
    монѣ: изведи Г(оспод)и изо ада и избави Г(оспод)и
    от мучителѧ Диавола!

97. И рече Г(оспод)ь к Лазорю: аще бы не Д(а)в(ы)да
    раба моего възлюбленнаго, а Соломона быхъ искоре-
    нилъ во адѣ.

98. И сниде д(у)хомь на Адама и множество н(е)б(е)с-
    ныхъ вои с нимъ.

Copy "V"

104. Тогда сокрушитъ Г(о)с(под)ь врата меденаѧ и вереѧ желѣзныя сотре.

105. Гл(агол)а Г(о)с(под)ь Адаму: си тѧ создалъ от
вѣка, а си тѧ рукою изводить ис тлѧ .

106. Тогда въскр(е)съ Ис(у)съ, гл(агол)а ап(о)с(то)-
ломъ, шедши проповѣдите по всеи земли, кр(е)с-
тѧще во имѧ Отца и С(ы)на и С(вя)т(о)го Духа,
учаще я соблюсти.

107. А самъ възнесесѧ на н(е)б(е)са и сѣде о дѣсную
Отца.

108. По всеи земли слава его, яко тому подобает
всѧ кӓ слав(а).

Copy "Z2"

105. И рече Г(оспод)ь Адаму: [6] сиа ти десница создала,
сиа же та възведе, внидете паки в рай.

Copy "Z"

СЛОВО С(ВЯ)ТЫХ АП(ОСТО)Л ИЖЕ ОТ АДАМА ВЪ АДѢ

К ЛАЗОРЮ. БЛ(АГОСЛО)ВИ ОТЧЕ.

6. Въспоим дружино пѣсньми днесь а плачь отложимъ и
   утѣшимсѦ.

7. Удари, рече Д(а)в(ы)дъ, в гусли, и възложи персты
   своѦ на живыѦ струны и иныѦ накладаѦ, а сѣдѦ в преисподнемъ адѣ.

8. Се бо времѦ весело наста, и се приспѣ д(е)нь сп(а)-
   сениа.

9. Уже бо слышу; пастыри свирѦ ютъ у вертепа, а глас
   ихъ проходит адова врата, и в мои уши приходитъ.

10. И уже слышу топотъ конь перьскихъ, иже дары принос
    с тъ ему волсви от своихъ ц(ѣса)рей[1] н(е)б(е)сному
    ц(ѣса)р(е)ви, днес на земли рожщусѦ.

11. А того есми дружино многи дни жадали.

12. И тому бо есть н(е)бо пр(ѣс)т(о)лъ, а землѦ подно-
    жие ногу его.

COPY "U"

СЛОВ(О) С(ВЯ)ТЫХ АП(О)С(ТО)Лъ ИЖЕ ОТ АДАМА ВЪ АДѢ
К ЛАЗОРЮ. БЛ(АГО)С(ЛО)ВИ О(Т)Ч(Е).

6. Въспоем(ъ) дружино п(ѣснь)ми дн(е)сь, а плач отложимъ утешимсѧ.

7. И реч(е) Д(а)в(ы)дъ, и ударимъ в гусли, възложимъ
   персты¹ своѧ на живыа струны, и иныѧ накладаа, а
   седѧ в преисподнем адѣ.

8. Се бо времѧ весело наста, се приспе д(е)нь сп(а)-
   с(е)ниѧ.

9. Уж бо слышю пастырѧ ; свирѧ ют у вертепа а глас их
   проходѧт² адова врата, а в мои уши приходит.

10. А уж слышю топот ног конь перьскых, иже дары несут
    ему волсви от своих ц(ѣса)р(е)въ н(е)б(е)сному
    ц(ѣса)р(е)ви, дн(е)сь на земли рождьщусѧ.

11. А того есмѧ дружино мнози дни жадали.

12. Тому бо ес(ть) н(е)бо пр(ѣ)ст(о)лъ а землѧ подножие
    ногу его.

Copy "P"[1]

СЛОВО С(ВЯ)ТЫХ АП(ОСТО)ЛЪ ИЖ(Е) ОТ АДАМА ВО АДѢ
К ЛАЗАРЮ. Г(ОСПОД)И.

6. Воспоемъ дружино пѣс(нь)ми дн(е)сь, а плач отло-
   жим, утѣшимсѦ.

7. Удари, реч(е) Д(а)в(ы)дъ, в гусли, възложи персты
   своа на живыя струны иныи накладая, а седѦ в преисподнемъ аде.

8. Се бо времѦ весело наста, се приспѣ д(е)нь сп(а)-
   сениѦ.

9. Уже бо слышю; пастыри свирають у вѣртепа, а глас их
   проходить адова врата, а в мои уши приходитъ.

10. А уже слышю топотъ ногъ перскых коне,[2] иж даръ не-
    суть ему вълъсви от своих ц(ѣса)р(е)въ н(е)б(ес)ному[3]
    ц(ѣса)р(е)ви, дн(е)сь на земли рождьщусѦ.

11. А того есми дружино мнози дни жадали.

12. Тому бо есть н(е)бо пр(ѣ)ст(о)лъ, а землѦ подножие
    ногу его.

74

Copy "Z"

13. Того бо м(а)ти д(ѣ)в(и)ца, повивши в пелены повивающаго н(е)бо облаки а землю мглою, приникши к нему, гл(агол)аше:

14. О, ц(ѣса)рю великии н(е)б(е)сныи, что ти сѧ въсхотѣло к намъ нищимъ снити на землю?

15. Сиа ли пещеры въсхотѣлъ еси, или сихъ яслеи в них же н(ы)нѣ лежиши?

16. А се скоро Ирод безумныи шатаѧ сѧ остритъ на тѧ мечь и хощетъ тѧ убити.

17. И гл(агол)а Адам сущимъ въ адѣ:

18. Приидѣте пр(о)р(о)цы и вси праведнии.

19. И пошлемъ вѣсть ко Вл(а)д(ы)цѣ Х(рист)у со слезами на живыи онъ вѣкъ - хощетъ ли насъ избавити от муки сеѧ.

20. А Исаиа и Еремиа ругающесѧ Адови и немощьнеи его силѣ и рекоста къ Д(а)в(ы)ду:

21. А кто можетъ отселѣ тамо вѣсть донести?

22. А врата мѣдѧнаѧ и вереѧ желѣзнаѧ а замки каменныѧ и твердо запечатано.

23. Тогда Д(а)в(ы)дъ к нимъ изрече велми ясно:

24. А се заутра от насъ поидетъ Лазорь, четверодневныи другъ х(ри)с(то)въ.

25. И тои от насъ к нему донесеть вѣсть.

Copy "U"

13. Того м(а)ти д(ѣ)в(и)це,³ повивши в пелены повивающе
    н(е)бо облакы а землю мъглою, приникши к нему, гл(а-
    гола)ше:

14. О, ц(ѣса)рю великыи н(е)б(е)сныи, что ти са въсхо-
    тело к нам нищим снити на землю?

15. Сиа ли пещеры въсхотѣлъ еси, или сих ли ясли в
    них же н(ы)нѣ лежиши?

16. Се скоро Иродъ безумны шатаяса острит на та мечь и
    хощет та убити.

17. И гл(агол)а Адам сущимъ въ адѣ:

18. Приидетѣ⁴ прор(о)цы и вси праведнии.

19. Послемъ вѣсть къ Вл(а)д(ы)це Х(рист)у съ слезами
    на живыи онъ вѣкъ - хощет ли нас от мукы сиа изба-
    вити.

20. А Исаа и Еремѣа ругающиса Адови и немощнои силѣ
    ег(о) и р(е)коста ко Д(а)выду:

21. А кто может отселѣ тамо от нас вѣсть донести?

22. А врата меда наа и вѣрѣа желѣзныа а замкы камены
    и твердо запечатано.

23. Тогда Д(а)в(ы)дъ к ним ясно рече:

24. А се заутра от нас поидет Лазорь, д-роднѣвъныи
    другъ х(ри)с(то)въ.

25. Тъ от нас к нѣму донесет вѣсть.

76

13. Того бо м(а)ти д(ѣ)в(и)ца, повивши в пелены повивающа н(е)бо облакы а землю мглою, приникши к нему, гл(агола)ше:

14. О, ц(ѣса)рю великыи н(е)б(е)сныи, что ти са въсхотѣло к намъ снити нищимъ на землю?

15. Сиа ли пещеры въсхотѣлъ еси, или сих яслеи в них же н(ы)нѣ лежиши?

16. А се скоро Ирод безумныи шатаяса острить на та мечь и хощеть та убити.

17. И гл(агол)а Адам сущимъ въ аде:

18. Приидете пр(о)роци и вси праведнии.

19. Послемъ вѣсть ко Вл(а)д(ы)це Х(рист)у съ слезами на живыи онъ вѣкъ - хощеть ли нас от мукы сеа избавити.

20. А Исаиа и Еремеи ругающис(а)[4] Адови и немощнои силѣ его, рекоста Д(а)в(ы)ду:

21. А кто мож(е)ть отселе тамо от нас вѣсть донести?

22. А врата меда наа и вереа железныа а замкы каменыа, а твердо запечатано.

23. Тогда Д(а)в(ы)дъ к нимъ ясно реч(е):

24. А се заутра от нас поидеть Лазорь четверодневныи другъ х(ристо)въ.

25. Тъи от нас к нему донесеть вѣсть.

Copy "Z"

26. И се слышавъ Адам первозданныи чл(овѣ)къ, и нача
    бити руками по лицу своему, тѧжко въпиаше и
    гл(агол)ѧ:

27. Повѣдаи о мнѣ Вл(а)д(ы)цѣ Х(рист)у, свѣтлыи друже
    х(ристо)въ Лазоре.

28. А се ти въпиетъ твои первозданныи Адамъ.

29. На се ли мѧ еси Г(оспод)и создал на короткии[2]
    вѣкъ на земли сеи быти?

30. А се и мѧ осуди во адѣ многа лѣта быти и мучитисѧ?

31. Того ли ради наполнихъ землю?

32. О, Вл(а)д(ы)ко, а се н(ы)нѣ твои възлюбленнии вну-
    цы во тмѣ седѧтъ въ дне адовѣ мучимы от Сотоны.

33. Скорбию и тугою с(е)рдце тѣшат, и слезами своими
    очи и зѣницы омывают, и памѧти желающе велми
    уныли суть.

34. Се бо на земли сеи толко[3] в малъ часъ видѣхомъ
    добра, и се уже в муки сеи многа лѣта въ обидѣ
    есмѧ.

35. В малѣ[4] часъ аз ц(ѣса)рь быхъ всѣмъ тваремъ б(о)-
    жиимъ, а н(ы)нѣ многи дни рабъ быхъ Аду, а бѣсомъ
    его полонѧникъ есмъ.

36. В мало времѧ свѣтъ твои видѣхомъ.

37. А се уже с(о)лнца твоего не вижу пресвѣтлаго на
    многа лѣта, ни бурѧ вѣтрѧнѧа не слышу, Г(оспод)и.

Copy "U"

26. И се слышавъ Адамъ первозданныи чл(овѣ)къ, и нача
    бити рукама по лицю своему, тѧжко вопиа, гл(аго-
    ла)ше:

27. Повѣдаи о мнѣ Вл(а)д(ы)цѣ Х(рист)у, свѣтлыи друже
    х(ристо)въ Лазорю.

28. А се ти въпиеть твои первозданныи Адамъ.

29. На се ли мѧ еси Г(о)с(под)и создалъ на к(о)роткыи[5]
    вѣкъ на земли сеи быти?

30. А се и мѧ осуди въ адѣ многа лѣта быти и мучитися?

31. Того ли ради наполних землю?

32. О, Вл(а)д(ы)ко, а се н(ы)нѣ твои възлюблении внуци
    въ тмѣ седѧт, въ днѣ адовѣ мучимы от Сотоны.

33. Скорбию и тугою с(е)рдце тешат и слезами своими
    очи и зеница омывают, и памѧти желающе велми уны-
    ли сут.

34. Се бо на земли сеи толкы[6] в мал час видѣхомъ доб-
    ра, и се уже в тузе сеи многа лѣта въ обидѣ есмѧ.

35. Азъ в малъ час ц(ѣса)рь быхъ всем тварем б(о)ж-
    иим, а н(ы)нѣ въ многи дни рабъ бых Аду, а бесом
    его полонѧникъ.

36. В мало времѧ свѣт твои видѣх.

37. А се уже с(о)лнца твоег(о) пресвѣтлаго не вижю на
    многа лѣта, ни бурѧ вѣтрѧ ныѧ не слышю.

Copy "P"

26. И се услышавъ Адамъ первозданны чл(овѣ)къ, и нача
битисѧ рукама своима по лицу своему, тѧжко въпияше
и гл(агола)ше:

27. Повѣдаи от менѣ Вл(а)д(ы)це, свѣтлыи друж(е) х(ристо)въ Лазорю.

28. А се ти въпиеть твои первозданныи Адамъ.

29. На се ли мѧ еси Г(оспод)и създалъ на короткыи вѣкъ
на земли сеи быти?

30. А се и мѧ осуд(и) въ адѣ многа лѣта быти мучитисѧ?

31. Того ли рад(и) наполних земьлю?

32. О, Вл(а)д(ы)ко, а се н(ы)нѣ тво(и) възлюбленнии
внуци въ тмѣ седѧть въ дне адовѣ мучимы от Сотоны.

33. И скорбию и тугою с(е)рдце тешать и слезами своими
очи и зеница омывають, и памѧти желающе велми уныли суть.

34. Се бо на земли сеи только в малѣ час видихом добра,
и се уже в тузе сеи многа лѣта въ обиде есме.

35. Въ малъ час азъ ц(ѣса)рь быти[5] всѣмъ тваремъ б(о)-
жиимъ, а н(ы)нѣ въ многы дни рабъ бых Аду, а бесомъ
его полонѧникъ.

36. В мало времѧ свѣтъ твои видѣхъ.

37. А се уже с(о)лнца твое[6] пресвѣтлаго не вижю на многа лѣта, ни бурѧ вѣтренѧя не слышю, Г(оспод)и.

Copy "Z"

38. Аще, Г(оспод)и, азъ согрѣшихъ паче всѣхъ чл(овѣ)къ,
    то по дѣломъ моимъ въздалъ ми еси муку сию; не жа-
    луюсѧ , Г(оспод)и, но сего ради жал ми, Г(оспод)и,
    азъ бо по твоему образу сотворенъ есмъ.

39. А н(ы)нѣ Диаволъ ругает ми сѧ и мучит мѧ злѣ и
    нудѧ мѧ , Г(оспод)и.

40. Аз бо в породѣ живаѧ [5] твою б(о)ж(ест)венyю[6] запо-
    вѣдь преступихъ.

41. А се ти Г(оспод)и первыи патриархъ Авраамъ а твои
    другъ, иже тебе ради хотѧ[7] заклати с(ы)на свое(го)
    възлюбленнаго Исаака.

42. Ты же, Г(оспод)и, рекъ ему: тобою Аврааме бл(аго)-
    с(ло)вѧтсѧ всѧ колѣна земнаѧ .

43. То и тои, Г(оспод)и, что согрѣши?

44. И здѣ въ адѣ семь мучитсѧ и тѧжко въздыхаетъ и
    Ной праведныи иже избавленъ бы(с)тъ, Г(оспод)и, то-
    бою лютаго потопа.

45. То Ада ли, Г(оспод)и, не можеши избавити, то аще
    будетъ сей согрѣшилъ якоже азъ.

46. А се великии прор(о)къ Моисей.

47. А тои, Г(оспод)и, согрѣшилъ есть что; и тои здѣ се-
    дитъ с нами въ тмѣ адовѣ.

Copy "U"

38. Г(о)с(под)и, аще азъ согрѣших пач(е) всех чл(о-
вѣ)къ, то по дѣлом моим възда(лъ) ми еси муку сию;
не жалуюсѧ, Г(о)с(под)и, но сего ради жалость ми
Г(о)с(под)и, азъ по твоему образу створенъ есмь.

39. А н(ы)нѣ Дьѧволъ ругаеть ми сѧ, а по твоему образу
створена мучит мѧ злѣ, нудѧ мѧ, Г(о)с(под)и.

40. Азъ ж(е) в породѣ живѧа твою б(о)ж(е)ственую[7] за-
повед преступих.

41. А се ти Г(о)с(под)и первыи патриархъ Авраамъ а
твои друг, иже тебѣ ради хотѧ[8] заклати с(ы)на сво-
ег(о) Исака възлюблѣн(н)аг(о).

42. И ты реч(е) ему: тобою Авраамѣ бл(аго)с(ло)вѧтсѧ всѧ
колѣна земнаа.

43. То тъ что согрѣши?

44. Въ адѣ семь мучитсѧ[9] и тѧжко въздышет и Ной пра-
ведньи иже тобою Г(о)с(под)и избавленъ быс(тъ) от
лютаг(о) потопа.

45. И то Ада ли не можеши избавити, то аще будут сии
согрѣшили якож(е) и азъ.

46. А се великыи прор(о)къ Моисе.

47. А тъи Г(о)с(под)и, что согрѣшилъ ес(ть); то и тъ
ж(е) здѣ седить с нами въ тмѣ адовѣ.

82

38. Аще азъ съгрѣших, Г(оспод)и, паче всѣх чл(овѣ)къ,
    то по дѣломъ моимъ въздал ми еси муку сию; не жа-
    люусѧ, Г(оспод)и, но сего рад(и) жаль ми, Г(ос-
    под)и, азъ по твоему образу сътворенъ есмь.

39. А н(ы)нѣ Диаволъ ругаеть ми сѧ, а по твоему об-
    разу сътворена м мучить злѣ нудѧ мѧ, Г(оспод)и.

40. Азъ ж(е) в порѣдѣ[7] живѧ, а твою б(о)ж(е)ственую
    заповѣд преступих.

41. А се ти Г(оспод)и первыи патриархъ Аврамъ а твои
    другъ, иже тебѣ ради хотѧ заклати с(ы)на своег(о)
    Исака възвюбленаго.

42. И тъи рече ему, Г(оспод)и,: тобою Авраме бл(а)гос-
    ловѧтсѧ всѧ колѣна земьная.

43. То тъи что съгрѣши?

44. А тои зде въ адѣ семь мучитсѧ и тѧжко въздышеть;
    и Нои правѣдны(и) иж(е) избавленъ быс(ть) тобою,
    Г(оспод)и, от лютаго потопа.

45. Ада ли не можеши избавити, то аще будут сии съгрѣ-
    шили яко и азъ.

46. А се великыи пророкъ Моисеи.

47. А то, Г(оспод)и, что съгрѣшилъ есть, то и тъи здѣ
    ж(е) седить с нами въ тмѣ адовѣ.

Copy "Z"

60. А Д(а)в(ы)да, Г(оспод)и, прославилъ еси на земли и
даль еси ему ц(ѣ)с(а)рствовати надо многими.

61. А той составилъ псалтырь и гусли.

62. То что Г(оспод)и тои согрѣшилъ?

63. И здѣ и во адѣ мучитса, часто стона, въздыхаетъ:

64. Аще ли будетъ такоже согрѣшилъ яко и азъ.

65. А се великии во прор(о)цѣхъ Иоан предотеча и кр(е)-
стит(е)ль г(оспода)нь, иже родиса от бл(а)говѣщениа
архагг(е)ла Гаврила.

66. В пустыни въспитаса о(т) уности ядыи медъ дивии.

67. И тои от Ирода поруганъ бысть.

68. Но что Г(оспод)и тои согрѣшилъ есть?

69. А здѣ и тои с нами мучитса въ адѣ семъ.

70. Но сего желаютъ пророцы твои.

71. Илья бо Иенохъ угодиша тебѣ паче всѣхъ праведникъ
на земли.

72. То грѣх ли ради Г(оспод)и нашихъ не хощеши помиловати насъ, или своего времени ждеши, или самъ
хощеши к намъ снити, ты свѣдыи единъ.

74. Но мы чл(овѣ)цы есми тощави,[8] а ты еси долготер-
пѣливъ.

75. Но прииди по нас вскорѣ и избави ада и свяжи
Г(оспод)и Диавола и да тя увѣдатъ Б(о)га истин-
наго буя выя жидовѣ.

84

Copy "U"

60. А Д(а)в(ы)да, Г(о)с(под)и, прославил еси на земли
    и дал еси ему ц(ѣса)рствовати надо многими.

61. А тъ составил пс(а)лт(ы)рь[10] и гусли.

62. То что тъ Г(о)с(под)и съгрѣшил?

63. А тои с нами здѣ въ адѣ сем мучитсѧ , часто стонѧ ,
    въпиаше:

64. Аще ли будет також(е) съгрѣшил яко и азъ.

65. А се великы(и) въ прор(о)цѣ[11] Иоан(нъ) прѣдътечь[12]
    кр(е)ст(ите)ль г(о)с(поде)нь, иже родитсѧ от
    бл(аговѣ)щ(е)ниѧ архагг(е)ла Гаврила.

66. В пустыни въспитасѧ от уности ядыи мед дивыи.

67. И то[13] от Ирода поруганъ быс(ть).

68. Но что тъ Г(о)с(под)и согрѣшилъ ес(ть)?

69. А здѣ с нами въ адѣ семь мучитсѧ.[14]

70. Но и сего желають прор(о)ци твои.

71. Ильѧ и Енохъ угод(и)ша тобѣ пач(е) всѣхъ праведникъ
    на земли.

72. То грѣх ли рад(и)[15] наших не хощеши помиловати
    нас, или своег(о) времени жидеши, или самъ хощеши
    к нам снити. но сам веси един.

74. Но мы чл(овѣ)ци есмѧ тощливы,[16] а ты Г(о)с(под)и
    долготрьпеливъ.

75. Но прииди по нас воскорѣ и избави ада и свѧжи
    Диавола и да тѧ уведѧт буѧвии жидовѣ.

Copy "P"

60. А Д(а)в(ы)да, Г(оспод)и, прославилъ еси на земли и
далъ еси ему ц(ѣ)с(арс)твовати надо многыми.

61. А тои съставилъ пс(а)лт(ы)рь и гусли.

62. То что тои Г(оспод)и съгрѣшилъ?

63. А и то(и) здѣ же с нами въ адѣ семь мучитьс(А),
часто стонА, въздышеть:

64. Аще ли будуть також(е) съгрѣшили якож(е) и азъ.

65. А се великыи въ прор(о)цѣх Иоан пр(ѣ)дт(е)чА кр(е)-
ст(ите)ль г(о)с(поде)нь, иже родисА от бл(а)говѣ-
щениа агг(е)л(о)ва гаврилова.

66. В пустыни въспитас(А) от уности ядыи мед дивии.

67. И тои от Ирода поруганъ быс(ть).

68. Но что тои Г(оспод)и съгрѣшилъ ес(ть)?

69. А здѣ с нами въ адѣ семъ мучимъ есть.

70. Но и сего желають пророци твои.

71. Илья и Енох угодиша тобѣ паче всѣх праведникъ на
земли.

72. То грѣх ли рад(и) наших не хощеши помиловати нас,
или своего времени жидеши, ли[8] самъ хощеши[9] свѣси
единъ.

74. Но мы чл(о)в(ѣ)ци есме тощливи, а ты еси, Г(оспод)и, долъготръпѣливъ.

75. Но прииди по нас въскоре и избави ада и свАжи Диавола и да тА увѣдАть буАвии жидове.

86

Copy "Z"

76. А мы вси чл(овѣ)цы бл(а)говѣрнии покланѧ емсѧ тобѣ
    Х(рист)е, имени твоему с(вя)тому, славѧ ще с(вя)-
    тую Тро(и)цу, Отца и С(ы)на и С(вя)т(о)го Духа.

Copy "U"

76. А мы вси чл(овѣ)ци бл(а)говѣрнии поклонимсѧ тебѣ

   Х(рист)е, имени твоем(у) с(вя)т(о)му, славѧще

   с(вя)тую Тро(и)цю,[17] Отца и С(ы)на и С(вя)т(о)го

   Д(у)ха, н(ы)нѣ и пр(и)сно.

Copy "P"

76. А мы вси чл(овѣ)ци благовѣрнии полонимъс(ѧ)[10]
    тобѣ, Х(рист)е, имени твоему с(вя)тому, славѧще
    с(вя)тую Тро(и)цу, О(т)ца, и С(ына).

NOTES

Copy "V"

1. sic - dittography.
2. two letters crossed out after ste-.
3. two letters crossed out after ja-.
4. for struny.
5. sic.
6. for Bogom".
7. for blagopriatno.
8. sic.
9. for nyně?
10. for a, but apparently corrected.
11. sic, for nyně?
12. sic.
13. note lacking vocatives.
14. sic, for Isaakom".
15. sic, for iz.
16. sic.
17. sic.
18. ?
19. sic.
20. copy reads vidimě.

Copy "Z2"

1. sic.
2. sic.
3. sic.
4. sic, for učenikom".
5. sic.
6. sic.

Copy "V"

21. copy reads svĕtazarnag$_o$.

22. copy reads podosta.

23. sic.

24. for proroci.

25. copy reads potriarx".

26. copy reads Isakam".

27. sic, for Samuil".

28. sic, for Raguel"?

29. copy reads Nafonail".

30. sic.

31. sic.

32. kto written in the margin of the ms.

Copy "Z"	Copy "U"
1. sic.	1. in copy <u>perty</u>.
2. <u>po</u> written very small above the line, possibly by a later scribe.	2. sic.
	3. sic.
	4. sic.
3. sic.	5. copy reads <u>krotkyi</u>.
4. sic.	6. sic.
5. <u>živyi</u> written in the left margin.	7. sic.
	8. for <u>xotě</u>?
6. sic.	9. copy reads <u>mučitsě</u>.
7. for <u>xotě</u>?	10. in the copy <u>p</u>... is written.
8. for <u>toščivy</u>?	11. sic.
	12. sic.
	13. or <u>toi</u>; the super-script is difficult to read.
	14. the copy reads <u>mučie</u>.
	15. the copy perhaps reads <u>ra^{di}</u>.
	16. for <u>toščivy</u>?
	17. the copy may also read <u>tr^oju</u>.

Copy "P"

1. the notes are my own, as are the punctuation and
   capitalization; the original manuscript has not
   been examined, the text being that of Pypin's
   edition from Kušelev-Bezborodko, G. (ed.), _Pamjat-_
   niki starinnoj russkoj literatury, vol. 3 (St.
   Petersburg, 1862), pp. 11-12.

2. sic.

3. an additional _n_ is printed under the tittle in
   Pypin's edition.

4. sic.

5. sic.

6. sic.

7. sic.

8. for _ili_?

9. clause apparently incomplete.

10. sic, as printed by Pypin.

IX

GLOSSARY

The glossary here compiled is a full listing of all
the words found in the copies. Each entry designates
the part of speech, grammatical form, location of the
word as well as the diacritics employed in conjunction
with that word. Nouns with endings in -_"_, -_'_, and -_i_
are assumed to be masculine, unless otherwise designa-
ted. Nouns with endings in -_a_ and -_ja_ are feminine,
while nouns in -_o_, -_e_, and -_mja_ are neuter. The alpha-
betic order adhered to is that of the Cyrillic alpha-
bet. The superscript numbers denote the time that the
entry occurs in a given line; if no superscript number
is given, then it is to be assumed that the entry
occurs either only once or for the first time in that
line.

The chief sources in the compilation of this glossary have been historical dictionaries and to a lesser
extent etymological dictionaries and lexical monographs.
The main sources have been Berneker, E., Slavisches
etymologisches Wörterbuch, 2 vols. (incompl.) (Heidelberg, 1924), 2nd ed.; Kurz, J., (ed.), Slovník jazyka

94

staroslověnského (Prague, 1959-   ); Miklosich, F.,

Lexicon palaeoslovenico-graeco-latinum (Vienna, 1862-

65); Sadnik, L. and Aitzetmüller, R., Handwörterbuch

zu den altkirchenslavischen Texten, SPR, 6 (Hague,

1955); Sreznevskij, I., Materialy dlja slovarja drevne-

russkogo jazyka, 3 vols., 1 suppl. (St. Petersburg,

1893-1909, 1912, reprint, Moscow-Leningrad, 1959);

Vasmer, M., Russisches etymologisches Wörterbuch,

3 vols. (Heidelberg, 1950-59).

A

a̲ - but, and (conj.) - V4 (a), V5 (a), V6,7 (a), V15,12

(â), V15,12^2 (á), V22 (â), V22^2 (â), V29,30 (a), V41

(a), V41^2 (a), V46 (ǎ), V47 (ǎ), V48 (â), V49 (á), V51

(a), V52 (ǎ), V53a (a), V56 (a), V97 (a), V105 (ǎ),

V107 (a); Z2-4 (ǎ), Z2-15,12 (a), Z2-24 (ǎ), Z2-41 (a),

Z2-46 (ǎ), Z2-48 (ǎ), Z2-51 (ǎ), Z2-52,53 (ǎ), Z2-56

(ǎ), Z2-71 (ǎ), Z2-74 (ǎ), Z2-97 (ǎ); Z6 (ǎ), Z7 (ǎ),

Z9 (ǎ), Z11 (ǎ), Z12 (ǎ), Z13 (ǎ), Z16 (ǎ), Z20 (ǎ),

Z21 (ǎ), Z22 (ǎ), Z22^2 (ǎ), Z24 (ǎ), Z28 (ǎ), Z30 (ǎ),

Z32 (ǎ), Z35 (ǎ), Z35^2 (ǎ), Z37 (ǎ), Z39 (ǎ), Z40 (ǎ),

Z41 (ǎ), Z46 (ǎ), Z47 (ǎ), Z60 (ǎ), Z61 (ǎ), Z65 (ǎ),

Z69 (ǎ), Z74 (ǎ), Z76 (ǎ); U6 (ǎ), U7 (â), U9 (ǎ), U9^2

(ǎ), U10 (a), U11 (ǎ), U12 (ǎ), U13 (ǎ), U20 (ǎ), U21

(â), U22 (â), U22^2 (â), U24 (â), U28 (ǎ), U30 (â), U32

(â), U35 (â), U35^2 (â), U37 (â), U39 (â), U39^2 (â),

U41 (â), U41^2 (a), U46 (â), U47 (a̓), U60 (a̓), U61 (a̓),

U63 (â), U65 (â), U68 (â), U74 (â), U76 (â); P6 (a̓), P7

(a̓), P9 (a̓), P9^2 (a̓), P10 (a̓), P11 (a̓), P12 (a̓), P13

(a̓), P16 (a̓), P20 (a̓), P21 (a̓), P22 (a̔), P22^2 (a̓), P22^3

(a̓), P24 (a̓), P28 (a̓), P30 (a̓), P32 (a̓), P35 (a̓), P35^2

(a̓), P37 (a̓), P39 (a̓), P39^2 (a̓), P40 (a̓), P41 (a̔), P41^2

(a̓), P44 (a̓), P46 (a̓), P47 (a̓), P60 (a̓), P61 (a̓), P63

(a̓), P65 (a̓), P69 (a̓), P74 (a̓), P76 (a̓).

abie - right away, immediately (adv.) - Z2-92 (abie).

Avvakum" - Habbakuk, Avvakum (pr. noun) - V23a (Avvakum") n.

Avraam" - Abraham (pr. noun) - V23a (Avraáme) v., V41

(Avram") n., V42a (Avráâma) g., V43 (Avraâm") n., V95

(Avraam") n.; Z2-41 (Avráâm") n.; Z42 (Avraáme) v.;

U41 (Avraâm") n., U42 (Avraâmě) v.; P41 (Avrám") n.,

P42 (Avrame) v.

Adam" - Adam (pr. noun) - V23a (Adam") n., V26 (Adam")

n., V39,40 (Adam") n., V86 (Adama) a., V95 (Adam") n.,

V105 (Adamǘ) d.; Z2-26 (Adám") n., Z2-86 (Adáma) a.,

Z2-95 (Adam") n., Z2-98 (Adáma), a., Z2-105 (Adamu), d.;

Z title (Adáma) g., Z17 (Adám) n., Z26 (Adam) n., Z28

(Adam") n.; U title (Adama) g., U17 (Adam) n., U26

(Adam") n., U28 (Adam") n.; P title (Adama) g., P17

(Adam) n., P26 (Adam") n., P28 (Adam") n.

adov" - of Hell, of Hades (poss. adj.) - Z9 (ádova) ntr. a. pl., Z32 (ádově) ntr. p. sg., Z47 (ádově) f. p. sg.; U9 (ádova) ntr. a. pl., U32 (ãdově) ntr. p. sg., U47 (adově) m. p. sg.; P9 (ádova) ntr. a. pl., P32 (ádově) ntr. p. sg., P47 (ádově) f. p. sg.

ad" - Hell, Hades (pr. noun) - V6,7 (ãdě) p., V20 (Adu) d., V23a (adu) p., V29,30 (adě) p., V39,40 (Ad") n., V41 (adě) p., V49 (adě) p., V52 (adě) p., V77 (adě) p., V86 (Ãd") n., V94 (ãdu) g., V95 (ãdu) p., V96 (ãdu) g., V97 (adu) p., V98 (Ada) a., V100 (Ãd") n.; Z2-6,7 (adě) p., Z2-20 (Adu) d., Z2-21 (ada) g., Z2-39 (Ad") n., Z2-41 (adě) p., Z2-47 (adě) p., Z2-49 (adě) p., Z2-52,53 (adě) p., Z2-59 (adě) p., Z2-71a (adě) p., Z2-71a^2 (adě) p., Z2-75 (ada) g., Z2-86 (Ad") n., Z2-94 (ada) g., Z2-95 (adě) p., Z2-96 (ada) g., Z2-97 (adě) p.; Z title (adě) p., Z7 (adě) p., Z17 (adě) p., Z20 (Adovi) d., Z30 (adě) p., Z35 (Adu) d., Z45 (Ada) g., Z63 (adě) p., Z69 (adě) p., Z75 (Ada) g.; U title (Adě) p., U7 (adě) p., U20 (Adovi) d., U30 (adě) p., U35 (Adu) d., U44 (ãdě) p., U45 (Ãda) g., U63 (adě) p., U69 (ãdě) p., U75 (Ãda) g.; P title (adě) p., P7 (ade) p., P17 (ade) p., P20 (Ãdovi) d., P30 (adě) p., P35 (Adu) d., P44 (ãdě) p., P45 (Ada) g., P63 (adě) p., P69 (ãdě) p., P75 (Ãda) g.

az" - I (pronoun) - V3 (mene) g., V3^2 (mene) g., V5 (az") n., V27 (mja) a., V38 (mně) d., V38 (az") n., V38 (mi) d., V39,40 (az") n., V86 (mi) d.; Z2-3 (mene) g.,

Z2-3 (mja) a., Z2-5 (áz") n., Z2-27 (menè) g., Z2-29
(mjà) a., Z2-38 (az") n., Z2-38 (mi) d., Z2-40 (áz")
n., Z2-40 (mi) d., Z2-43 (áz") n., Z2-47 (áz") n.,
Z2-50 (áz") n., Z2-86 (mi) d.; Z2-91 (mjà) a.; Z27
(mnĕ) p., Z29 (mjà) a., Z30 (mjà) a., Z35 (az) n., Z38
(áz") n., Z38 (mi) d., Z38^2 (mi) d., Z38^2 (áz") n.,
Z39 (mi) d., Z39 (mja) a., Z39^2 (mja) a., Z40 (áz")
n., Z45 (áz") n., Z64 (áz") n.; U27 (mnĕ) p., U29 (mja)
a., U30 (mja) a., U35 (âz") n., U38 (āz") n., U38 (mi)
d., U38^2 (mi) d., U38^2 (âz") n., U39 (mi) d., U39 (mja)
a., U39^2 (mja) a., U40 (áz") n., U45 (áz") n., U64 (âz")
n.; P27 (menĕ) g., P29 (mja) a., P30 (mja) a., P35 (âz")
n.; P38 (áz") n., P38 (mi) d., P38^2 (mi) d., P38^2
(áz") n., P39 (mi) d., P39 (mja) a., P39^2 (mja) a., P40
(áz") n., P45 (áz") n.

angelov" - of the (an) angel (poss. adj.) - P65 (aǵglva)
ntr. g. sg.

angel" - angel (noun) - V98 (angĺi) n. pl., V101 (angĺi)
n. pl.

apostol" - apostle (noun) - V106 (apĺom") d. pl.;
Z title (apĺ") g. pl.; U title (ap^{s}l") g. pl.; P title
(apĺ") g. pl.

Aron" - Aaron (pr. noun) - V23a (Áron") n.

arxangel" - archangel (noun) - Z65 (árxaǵgla) g. sg.;
U65 (árxáǵgla) g. sg.

ašče - if, whether (conj.) - V39,40 (ašče), V57 (ašče),
V83 (ašče), V97 (ašče); Z2-40 (ašče), Z2-79 (ašče),
Z2-83 (ašče), Z2-83[2] (ašče), Z2-91 (ašče), Z2-97 (ašče);
Z38 (ašče), Z45 (ašče), Z64 (ašče); U38 (ašče), U45
(ašče), U64 (ašče); P38 (ašče), P45 (ašče), P64 (ašče).

B

bezum'n" - mad, senseless (adj.) - V16 (bezumnyi) m. n.
sg. lg.; Z2-16 (bezumnyi) m. n. sg. lg.; U16 (bezumny)
m. n. sg. lg.; Z16 (bezumnyi) m. n. sg. lg.; P16 (bezumnyi) m. n. sg. lg.

bes"m'rt'n" - deathless, immortal (adj.) - Z2-14 (bes-
mertnyi) m. n. sg. lg.

biti - to beat, strike (vb.)impf Z2-26 (bijušči) pr. act.
pt., f. n. sg.!; Z26 (biti) inf.; U26 (biti) inf.

biti sja - to beat, strike(vb.)impf. P26 (bitisja) inf.

blagověr'n" - faithful,pious-Z76(blgověrnii)m.n.lg.,U76
(blgověrnii) m. n. pl. lg.; P76 (blagověrnii) m. n.
pl. lg.

blagověščenie - annunciation (noun) - Z65 (blgověščenia)
g. sg.; U65 (blščnija) g. sg.; P65 (blgověščenia) g.
sg.

blagodar'n" - thankful, grateful (adj.) - Z2-73 (blgo-
darnago) m. g. sg. lg.

blagodat'n" - beneficial, blissful, having grace (adj.)
- V73 (blg[d]tnago) m. g. sg. lg.

blagoprijat'n" - favorable, propitious, auspicious
(adj.) - V8 (blg̑opriátna) ntr. n. sg.; Z2-8 (blǵo-
priátno) ntr. n. sg.

blagosloviti - to bless (vb.), pf. - V title (blg̑v̑i)
2 sg. impv.; Z title (blv̑i) 2 sg. impv.; U title (blv̑i)
2 sg. impv.

blagosloviti sja - to be blessed (vb.), pf. - Z42
(blv̑jatsja) 3 pl. pr.; U42 (blv̑jatsja) 3 pl. pr.; P42
(blǵoslovjatsja) 3 pl. pr.

bo - for (conj.) - V8 (bo), S10 (bo), V15,12 (bo), V22
(bo), V38 (bo), V38^2 (bo), V73 (bo), V86 (bo), V101 (bo),
Z2-8 (bo), Z2-10 (bo), Z2-38 (bo), Z2-73 (bo), Z2-90 (bo);
Z8 (bo), Z9 (bo), Z12 (bo), Z13 (bo), Z34 (bó), Z38
(bo), Z39 (bo), Z71 (bo); U8 (bo), U9 (bo), U12 (bo),
U34 (bo); P7 (bo), P9 (bo), P12 (bo), P13 (bo), P34
(bo).

Bog" - God (noun) - V6,7 (B̑gam") i. sg., V57 (B̑") n.;
Z75 (Bga) a.

božii - God's (poss. adj.) - Z2 title (bži̇a) m. g. sg.,
Z2-24 (bži̇i) m. n. sg., Z2-91 (bži̇ju) f. a. sg.; Z35
(bži̇im") f. d. pl. lg.; U35 (bži̇i^m) f. d. pl. lg.; P35
(bži̇im") f. d. pl. lg.

bož'stv'n" - divine (adj.) - Z40 (bž̑tvenuju) f. a. sg.
lg.; U40 (bž̑ᵗvenuju) f. a. sg. lg.; P40 (bž̑ᵗvenuju) f.
a. sg. lg.

bran' - f., battle (noun) - V101 (branĕx") p. pl.

100

brat" - brother (noun) - V83 (brat") n. sg., V85 (brat")
n. sg.; Z2 title (bráta) g. sg., Z2-83 (brát") n. sg.,
Z2-83^2 (brát") n. sg.

burja - storm (noun) - Z37 (búrja) g. sg.; U37 (burja)
g. sg.; P37 (burja) g. sg.

bujav" - foolish, stupid (adj.) - Z75 (bujávyja) m. a.
pl. lg.¡; U75 (bujávii) m. n. pl. lg.; P75 (bujávii) m.
n. pl. lg.

byst' - see byti

byti - to be (vb.), impf. - V15,12 (sut') 3 pl. pr.,
V29,30 (ĕsi) 2 sg. pr., V29,30 (byti) inf., V57 (budet')
3 sg. fut., V73 (e^{s}my) 1 pl. pres., V83 (by) 2 sg. pf.
aor., V83 (byl") res. pt. m. sg., V83^2 (by) 3 sg. pf.
aor., V86 (ĕst') 3 sg. pr., V86 (e^{s}m') 1 sg. pr., V97
(by) 3 sg. pf. aor., V97 (byx") 1 sg. pf. aor., V100
(byti) inf., V101 (e^{s}t') 3 sg. pr., V102 (bĕx") 1 sg.
impf. aor.; Z2-29 (ĕsi) 2 sg. pr., Z2-38 (ĕsm') 1 sg.
pr., Z2-40 (ĕsi) 2 sg. pr., Z2-51 (býst') 3 sg. pf.
aor., Z2-73 (ĕsmjà) 1 pl. pr., Z2-83 (by) 3 sg. pf.
aor., Z2-83 (býl") res. pt. m. sg., Z2-83^2 (by) 3 sg.
pf. aor., Z2-86 (ĕst') 3 sg. pr., Z2-86 (ĕsmi) 1 pl.
pr., Z2-90 (ĕst') 3 sg. pr., Z2-97 (by) 3 sg. pf. aor.;
Z11 (ĕsi) 1 pl. pr., Z12 (ĕst') 3 sg. pr., Z15 (ĕsi)
2 sg. pr., Z17 (suščim") pr. act. pt. m. d. pl. lg.,
Z29 (ĕsi) 2 sg. pr., Z29 (býti) inf., Z30 (býti) inf.,
Z33 (sút') 3 pl. pr., Z34 (ĕsmjà) 1 pl. pr., Z35 (býx")

1 sg. pf. aor., Z35^2 (byx") 1 sg. pf. aor., Z35 (ẻsm")
1 pl. pr., Z38 (ẻsi) 2 sg. pr., Z38 (ẻsm") 1 pl. pr.,
Z44 (bŷt') 3 sg. pf. aor., Z45 (budet") 3 sg. fut., Z47
(ẻst') 3 sg. pr., Z60 (ẻsi) 2 sg. pr., Z60^2 (ẻsi) 2 sg.
pr., Z64 (búdet") 3 sg. fut., Z67 (býst') 3 sg. pf.
aor., Z68 (ẻst') 3 sg. pr., Z74 (ẻsmi) 1 pl. pr., Z74
(ẻsi) 2 sg. pr.; U11 (ẻsmja) 1 pl. pr., U12 (ê̂) 3 sg.
pr., U15 (êsi) 2 sg. pr., U17 (suš̆čim") pr. act. pt.,
m. d. pl. lg., U29 (êsi) 2 sg. pr., U29 (byti) inf.,
U30 (byti) inf., U33 (sủᵗ) 3 pl. pr., U34 (ẻsmja) 1 pl.
pr., U35 (byx") 1 sg. pf. aor., U35^2 (bỷˣ) 1 sg. pf.
aor., U38 (êsi) 2 sg. pr., U38 (êsm') 1 pl. pr., U44
(bỷ̂) 3 sg. pf. aor., U45 (budủᵗ) 3 pl. fut., U47 (ê̂)
3 sg. pr., U60 (êsi) 2 sg. pr., U60^2 (ẻsi) 2 sg. pr.,
U64 (budẻᵗ) 3 sg. fut., U67 (bỷ̂) 3 sg. pf. aor., U68
(ê̂) 3 sg. pr., U74 (ẻsmja) 1 pl. pr.; P11 (ẻsmi) 1 pl.
pr., P12 (ẻst') 3 sg. pr., P15 (ẻsi) 2 sg. pr., P17
(suš̆čim") pr. act. pt., m. d. pl. lg., P29 (êsi) 2 sg.
pr., P29 (byti), inf., P30 (byti) inf., P33 (sut')
3 pl. pr., P34 (ẻsme) 1 pl. pr., P35 (byti) inf.!,
P35 (byˣ) 1 sg. pf. aor., P38 (ẻsi) 2 sg. pr., P38
(ẻsm") 1 sg. pr.!, P44 (bỷ̂) 3 sg. pf. aor., P45
(budủᵗ) 3 pl. fut., P47 (ẻst') 3 sg. pr., P60 (ẻsi)
2 sg. pr., P60^2 (ẻsi) 2 sg. pr., P64 (budut') 3 pl.
fut., P67 (bỷ̂) 3 sg. pf. aor., P68 (ê̂) 3 sg. pr., P69
(ẻst') 3 sg. pr., P74 (ẻsme) 1 pl. pr., P74 (ẻsi) 2 sg. pr.

byx" - see byti

běs" - demon, devil (noun) - Z35 (bě́som") d. pl.; U35
(běso͞m) d. pl.; P35 (besom") d. pl.

běx" - see byti

va - you (two) (pro.) - V83 (vaju) g.

Vavilon" - Babylon (pr. noun) - V51 (Vaviloně) p.; Z2-51
(Vavilo͡ně) p.

vaš' - your, 2 pl. (poss. adj.) - Z2-83 (vaš") n.

velik" - great (adj.) - V51 (velikyï) m. n. sg. lg.,
V102 (velikyï) m. n. sg. lg.; Z2-51 (velíkii) m. n. sg.
lg.; Z14 (velíkii) m. n. sg. lg., Z46 (velíkii) m. n.
sg. lg., Z65 (velíkii) m. n. sg., lg.; U14 (velikyi) m.
n. sg. lg., U46 (velikyi) m. n. sg. lg., U65 (velikỳ) m.
n. sg.!; P14 (velikyi) m. n. sg. lg., P46 (velikyi) m.
n. sg. lg., P65 (velikyi) m. n. sg. lg.

vel'mi - very, quite (adv.) - Z23 (velmi); Z33 (velmi);
U33 (velmi); P33 (velmi).

veréja - bolt (noun) - V22 (vereja) n. sg., V103 (vereja) n. pl., V104 (vereja) n. pl.; Z22 (vereja) n. sg.;
U22 (věréja) n. pl.; P22 (verea) for n. pl.

vesel" - gay, merry (adj.) - V6,7 (vesel'ja) for f. a.
pl. lg.; Z2-6,7 (vesely) f. a. pl.; Z8 (véselo) ntr. n.
sg., U8 (veselo) ntr. n. sg.; P8 (veselo) ntr. n. sg.

viděti - to see (vb.), impf. - V73 (vidim") 1 pl. pr.;
Z2-73 (vidim") 1 pl. pr.; Z34 (viděxom") 1 pl. aor.,

Z37 (vižu) 1 sg. pr.; U34 (viděxo^m) 1 pl. aor., U36

(viděˣ) 1 sg. aor., U37 (vižju) 1 sg. pr.; P34 (vidixo^m)

1 pl. aor., P36 (viděx") 1 sg. aor., P37 (vižju) 1 sg.

pr.

Vifanija, Vitanija - Bethany (pr. noun) - V81 (Vifani-

ju) a.; Z2-80 (Vifaniju) a., Z2-81 (Vifániju) a.

Vladyka - Lord, Ruler (noun) - V21 (vlče) d., V22a

(vlče) d., V24 (vlce) d., V25 (vlce) d., V27 (vlce) d.;

Z2-21 (vlce) d., Z2-27 (vlce) d., Z2-74 (vlko) v.;

Z19 (vlce) d., Z27 (vlce) d., Z32 (vlko) v.; U19 (vlce)

d., U27 (vlce) d., U32 (vlko) v.; P19 (vlce) d., P27

(vl^{d}ce) d., P32 (vl^{d}ko) v.

vlas" - hair (noun) - Z2-82 (vlasy) i. pl.

voin" - warrior, host (noun) - Z2-98 (voi) g. pl.

vol" - ox (noun) - V4 (vol") n. sg.

volja - will (noun) - V97 (voleju) i. sg.

vrata - ntr. pl., gate(s) (noun) - V22 (vrata) n., V41

(vratex") p., V99 (vrata) a., V103 (vrata) n., V104

(vrata) a.; Z9 (vrata) a., Z22 (vrata) n.; U9 (vra)

a., U22 (vra^{ta}) n.; P9 (vrata) a., P22 (vrata) n.

vrěmja - time (noun) - V8 (vremja) n. sg.; Z2-8 (vré-

mja) n. sg., Z2-71a (vremena) a. pl.; Z8 (vrémja) n.

sg., Z36 (vremja) a. sg., Z72 (vremeni) g. sg.!; U8

(vrémja) n. sg., U36 (vremja) a. sg., U72 (vremeni)

g. sg.!; P7 (vremja) n. sg., P36 (vremja) a. sg.,

P72 (vremeni) g. sg.!

<u>v"</u> - to, in (prep.), + a. or p. - V6,7 (v") + p., V15,12
(v") + p., V22 (v) + p., V23a (vo) + p., V26 (v) + a.,
V29,30 (v") + p., V38 (v) + p., V41 (v") + p., V41^2
(v") + p., V46 (v) + p., V48 (v") + a., V49 (vo) + p.,
V51 (v) + p., V51^2 (v) + a., V52 (v") + p., V56 (v") +
p., V57 (vo) + a., V58 (v) + a., V77 (v") + p., V81 (v)
+ a., V95 (v") + p., V97 (v") + p., V101 (v") + p.,
V102 (v") + p., V106 (vo) + a.; Z2 title (v) + a., Z2-4
(vo) + p., Z2-6,7 (v") + p., Z2-15,12 (v") + p., Z2-26
(v) + a., Z2-29 (vo) + p., Z2-38 (v) + p., Z2-41 (v) +
p., Z2-41^2 (v̓) + p., Z2-46 (v) + p., Z2-47 (v") + p.,
Z2-48 (vo) + a., Z2-49 (v") + p., Z2-51 (v) + p., Z2-51
(vo) + a., Z2-51^2 (v) + a., Z2-52,53 (vo) + p., Z2-56
(v") + p., Z2-59 (v") + p., Z2-71a (v") + p., Z2-71a^2
(v") + p., Z2-80 (vo) + a., Z2-81 (v) + a., Z2-84 (v) +
a., Z2-86 (v) + a., Z2-91 (v) + a., Z2-95 (v") + p.,
Z2-97 (vo) + p., Z2-105 (v) + a.; Z title (v") + p.,
Z7 (v) + a., Z9 (v̓) + a., Z13 (v) + a., Z15 (v) + p.,
Z17 (v") + p., Z30 (vo) + p., Z32 (vo) + p., Z32 (v")
+ p., Z34 (v) + a., Z34^2 (v) + p., Z34 (v") + p., Z35
(v̓) + a., Z36 (v̓) + a., Z40 (v) + p., Z47 (v") + p.,
Z63 (vo) + p., Z65 (vo) + p., Z66 (v) + p., Z69 (v")+
p.; U title (v") + p., U7 (v) + a., U7^2 (v) + p., U9
(v) + a., U13 (v) + a., U15 (v) + p., U17 (v") + p.,
U30 (v") + p., U32 (v") + p., U32^2 (v") + p., U34 (v) +

a., U34^2 (v) + p., U34 (v") + p., U35 (v) + a., U35

(v") + a., U36 (v) + a., U40 (v) + p., U44 (v") + p.,

U47 (v") + p., U63 (v") + p., U65 (v") + p., U66 (v)

+ p., U69 (v") + p.; P title (vo) + p., P7 (v́) + a.,

P7^2 (v̀) + p., P9 (v̀) + a., P13 (v̀) + a., P15 (v) + p.,

P17 (v") + p., P30 (v") + p., P32 (v") + p., P32^2 (v")

+ p., P34 (v́) + a., P34^2 (v̀) + p., P34 (v") + p., P35

(v") + a., P35^2 (v") + a., P36 (v̀) + a., P40 (v̀) + p.,

P44 (v") + p., P47 (v") + p., P63 (v") + p., P65 (v")

+ p., P66 (v̀) + p., P69 (v") + p.

v"vrěšči - to throw in (vb.), pf. - V51 (vverž̇en") past

pass. pt., m. n. sg.; Z2-51 (vvérž̇en") past pass. pt.,

m. n. sg.

v"zbiti sja - to beat upon (vb.), pf. - V26 (vozbisja)

3 sg. aor.

v"zvesti - to lead up (vb.), pf. - Z2-105 (v"zvede)

3 sg. aor.

v"zdati - to give up (vb.), pf. - Z2-40 (v"zdal") res.

pt., m. sg.; Z38 (v"zdál") res. pt., m. sg.; U38

(v"z^{d}a) for res. pt., m. sg.; P38 (v"z^{d}al̀) res. pt.,

m. sg.

v"zdvignuti - to lift, raise up (vb.), pf. - Z2-80

(v"zdvígnuti) inf.

v"zdyxanie - sigh (noun) - Z2-75 (v"zdyxánie) a. sg.

v"zdyxati - to sigh (vb.), impf. - Z44 (v"zdyxáet')

3 sg. pr., Z63 (v"zdyxaet") 3 sg. pr.; U44 (v"zdyše^t)

3 sg. pr.; P44 (v"zdyšet') 3 sg. pr., P63 (v"zdyšet')

3 sg. pr.

v"zlo**ž**iti - to lay upon, put upon (vb.), pf. - Z7
(v"zlo**ž**i) 3 sg. aor.; U7 (v"zlo**ž**im") 1 pl. pr./fut.;
P7 (v"zlo**ž**i) 3 sg. aor.

v"zljublen" - beloved (adj.) - V97 (vozljublenago) m.
g. sg. lg.; Z2-97 (v"zljublennago) m. g. sg. lg.; Z32
(v"zljublennii) m. n. pl. lg., Z41 (v"zljublennago) m.
a. sg. lg.; U32 (v"zljublenii) m. n. pl. lg., U41 (v"z-
ljublena) m. a. sg. lg.; P32 (v"zljublennii) m. n. pl.
lg., P41 (v"zljublenago) m. a. sg. lg.

v"zmetati - to throw up, lift up (vb.), pf. - V99 (v"z-
měte) for 2 pl. impv.

v"znesti - to carry up, raise up (vb.), pf. - V2 (v"z-
nesox") 1 sg. aor., V48 (v"znes") past act. pt., m. n.
sg., V107 (v"znese) 3 sg. aor.; Z2-2 (v"znesox") 1 sg.
aor., Z2-48 (v"znesén") past pass. pt., m. n. sg.

v"znesti sja - to be carried up, raised up, to rise
(vb.) pf. - V58 (v"znesostasja) 3 du. aor.!

v"z'rěti - to look up (vb.), pf. - Z2-91 (v"zre̋v")
past act. pt., m. n. sg.

v"lxv" - magus, magician, wizard (noun) - V10 (volx-
vov") g. pl.; Z10 (volsvi) n. pl.; U10 (volsvi) n. pl.;
P10 (v"l"svi) n. pl.

v"niti - to enter (vb.), pf. - V99 (vnidet') 3 sg.
pr./fut.; Z2-105 (vnidete) 2 pl. impv.

v"nuk" - grandson, descendant (noun) - V41 (vnuci) n.
pl., V41 (vnukom") i. sg., V95 (vnukom') i. sg.; Z2-41

(vnukom") i. sg., Z2-95 (vnukom") i. sg.; Z30 (vnucy)
n. pl.; U32 (vnuci) n. pl.; P32 (vnuci) n. pl.

v"nušiti - to hearken to, pay attention to (vb.), pf.
- Vl (vnuši) 2 sg. impv.; Z2-1 (vnuši) 2 sg. impv.

v"n" - forth, out (adv.) - Z2-91 (von").

v"piti - to cry out, exclaim (vb.), impf. - V95 (vo-
pijut) 3 sg. pr., V96 (vopiet') 3 sg. pr.; Z2-26
(v"piaše) 3 sg. impf., Z2-96 (v"piet") 3 sg. pr.; Z26
(v"piaše) 3 sg. impf., Z2-95 (v"pijut") 3 pl. pr., Z28
(v"piet") 3 sg. pr.; U26 (vopia) pr. act. pt., m. n.
sg., U28 (v"piet') 3 sg. pr., U63 (v"piaše) 3 sg.
impf.; P26 (v"pijaše) 3 sg. impf., P28 (v"piet') 3 sg.
pr.

v"skorě - quickly (adv.) - Z75 (vskorě); U75 (voskorě);
P75 (v"skore).

v"skr'senie - resurrection (noun) - Z2 title (v"s-
krnie) a. sg.

v"skr'snuti - to rise, be resurrected (vb.), pf. -
V85 (v"skr^esnet') 3 sg. pres./fut., V94 (v"skr^sl")
res. pt., m. sg., V106 (v"s^krš") past act. pt., m. n.
sg.; Z2-83 (v"skrnet") 3sg. pres./fut., Z2-84 (v"skr^snet")
3sg. pres./fut., Z2-94 (v"skrs") past act. pt., m. n. sg.

v"spitati sja - to nourish oneself (vb.), pf. - Z66
(v"spitasja) 3 sg. aor.; U66 (v"spitasja) 3 sg. aor.;
P66 (v"spita^s) 3 sg. aor.

108

v"spěti - to sing, praise (vb.), pf. - V6,7 (v"spoem")
1 pl. pr./fut.; Z2-6,7 (v"spoem") 1 pl. pr./fut.; Z6
(v"spoim") 1 pl. impv.; U6 (vospoe^m) 1 pl. pr./fut.;
P6 (vospoem") 1 pl. pr./fut.

v"stati - to get up, stand up (vb.), pf. - Z2-92
(v"sta) 3 sg. aor.

v"sxotěti - to want, to desire (vb.), pf. - V15,12
(vosxotě) 2 sg. aor., V15,12^2 (vosxotě) 2 sg. aor.;
Z2-15,12 (v"sxotě) 2 sg. aor.; Z15 (v"sxotěl") res.
pt. m. sg., U15 (v"sxotel") res. pt. m. sg.; P15
(v"sxotěl") res. pt. m. sg.

v"sxotěti sja - to have the desire (vb.), pf. - V14
(sja vosxotě) 3 sg. aor.; Z2-14 (sja...v"sxotě) 3 sg.
aor.; Z14 (sja v"sxotělo) res. pt. n. sg.; U14 (sja
v"sxotělo) res. pt. n. sg.; P14 (sja v"sxotělo) res.
pt. n. sg.

vysok" - high (adj.) - V14 (vysokyi) m. n. sg. lg.;
Z2-14 (vysokii) m. n. sg. lg.

v'rt'p" - cave; garden (noun) - Z9 (vertepa) g. sg.;
U9 (vertepa) g. sg.; P9 (věrtepa) g. sg.

v'sak" - all, every kind of (pro.) - V108 (vsjaka) f.
n. sg.

v's' - all (pro.) - V23a (vsja) ntr. n. pl.?, V98
(vsi) m. n. pl., V98^2 (vsi) m. n. pl., V106 (vsei)
f. d. sg., V108 (vsei) f. d. sg.; Z2-18 (vsi) m. n.
pl., Z2-71a (vsi) m. n. pl., Z2-95 (vsi) m. n. pl.;
Z18 (vsi) m. n. pl., Z35 (vsěm") f. d. pl., Z38

(vsěx") m. g. pl., Z42 (vsja) ntr. n. pl., Z71 (vsěx")
m. g. pl., Z76 (vsi) m. n. pl.; U18 (vsi) m. n. pl.,
U35 (vse^m) f. d. pl., U38 (vse^x) m. g. pl., U42 (vsja)
ntr. n. pl., U71 (vsě^x) m. g. pl.; U76 (vsi) m. n.
pl.; P18 (vsi) m. n. pl., P35 (vsja) ntr. n. pl., P71
(vsě^x) m. g. pl., P76 (vsi) m. n. pl.

vě - we (two) (pro.) - V83 (naju) g., V85 (naju) g.

věděti - to know (vb.), impf. - V102 (vědax") 1 sg.
impf.; Z2-84 (věmy) 1 pl. pr.; U72 (vesi) 2 sg. pr.

věk" - age (noun) /ot" věka = ages ago, from time
immemorial/ - Z2-29 (věk") a. sg.; Z19 (věk") a. sg.,
Z29 (věk") a. sg.; U19 (věk") a. sg., U29 (věk") a.
sg.; P19 (věk") a. sg., P29 (věk") a. sg. /V105 (o^t
věka) g. sg./.

věn'c' - crown (noun) - Z2-71a (venéc") a. sg.

věra - faith (noun) - Z2-83 (věru) a. sg.
věrovati - to have faith in, believe in (vb.), impf.
Z2-91 (věruéte) 2 pl. pr.

věst' - news (noun) - V21 (věst') a. sg., V22a
(věst') a. sg., V25 (věst') a. sg., V27 (věst') a.
sg.; Z2-21 (věst') a. sg., Z2-27 (věst') a. sg.;
Z19 (věst') a. sg., Z21 (věst') a. sg., Z25 (věst')
a. sg.; U19 (vest') a. sg., U21 (věst') a. sg; P19
(věst') a. sg., P21 (věst') a. sg., P25 (věst') a.
sg.

větr" - wind, breeze (noun) - V73 (větra) g. sg.;
Z2-73 (větra) g. sg.

110

<u>větrjan"</u> - windy (adj.) - Z37 (větrjanjaa) for f. g.
sg. lg.; U37 (větrjanyjá) f. g. sg. lg.; P37 (větre-
njaja) for f. g. sg. lg.

<u>věč'n"</u> - eternal (adj.) - V99 (věčnyjá) a. pl.

<u>gavriilov"</u> - Gabriel's (poss. adj.) - P65 (gavrilova)
ntr. g. sg.

<u>Gavriil"</u> - Gabriel (pro. noun) - V98 (Gavril") n.; Z65
(Gavríla) g.; U65 (Gavrila) g.

<u>gdě</u> - where (adv.) - Z2-87 (gdě).

<u>glagolati</u> - to speak, say, talk (vb.),impf. - V1 (glâ)
3 sg. aor., V6,7 (glše) 3 sg. impf., V20 (glšči) for
pr. act. pt., m. n. pl., V21 (gli) 2 sg. impv., V22a
(gli) 2 sg. impv., V26 (glja) pr. act. pt., m. n. sg.,
V46 (glavyi) past act. pt., m. n. sg. lg., V57 (glše)
3 sg. aor., V82 (glšče) for pr. act. pt., f. n. pl.,
V85 (gla) 3 sg. aor., V86 (gla) 3 sg. aor., V97 (gla)
3 sg. aor., V100 (gla) 3 sg.aor., V101 (glaša) 3 pl.
aor., V105 (gla) 3 sg. aor., V106 (gla) 3 sg. aor.;
Z2-1 (glaše) 3 sg. impf., Z2-6,7 (glaše) 3 sg. impf.,
Z2-6,7² (glaše) 3 sg. impf., Z2-13 (glaše) 3 sg. impf.,
Z2-21 (gli) 2 sg. impv., Z2-26 (glaše) 3 sg. impf.,
Z2-46 (glav") past act. pt., m. n. sg., Z2-82 (gljušči) pr. act.
pt., f. n. du., Z2-83 (gla) 3 sg. aor., Z2-86 (gla) 3 sg. aor.,
Z2-94 (gla) 3 sg. aor.; Z13 (glaše) 3 sg. impf., Z17 (gla) 3 sg.
aor., Z26 (glja) pr. act. pt., m. n. sg; U13 (glše) 3 sg.
impf., U1i (gla) 3 sg. aor., U26

(glše) 3 sg. impf.; P13 (glše) 3 sg. impf., P17 (gla) 3

sg. aor., P26 (glše) 3 sg. impf.

glas" - voice, sound(noun)-V23 (glasom") i.sg., V23a

(glasa) g. sg.; Z2-23 (glasom") i.sg., Z2-23(glasa)g.sg.;

Z9(glă)n.sg.; U9(glă) n.sg.;P9 (glă) n. sg.

Gospodin" - Lord (noun) - V4 (Gña).

Gospod'-Lord (noun)-V title (Gi)v., V1 (G͡ᵖ)n., V6,7 (Gem')

i., V15,12 (Gi) v., V15,12² (Gi) v., V16 (Gi)v., V31 (Gi) v.

V38 (Gi)v., V38² (Gi) v., V38³ (Gi) v., V39,40(Gi)v., V42a (Gi)

v., V43 (Gi) v., V46 (Gi) v., V48 (Gi) v., V49 (Gi) v., V50 (Gi)

v., V52 (Gi) v., V53a (Gi) v., V55 (Gi) v., V73 (Gi) v., V77

(G') n., V85 (G') n., V94 (Gi) v., V96 (Gi) v., V97

(Gi) v., V101 (G') n., V104 (G') n., V105 (G') n.; Z2-2

(G') n., Z2-4 (Ga) a., Z2-6,7 (Gdem") i., Z2-15,12

(Gi) v., Z2-15,12² (Gi) v., Z2-16 (Gi) v., Z2-19

(Gdě) p!., Z2-38 (Gi) v., Z2-40 (Gi) v., Z2-47 (Gi) v.,

Z2-48 (Gi) v., Z2-49 (Gi) v., Z2-50 (Gi) v., Z2-52,53

(Gi) v., Z2-56 (Gi) v., Z2-71a (Gi) v., Z2-71a² (Gi)v.,

Z2-73 (Gi) v., Z2-74 (Gi) v., Z2-74² (Gi)v., Z2-75 (Gi)v.,

Z2-75 (G') n., Z2-78 (G') n., Z2-83 (Gi) v., Z2-83 (G') n.,Z2-84

(Gi) v., Z2-87 (G') n., Z2-89 (G') n., Z2-90 (Gi) v.,

Z2-91 (G') n., Z2-93 (G') n., Z2-94 (Gu) d., Z2-95

(Gi) v., Z2-96 (Gi) v., Z2-96² (Gi) v., Z2-96³ (Gi)

v., Z2-97 (G') n., Z2-105 (G') n.; Z29 (Gi) v., Z37

(Gi) v., Z38 (Gi) v., Z38² (Gi) v., Z38³ (Gi) v.,

Z39 (Gì) v., Z41 (Gì) v., Z42 (Gì) v., Z43 (Gì) v.,

Z44 (Gì) v., Z47 (Gì) v., Z60 (Gì) v., Z62 (Gì) v.,

Z68 (Gì) v., Z72 (Gì) v., Z75 (Gì) v.; U29 (Gî) v.,

U38 (Gî) v., U38^2 (Gî) v., U38^3 (Gî) v., U39 (Gî) v.,

U41 (Gî) v., U44 (Gî) v., U47 (Gî) v., U60 (Gî) v.,

U62 (Gî) v., U68 (Gî) v., U74 (Gî) v.; P title (Gì)

v., P29 (Gì) v., P37 (Gì) v., P38 (Gì) v., P38^2 (Gì)

v., P38^3 (Gì) v., P39 (Gì) v., P41 (Gì) v., P42 (Gì)

v., P44 (Gì) v., P47 (Gì) v., P60 (Gì) v., P62 (Gì)

v., P68 (Gì) v., P74 (Gì) v.

gospod'n' - Lord's, of the Lord (poss. adj.) - V24
(gñ') m. n. sg., V27 (gñ') m. n. sg., V82 (gñi) a.
pl.; Z2 title (gnja) for m. g. sg., Z2-27 (gn') m.
n. sg.; U65 (gñ') m. n. sg.; P65 (gñ') m. n. sg.;
Z65 (gn') m. n. sg.

grob" - tomb, grave (noun) - Z2-88 (grob") a. sg.,
Z2-89 (gróba) g. sg.

grěx" - sin (noun) - Z72 (grèx) g. pl.; U72 (grě^x)
g. pl.; P72 (grě^x) g. pl.

grjasti - to come, walk (vb.), impf. - Z2-91 (grja-
di) 2 sg. impv.

gusli - f. pl., gusli, stringed instrument (noun) -
Z7 (gúsli) a., Z61 (gúsli) a.; U7 (gusli) a., U61
(gusli) a.; P7 (gusli) a., P61 (gusli) a.

da - and, but, so that, let (conj.) - V5 (da), V25
(da), V28 (da), V42a (da), V99 (da); Z2-5 (da), Z2-19
(da), Z75 (dá); U75 (da); P75 (da).

<u>davydov"</u> - David's, of David (poss. adj.) - V-56
(dvd̂v") m. n. sg.; Z2-56 (dv̌d") m. n. sg.

<u>Davyd"</u> - David (pro. noun) - V6,7 (Dv̂d") n., V21 (Dv̂de)
v., V22 (Dv̂d") n., V22² (Dv̂d") n., V22a (Dv̂d") n., V23
(Dv̂d") n., V96 (Dv̂d") n., V102 (Dv̂d") n.; Z2-6,7 (Dv̌d")
n., Z2-20 (Dv̌du) d., Z2-21 (Dv̀de) v., Z2-23 (Dv̀d") n.,
Z2-96 (Dv̀d") n., Z2-97 (Dv̌da) g.; Z7 (Dv̌d") n., Z20
(Dv̌du) d., Z23 (Dv̌d") n., Z60 (Dv̀da) a.; U7 (Dv^d') n.,
U20 (Dv̌ẙ) d., U23 (Dv̌ẙ) n., U60 (Dv̌da) a.; P7 (Dv̌")
n., P20 (Dv̌du) d., P23 (Dv^d") n., P60 (Dv̌da) a.

<u>Daniil"</u> - Daniel (pro. noun) - V23a (Danil") n., V51
(Danil") n., V53 (Danil") n.; Z2-51 (Daníl") n.

<u>dar"</u> - gift (noun) - V10 (dary) a. pl.; Z2-10 (dáry)
a. pl.; Z10 (dáry) a. pl.; U10 (dary) a. pl.; P10
(dar") a. sg.

<u>dati</u> - to give (vb.), pf. - V5 (dam") 1 sg. pres./fut.;
Z2-5 (dam") 1 sg. pres./fut.; Z60 (dál") res. pt., m.
sg.; U60 (da^l') res. pt., m. sg.; P60 (dal") res. pt.,
m. sg.

<u>dv'ri</u> - f.pl.door (noun) - Z2-89 (dvérii) g.

<u>desnica</u> - right hand (noun) - Z2-46 (desniceju) i. sg.;
Z2-105 (desníca) n. sg.

<u>desn"</u> - right (adj.) - V107 (děsnuju) f. a. sg. lg.

<u>div"</u> - wild (adj.) - Z66 (dívii) m. a. sg. lg.; U66
(divyî) m. a. sg. lg.; P66 (divii) m. a. sg. lg.

Dijavol" - Devil (noun) - V21 (D'ja̋vole) v., V86
(D'ja̋volu) d., V100 (D'javolu) d.; Z2-39 (Diavolom")
i., Z2-59 (Diávola) g., Z2-75 (Diávola) a., Z2-86
(Diávolu) d., Z2-96 (Diávola) g.; Z39 (Diávol") n.,
Z75 (Diávola) a.; U39 (D'ja̍vol") n., U75 (Dia̍vola) a.;
P39 (Diavol") n., P75 (Diàvola) a.

dobro - good (noun) - Z34 (dobrá) g. sg.; U34 (dobra)
g. sg.; P34 (dobra) g. sg.

donesti - to bring to, carry to (vb.), pf. - Z21 (do-
nestì) inf., Z25 (doneset') 3 sg. pr./fut.; U21 (donesti) inf., U25 (donese^t) 3 sg. pr./fut.; P21 (donesti) inf., P25 (doneset') 3 sg. pr./fut.

drug" - friend (noun) - V24 (drug") n. sg., V27 (druže) v. (sg.); Z2 title (druga) g. sg., Z2-24 (drúg")
n. sg., Z2-27 (drúže) v. (sg.), Z2-41 (drúg") n. sg.;
Z2-78 (drúg") n. sg.; Z24 (drúg") n. sg., Z27 (druže)
v. (sg.), Z41 (drug") n. sg.; U24 (drű) n. sg., U27
(druže) v. (sg.), U41 (drų) n. sg.; P24 (drug") n. sg.,
P27 (drǔ) v. (sg.), P41 (drug") n. sg.

družina - družina, retinue (noun) - V6,7 (družina) n.
sg.; Z2-6,7 (družíno) v. (sg.); Z6 (drûžino) v. (sg.),
Z11 (drúžino) v. (sg.); U6 (družino) v. (sg.), U11
(družino) v. (sg.); P6 (družino) v. (sg.), P11 (družino) v.(sg.).

drěvjan" - wooden (adj.) - V54 (drevjany̋i) m. a. sg.
lg.; Z2-54 (drévjan") m. a. sg.

dux" - spirit (noun) - V98 (dx̂om") i. sg.; Z2-98
(dx̌om") i. sg. See also entry Svjatyi Dux".

duša - soul (noun) - V86 (dŝa) n. sg.; Z2-86 (dša) n.
sg.

d"va - two (numeral) - V56 (dv̂a) m. a.; Z2-56 (dv̀a) m.
a.

d"lgot'rpĕliv" - long-patient (adj.) - Z2-74 (dolgoterpĕlív") m. n. sg.; Z74 (dolgoterpĕlív") m. n. sg.;
U74 (dolgotr'peliv") m. n. sg.; P74 (dolgotr"pĕliv")
m. n. sg.

d"no - bottom (noun) - Z32 (dnè) pr. sg.; U32 (dně) pr.
sg.; P32 (dńe) pr. sg.

d'n' - day (noun) - Z2-8 (dń') n. sg., Z2-84 (dń') a.
sg.; Z8 (dǹ') n. sg., Z11 (dǹi) a. pl., Z35 (dńi) a.
pl.; U8 (dń') n. sg., U11 (dńi) a. pl., U35 (dńi) a.
pl.; P8 (dń') n. sg., P11 (dńi) a. pl., P35 (dńi) a.
pl.

d'n's' - today (adv.) - V6,7 (dn̂'); Z2-6,7 (dn̂');
Z6 (dnés'), Z10 (dn̂e); U6 (dn̂'), U10 (dn̂'); P6 (dn̂'),
P10 (dn̂')

dĕvica - maiden, virgin (noun) - V13 (dv̂ca) n. sg.;
Z2-13 (dv́ca) n. sg.; Z13 (dv̀ca) n. sg.; U13 (dv́ce) for
n. sg.; P13 (dv̀ca) n. sg.

dĕvič' - maiden's, virgin's (poss. adj.) - V48 (dv̌če)
ntr. a. sg.

děistvo - action, act (noun) - Z2-48 (děistvom") i. sg.

dělo - deed (noun) - V38 (dělěx") p. pl.; Z2-38 (dě-
lex") p. pl., Z2-40 (dělom") d. pl.; Z38 (dělom") d.
pl.; U38 (dělo^m) d. pl.; P38 (dělom")d. pl.

dělja - for the sake of (prep.) + g. - V31 (dělja),
V42a (dělja), V97 (delja).

egda - when (adv.,conj.) - Z2-94 (iegda).

edin" - alone - (pronoun) - Z72 (edin") m. n. sg.; U72
(edî) m. n. sg.; P72 (edin") m. n. sg.

Ezekija - Hezekiah (pro. noun) - V51 (Ezěkěja) g.;
Z2-51 (Ezekia) g.

emu - see on".

Enox" - Enoch (pro. noun) - Z71 (Ienox") n.; U71
(Enox") n.; P71 (Eno^x) n.

esi - see byti.

esm" - see byti.

esm' - see byti.

ž - see že.

žadati - to long for, thirst for (vb.), impf. - Z11
(žadali) res. pt. m. pl.; U11 (žadali) res. pt. m. pl.;
P11 (žadali) res. pt. m. pl.

žalovati sja - to complain (vb.), impf. - Z2-38 (žalujusja) 1 sg. pr.; Z38 (žalujusja) 1 sg. pr.; U38 (žalujusja) 1 sg. pr.; P38 (žalujusja) 1 sg. pr.

žalost' - f., pity, compassion (noun) - U38 (žalost')

n. sg.

žal' - pity (adv.) - V38 (žal'), V38^2 (žal'); Z2-38

(žál'), Z38 (žál); P38 (žal').

že - intensifying particle placed after word

strengthened - V6,7 (že), V13 (že), V15,12 (že), V24

(že), V39,40 (že), V58 (že), V82 (že), V96(že), V103

(že); Z2-13 (že), Z2-15,12 (že), Z2-20 (že), Z2-79

(že), Z2-80 (že), Z2-84 (že), Z2-96 (že); Z15 (že), Z42

(že); U15 (že), U40 ($^{\v{z}}$), U47 ($^{\v{z}}$); P15 (že), P39 ($^{\v{z}}$),

P47($^{\v{z}}$), P63 (že).

želati - to desire + g. (vb.), impf. - Z33 (želájušče)

pr. act. pt., m. n. pl., Z70 (želájut") 3 pl. pr.; U33

(želajušče) pr. act. pt., m. n. pl.; U70 (želajut') 3

pl. pr.; P33 (želajušče) pr. act. pt., m. n. sg., P70

(želajut') 3 pl. pr.

želězn" - iron (adj.) - V22 (želězna) f. n. sg., V103

(železny) f. n. pl., V104 (želěznyja) f. n. pl. lg.;

Z22 (želéznaja) f. n. sg. lg.; U22 (želěznyja) f. n.

pl. lg.; P22 (železnya) f. n. pl. lg.

želěnie - mourning (noun) - V73 (želěnia) g. sg.

život" - life (noun) - V102 (živote) pr. sg.

živ" - alive, living (adj.) - V6,7 (živyja) f. a. pl.

lg., V21 (živyi) m. a. sg. lg., V22a (živyi) m. a.

sg. lg., V24 (živyi) m. a. sg. lg., V25 (živyi) m. a.

sg. lg., V27 (živyi) m. a. sg. lg.; Z2-6,7 (živýja)

m. a. pl. lg., Z2-21 (živyi) m. a. sg. lg., Z2-27

(živyi) m. a. sg. lg.; Z7 (živýja) f. a. pl. lg., Z19

(živy̍i) m. a. s. lg.; U7 (živyâ) f. a. pl. lg., U19

(živyî) m. a. sg. lg.; P7 (živyjâ) f. a. pl. lg., P19

(živyî) m. a. sg. lg.

židovin" - Jew (noun) - Z2-46 (židóv") g. pl.; Z75

(žídově) n. pl.; U75 (žĭvě̍) n. pl.; P75 (židove) n. pl.

židov'sk" - Jewish (adj.) - Z2-88 (židóv"ska) m. g. sg.

žiti - to live (vb.), impf. - V29,30 (žiti) inf.; Z40

(živaja) pr. act. pt., m. n. sg.!; U40 (živjaa) pr.

act. pt., m. n. sg. !; P40 (živja) pr. act. pt., m. n.

sg.

ž'dati - to wait for (vb.), impf. - Z72 (ž'deši) 2 sg.

pr.; U72 (žideši) 2 sg. pr.; P72 (žideši) 2 sg. pr.

ž'zl" - rod, staff (noun) - V46 (žezlom") i. sg.

za - for (prep.) + a. or i.- Z2-54 (zá) +a.

zaklati - to stab, slaughter (vb.),pf.Z41 (zaklati) inf.;

U41 (zaklati) inf.; P41 (zaklati) inf.

zaključiti - to confine (vb.),pf.V22 (zaključen") past.

pass. part., m. n. sg.

zam"k" - lock (noun) - V22 (zjam"cě) p. sg.; Z22 (zam-

ki) n. pl.; U22 (zamky) n. pl.; P22 (zamky) n. pl.

zapečatati - to seal (vb.), pf. - Z22 (zapečátano)

past pass. pt., ntr. n. sg.; U22 (zapečatano) past

pass. pt., ntr. n. sg.; P22 (zapečatano) past pass pt.,

ntr. n. sg.

zapověd' - f., commandment (noun) - Z40 (zapověd') a.
sg.; U40 (zapově^{d}) a. sg.; P40 (zapově^{d}) a. sg.

zautra - tomorrow (adv.) - Z2-24 (zaútra); Z24 (zaútra); U24 (zaútra); P24 (zaútra).

zdě - see s'de.

zemlja - earth (noun) - V1 (zemle) v. (sg.), V5 (zemlju) a. sg., V14 (zemlju) a. sg., V15,12 (zemlja) n.
sg., V31 (zemlju) a. sg., V57 (zemli) pr. sg., V106
(zemli) d. sg., V108 (zemli) d. sg.; Z2-1 (zemljà) n.
sg., Z2-10 (zemlì) pr. sg., Z2-14 (zemlju) a. sg.,
Z2-15,12 (zemljà) n. sg., Z2-31 (zémlju) a. sg.; Z10
(zemlì) pr. sg., Z12 (zemlja) n. sg., Z13 (zémljù) a.
sg., Z14 (zemljù) a. sg., Z29 (zemlì) pr. sg., Z31
(zemlju) a. sg., Z34 (zemlì) pr. sg., Z60 (zemlì) pr.
sg., Z71 (zemlì) pr. sg.; U10 (zemlí) pr. sg., U12
(zemlja) n. sg., U13 (zemlju) a. sg., U14 (zemlju) a.
sg., U29 (zemlì) pr. sg., U31 (zemlju) a. sg., U34
(zemli) pr. sg., U60 (zemlí) pr. sg., U71 (zemli) pr.
sg.; P10 (zemli) pr. sg., P12 (zemlja) n. sg., P13
(zemlju) a. sg., P14 (zemlju) a. sg., P29 (zemli) pr.
sg., P31 (zem'lju) a. sg., P34 (zemli) pr. sg., P60
(zemli) pr. sg., P71 (zemli) pr. sg.

zem'n" - of the earth (adj.) - Z 42 (zemnàja) ntr. n.
pl. lg.; U42 (zemnaâ) ntr. n. pl. lg.; P42 (zem'najà)
ntr. n. pl. lg.

ži - sixteen (numeral) - V23a (ži) a.

zlat" - golden (adj.) - V51 (zlatoӗ) ntr. a. sg. lg.,
V56 (zlata) m. a. du.; Z2-51 (zlato) ntr. a. sg.,
Z2-56 (zláta) m. a. du.

zub" - tooth (noun) - V16 (zuby) a. pl.; Z2-16 (zúby)
a. pl.

z"lě - evilly (adv.) - Z39 (zlě); U39 (zlě); P39 (zlě).

zěnica - pupil of the eye (noun) - Z2-71 (zénicy) a.
du., Z33 (zěnicy) a. du.; U33 (zenica) a. pl.; P33
(zenica) a. pl.

i - and, also (conj.) - V2(ĭ), V3 (ĭ), V3^2 (ĩ), V4 (i),
V6,7 (ĭ), V6,7^2 (i), V20 (ĭ), V23a (i), V26 (ĭ), V38
(ĭ), V39,40 (ĭ), V41 (ĭ), V46 (i), V48 (ĭ), V51 (ĭ),
V51^2 (ĭ), V55 (i), V56 (ĭ), V56^2 (ĭ), V56^3 (ĭ), V57
(ĭ), V73 (ĭ), V81 (ĭ), V81^2 (ĭ), V82 (ĭ), V82^2 (ĭ),
V82^3 (ĭ), V85 (ĭ), V85^2 (ĭ), V86 (ĭ), V94 (ĭ), V95 (i),
V97 (i), V98 (ĭ), V98^2 (ĭ), V98^3 (ĭ), V98^4 (i), V100
(ĭ), V101 (ĭ), V101^2 (ĭ), V103 (ĭ), V104 (ĭ), V106 (ĭ),
V106^2 (ĭ), V107 (ĭ); Z2-1 (ĭ), Z2-2 (ĭ), Z2-3 (ĭ),
Z2-6,7 (ĭ), Z2-6,7^2 (ĭ), Z2-6,7^3 (ĭ), Z2-6,7^4 (ĭ),
Z2-8 (ĭ), Z2-10 (i), Z2-13 (ĭ), Z2-14 (ĭ), Z2-18 (ĭ),
Z2-20 (ĭ), Z2-26 (ĭ), Z2-31 (ĭ), Z2-39 (ĭ), Z2-41
(ĭ), Z2-43 (ĭ), Z2-46 (ĭ), Z2-47 (ĭ), Z2-47^2 (ĭ),
Z2-48 (ĭ), Z2-48^2 (ĭ), Z2-49 (ĭ), Z2-51 (ĭ), Z2-52,53
(ĭ), Z2-54 (ĭ), Z2-56 (ĭ), Z2-56^2 (ĭ), Z2-59 (ĭ),
Z2-71a (ĭ), Z2-71a^2 (ĭ), Z2-71a^3 (ĭ), Z2-71a^4 (ĭ),
Z2-75 (ĭ), Z2-75^2 (ĭ), Z2-75^3 (ĭ), Z2-75^4 (ĭ), Z2-78
(ĭ), Z2-81 (ĭ), Z2-81^2 (ĭ), Z2-81^3 (ĭ), Z2-82 (ĭ),

Z2-82^2 (i̇), Z2-82^3 (i̇), Z2-83 (i̇), Z2-83^2 (i̇), Z2-86 (i̇), Z2-87

(i̇), Z2-87^2 (i̇), Z2-88 (i̇), Z2-88^2 (i̇), Z2-89 (i̇), Z2-90 (i̇),

Z2-90^2 (i̇), Z2-91 (i̇), Z2-91^2 (i̇), Z2-91^3 (i̇), Z2-91^4

(i̇), Z2-92 (i̇), Z2-93 (i̇), Z2-94 (i̇), Z2-95 (i̇), Z2-

95^2 (i̇), Z2-96 (i̇), Z2-97 (i̇), Z2-98 (i̇), Z2-98^2 (i̇),

Z2-105 (i̇); Z6 (i̇), Z7 (i̇), Z7^2 (i̇), Z8 (i̇), Z9 (i̇),

Z10 (i̇), Z12 (i̇), Z16 (i̇), Z17 (i̇), Z18 (i̇), Z19 (i̇),

Z20 (i̇), Z20^2 (i̇), Z20^3 (i̇), Z22 (i̇), Z22^2 (i̇), Z25

(i̇), Z26 (i̇), Z26^2 (i̇), Z26^3 (i̇), Z30 (i̇), Z30^2 (i̇),

Z33 (i̇), Z33^2 (i̇), Z33 ^{3} (i̇), Z33 ^{4} (i̇), Z34

(i̇), Z39 (i̇), Z39^2 (i̇), Z43 (i̇), Z44 (i̇), Z44^2 (i̇),

Z44^3 (i̇), Z47 (i̇), Z60 (i̇), Z61 (i̇), Z63 (i̇), Z63^2 (i̇),

Z64 (i̇), Z65 (i̇), Z67 (i̇), Z69 (i̇), Z75 (i̇), Z75^2 (i̇),

Z75^3 (i̇), Z76 (i̇), Z76^2 (i̇); U7 (i̇), U7^2 (i̇), U16 (i̇),

U17 (i̇), U18 (i̇), U19 (i̇), U20 (i̇), U20^2 (i̇), U22 (i̇),

U22^2 (i̇), U26 (i̇), U26^2 (i̇), U30 (i̇), U30^2 (i̇), U33 (i̇),

U33^2 (i̇), U33^3 (i̇), U33^4 (i̇), U34 (i̇), U42 (i̇), U44 (i̇),

U44^2 (i̇), U45 (i̇), U45^2 (i̇), U47 (i̇), U60 (i̇), U61 (i̇),

U64 (i̇), U67 (i̇), U70 (i̇), U71 (i̇), U75 (i̇), U75^2 (i̇),

U75^3 (i̇), U76 (i̇), U76^2 (i̇), U76^3 (i̇); P16 (i̇), P17

(i̇), P18 (i̇), P20 (i̇), P20^2 (i̇), P22 (i̇), P26 (i̇), P26^2

(i̇), P26^3 (i̇), P30 (i̇), P33 (i̇), P33^2 (i̇), P33^3 (i̇),

P33^4 (i̇), P34 (i̇), P42 (i̇), P44 (i̇), P44^2 (i̇), P45 (i̇),

P47 (i̇), P60 (i̇), P61 (i̇), P63 (i̇), P67 (i̇), P70 (i̇),

P71 (i̇), P75 (i̇), P75^2 (i̇), P75^3 (i̇), P76 (i̇).

<u>Iezekil'</u> - Ezekiel (pro. noun) - V23a (Iezĕkel') n.

Ieremija - Jeremiah (pro. noun) - V20 (Erěměja) n.,
V23a (Irěměja) n., V53a (Erěměja) n.; Z2-20 (Ieremě-
ja) n., Z20 (Eremia) n.; U20 (Ereměa) n.; P20 (Ere-
mei) n.

Ierusalim" - Jerusalem (pro. noun) - V56 (Ierusaliмě)
p., Z2-56 (Ierliмě) p.

iže - he who, they who (pro. and conj.) - Z2-38 (iže)
m. n. sg., Z2-46 (iže) m. n. sg., Z2-54 (iže) m. n.
sg., Z2-71a (iže) m. n. sg.; Z title (iže) for ntr. n.
sg., Z10 (iže) m. n. pl., Z41 (iže) m. n. sg., Z44
(iže) m. n. sg., Z65 (iže) m. n. sg.; U title (iže)
for ntr. n. sg., U10 (iže) m. n. pl., U41 (iže) m. n.
sg., U44 (iže) m. n. sg., U65 (iže) m. n. sg.; P title
(iž) for ntr. n. sg., P10 (iž) m. n. pl., P41 (iže)
m. n. sg., P44 (iž) m. n. sg., P65 (iž) m. n. sg.

iz - from, out of (prep.), + g. - V48 (is), V94 (iz'),
V96 (iz"), V105 (is); Z2-21 (izo), Z2-48 (iz'), Z2-75
(izo), Z2-94 (izo), Z2-96 (izo).

izbaviti - to deliver (vb.), pf. - Z2-21 (izbaviti)
inf., Z2-96 (izbavi) 2 sg. impv.; Z19 (izbaviti) inf.,
Z44 (izbavlen") past pass. pt., m. n. sg., Z45 (izbaviti) inf., Z75 (izbavi) 2 sg. impv.; U19 (izbaviti)
inf., U44 (izbavlen") past pass. pt., m. n. sg., U45
(izbavti) inf., U75 (izbavi) 2 sg. impv.; P19 (izbaviti) inf., P44 (izbavlen") past pass. pt., m. n. sg.,
P45 (izbaviti) inf., P75 (izbavi) 2 sg. impv.

izvesti - to lead out of (vb.), pf. - V96 (izvedi) 2

sg. impv.; Z2-75 (izvedi) 2 sg. impv., Z2-96 (izve-

di) 2 sg. impv.

izvoditi - to lead out of (vb.), impf. - V105 (izvo-

dit') 3 sg. pr.

izvolenik" - chosen one (noun) - V41 (izvolnici) n. pl.

izvoliti - to choose (vb.), pf. - Z2-41 (izvolnyi)

past pass. pt., m. n. pl. lg.

iziti - to go out, leave (vb.), pf. - V24 (iziti)

inf.; Z2-24 (izydet") 3 sg. pr./fut.

Izmail" - Ishmael (pro. noun) - V98 (Izmail") n.

iznesti - to carry out (vb.), pf. - V21 (izneset')

3 sg. pres./fut., V22a (izneset') 3 sg. pres./fut.,

V25 (izneset") 3 sg. pres./fut., V26 (iznesi) 2 sg.

impv.; Z2-21 (izneset") 3 sg. pres./fut., Z2-27 (iz-

nesi) 2 sg. impv.

izrešči - to utter, pronounce (vb.), pf. - Z23 (iz-

reče) 3 sg. aor.

ili - or (conj.) - V15,12 (ili), V43 (ili), V50

(ili), V53 (ili), V55 (ili); Z2-15,12 (ili), Z2-

43 (ili), Z2-47 (ili), Z2-50 (ili); Z15 (ili),

Z72 (ili), Z72^2 (ili); U15 (ili), U72 (ili), U72^2

(ili); P15 (ili), P72 (ili).

Ilija - Elijah (pro. noun) - Z71 (Il'ja) n.; U71

(Il'ja) n.; P71 (Il'ja) n.

imati - to have (vb.), impf. - Z2-83 (imaete) 2 pl. pres.

imja - name(noun) - V106 (imja) a. sg.; Z76 (imeni)

d. sg.; U76 (imeni) d. sg.; P76 (imeni) d. sg.

in" - other, one of, a certain, only (pro.) - V5

(inomu) m. d. sg. lg.; Z2-5 (inomu) m. d. sg. lg.;

Z7 (inyja) m. a. pl. lg.; U7 (inyja) m. a. pl. lg.;

P7 (inyi) for m. a. pl. lg.

Ioan" - John (pro. noun) - Z65 (Io) n.; U65 (Ioa)

n.; P65 (Ioa) n.

Irod" - Herod (pro. noun) - V16 (Irod") n.; Z2-16

(Irod") n., Z16 (Iro) n., Z67 (Iroda) g.; U16 (Iro)

n.; U67 (Iroa) g.; P16 (Iro^d) n., P67 (Iroda) g.

Isaak" - Isaac (pro. noun) - V23a (Isače) v., V41

(Isaakam") i.!, V95 (Isakam") i.!; Z2-41 (Isaakom")

i.; Z41 (Isaaka) a.; U41 (Isaka) a.; P41 (Isaka) a.

Isaija - Isaiah (pro. noun) - V20 (Isaija) n., V23a

(Isaija) n., V48 (Isaija) n., V50 (Isaija) n.; Z2-20

(Isaia) n., Z2-48 (Isaia) n.; Z20 (Isaia) n.; U20

(Isaa) n.; P20 (Isaia) n.

izkoreniti - to uproot, eradicate (vb.), pf. - V97

(iskorenil") res. pt. m. sg.; Z2-97 (iskorenil")

res. pt. m. sg.

istin'n" - true (adj.) - Z75 (istinnago) m. a. sg.

lg.

isusov" - of Jesus (poss. adj.) - Z2-82 (isovymi) f.

i. pl. lg.

Isus" - Jesus (noun) - V106 (Is") n.; Z2-16 (Ise)

p., Z2-80 (Is") n.

iti - to go (vb.), impf. - V98 (idut') 3 pl. pr.,

V106 (šeši) past act. pt., m. n. pl.!; Z2-80 (idem")

1 pl. pr., Z2-88 (idosta) 3 du. aor.

ix" - see on".

Ijakov" - Jacob, James (pro. noun) - V23a (Ijakove)

v., V41 (Iakovom") i., V95 (Ijakovom") i.; Z2 -

title (Iakova) g., Z2-41 (Iakovom") i., Z2-95 (Ja-

kovom") i.

K

kamen' - stone (noun) - Z2-89 (kamen') a. sg.

kaměn" - stone (adj.) - V22 (kamene) m. p. sg.;

Z22 (kamennyja) for m. n. pl. lg.; U22 (kameny) m.

n. pl.; P22 (kamenyja) for m. n. pl. lg.

koz'l" - yoke (noun) - V54 (kozel") a. sg.; Z2-54

(kozel") a. sg.

koli - when (adv.) - V102 (koli).

koléno - generation (noun) - Z42 (koléna) n. pl.;

U42 (koléna) n. pl.; P42 (koléna) n. pl.

kon' - horse (noun) - V10 (kon') g. pl.; Z2-10

(kon') g. pl.; Z10 (kon') g. pl.; U10 (kon') g. pl.;

P10 (kone) g. pl.!

krat"ko - for a short time, shortly (adv.) - V29,30

(korotko).

krat"k" - short (adj.) - Z2-29 (korotkii) m. a. sg.

lg.; Z29 (kotkii) m. a. sg. lg.; U29 (krokyi) m. a.

sg. lg.; P29 (korotkyi) m. a. sg. lg.

kr'stitel' - baptist (noun) - Z65 (kr̂tl') n.; U65

(kr̂tl') n.; P65 (kr̂tl') n.

kr'stiti - to baptize (vb.), impf. - V106 (kr̂tjašče)

pr. act. pt., m. n. pl.

kr'st" - cross (noun) - V98 (kr̂tom") i. sg.

kupina - bush (noun) - V46 (kupině) p. sg.; Z2-46

(kupině) p. sg.

k" - to, toward (prep.) + d. - V13 (k), V14 (k), V21

(ko), V22a (ko), V24 (ko), V25 (ko), V27 (ko), V51

(ko), V81 (k), V85 (k), V86 (ko), V97 (k), V100 (k");

Z2-13 (k), Z2-14 (k), Z2-20 (k"), Z2-21 (k"), Z2-27

(k"), Z2-51 (ko), Z2-79 (k), Z2-86 (k"), Z2-94 (k),

Z2-97 (k), Z title (k), Z13 (k), Z14 (k), Z19 (ko),

Z20 (k"), Z23 (k), Z25 (k), Z72 (k); U title (k),

U13 (k), U14 (k), U19 (k"), U20 (ko), U23 (k), U25

(k), U72 (k); P title (k), P13 (k), P14 (k), P19

(ko), P23 (k), P25 (k).

k"to - who (pro.) - V21 (kto) n., V22 (kto) n., V100

(kto) n.; Z2-21 (kto) n.; Z21 (kto) n.; U21 (kto)

n.; P21 (kto) n.

L

lazorev" - of Lazarus (poss. adj.) - V81 (lazorevě)

f. d. sg.!; Z2-81 (lazorevy) for f. n. du., Z2-88

(lazorev") m. a. sg.

Lazor' - Lazarus (pro. noun) - V24 (Lazar') n., V27

(Lazorju) v., V83 (Lazor') n., V85 (Lazor') n., V86

(Lazorja) a., V94 (Lazor') n., V97 (Lazorju) d.; Z2

title (Lázorja) g., Z2-24 (Lázor') n., Z2-27 (Lázar-

ju) v., Z2-78 (Lázar') n., Z2-80 (Lázorja) a., Z2-83

(Lázor') n., Z2-83^2(Lázor')n., Z2-86 (Lázorja) a., Z2-91(Lázor')

n., Z2-92 (Lázor') n., Z2-94 (Lázor') n., Z2-97 (Lázorju) d; Z

title (Lázorju)d., Z24 (Lázor') n., Z27 (Lázore) v.; U title

(Lazorju) d., U24 (Lazor') n., U27 (Lazorjŭ) v. P title

(Lazorju) d., P24 (Lazor') n., P27 (Lazorju)

v.

ležati - to lie (vb.), impf. - Z15 (ležiši) 2 sg. pr.;

U15 (leži śi) 2 sg. pr.; P15 (ležiśi) 2 sg. pr.

li - whether, if (particle) - V29,30 (li); Z2-15,12

(li), Z2-21 (li), Z2-29 (li), Z2-31 (li); Z15 (li),

Z19 (li), Z29 (li), Z30 (li), Z45 (li), Z64 (li),

Z72 (li); U15 (li), U15^2 (li), U29 (li), U31 (li),

U45 (lĩ), U64 (^{li}), U72 (li); P15 (li), P19 (li),

P29 (li), P31 (li), P45 (li), P64 (li), P72 (li),P72^2

(li).

lice - face (noun) - V26 (lice) a. sg.; Z26 (licu) d.

sg.; U26 (licju) d. sg.; P26 (licu) d. sg. /licem"

k" licu - face to face - V46 (licem" k licju); Z2-46

(licem" k" licu)/.

l'v" - lion (noun) - V57 (lvom") d. pl.; Z2-51 (lvom")

d. pl.

l'st' - f., delusion, deceit, enticement (noun) - V5

(l'sti) g. sg.; Z2-5 (l'ti) g. sg.

lěto - year (noun) - V29,30 (lěta) a. pl.; Z2-71a

(lěta) a. pl.; Z30 (lĕtá) a. pl., Z34 (lěta) a. pl.,
Z37 (lěta) a. pl.; U30 (lěta) a. pl., U34 (lěta) a.
pl., U37 (lěta) a. pl.; P30 (lěta) a. pl., P34 (lěta) a. pl., P37 (lěta) a. pl.

<u>ljubov'</u> - f., love (noun) - V13 (ljubov'ju) i. sg.

<u>ljudie</u> - m. pl., people (noun) - V3 (ljue) n., V5
(ljudi) a.; Z2-3 (ljudie) n., Z2-5 (ljudi) a.

<u>ljut"</u> - fierce, wild (adj.) - Z44 (ljutago) m. g. sg.
lg., U44 (ljutag) m. g. sg. lg.; P44 (ljutago) m. g.
sg. lg.

<u>mal"</u> - little, short (adj.) - Z34 (mal") m. a. sg.,
Z35 (malě) for m. a. sg., confusion between <u>v" malě</u>
(for a short time) and <u>v" mal" čas"</u> (for a short time),
Z36 (malo) ntr. a. sg.; U34 (ma) m. a. sg., U35 (mal")
m. a. sg., U36 (malo) ntr. a. sg.; P34 (malě) for m.
a. sg. (as Z35), P35 (mal") m. a. sg.; P36 (malo) ntr.
a. sg.

<u>Marija</u> - Mary (pro. noun) - V81 (Mr'e) d., V82 (Mr'ja)
n., V85 (Mr'e) d.; Z2-81 (Maria) n., Z2-83 (Márii) d.,
Z2-87 (Márii) d., Z2-90 (Mária) n.

<u>Marfa</u>, <u>Marta</u> - Martha (pro. noun) - V81 (Marfě) d.,
V82 (Marfa) n., V85 (Marfě) d.; Z2-81 (Márfa) n., Z2-83
(Márfe) d., Z2-87 (Márfě) d., Z2-90 (Marfa) n.

<u>mater'n"</u> - maternal (adj.) - V48 (mtrnja) ntr. g. sg.;
Z2-48 (mtrnja) ntr. g. sg., Z2-48 (mtrně) for ntr. a.
sg.

mati - f., mother (noun) - V13 (m̂ti) n. sg.; Z2-13
(mťi) n. sg.; Z13 (mťi) n. sg.; U13 (mťi) n. sg.;
P13 (mťi) n. sg.

med" - honey (noun) - Z66 (méd") a. sg.; U66 (me^d)
a. sg.; P66 (me^d) a. sg.

mene - see az".

meč' - sword (noun) - Z16 (meč') a. sg.; U16 (meč') a.
sg., P16 (meč') a. sg.

mi - see az".

mir" - world (noun) - Z2-54 (mir") a. sg.

Mixail" - Michael (pro. noun) - V98 (Mixail") n.

moi - my (pro.) - V3 (moï) m. n. pl., V5 (moëja) f. g.
sg., V5 (moë) ntr. a. sg., V6,7 (moja) f. n. sg., V23a
(moëgo) m. g. sg., V41 (moï) m. n. pl., V86 (moja) f.
n. pl., V97 (moëgo) m. g. sg.; Z2-3 (moì) m. n. pl.,
Z2-5 (moeja) f. g. sg., Z2-5 (moë) ntr. a. sg., Z2-23
(moëgo) m. g. sg., Z2-40 (moìm") ntr. d. pl., Z2-86
(mojà) f. n. sg., Z2-97 (moëgo) m. g. sg.; Z9 (moì)
ntr. a. du., Z38 (moìm") ntr. d. pl.; U9 (moî) ntr. a.
du., U38 (moî) ntr. d. pl.; P9 (moì) ntr. a. du., P38
(moìm") ntr. d. pl.

Moiséi - Moses (pro. noun) - V46 (Moïsii) n., V47
(Moisěi) n.; Z2-46 (Moisei) n.; Z46 (Moiséi) n.; U46
(Moise) n.; P46 (Moisei) n.

molitva - prayer (noun) - Z2-75 (mĺtvu) a. sg.

mošči - to be able (vb.), impf. - Z21 (možet") 3 sg.
pr., Z45 (možeši) 2 sg. pr.; U21 (može) 3 sg. pr.,

U45 (možeši) 2 sg. pr.; P21 (mo$^{\check{z}}$t') 3 sg. pr., P44 (možeši) 2 sg. pr.

muka - torment (noun) - Z2-40 (muku) a. sg.; Z19 (múki) g. sg., Z34 (múki) for pr. sg., Z38 (múku) a. sg.; U19 (muky) g. sg., U38 (muku) a. sg.; P19 (muky) g. sg., P38 (muku) a. sg.

mučitel' - tormentor (noun) - Z2-96 (mučitelja) g. sg.!

mučiti - to torment (vb.), impf.- V29,30 (mučenu) past pass. pt., m. d. sg.; Z2-47 (múčim") pr. pass. pt., m. n. sg., Z2-71a (múčimy) pr. pass. pt., m. n. pl.; Z32 (múčimy) past pass. pt., m. n. pl., Z39 (múčit) 3 sg. pr.; U32 (mučimy) pr. pass. pt., m. n. pl., U39 (mučit^{t}) 3 sg. pr.; P32 (mučimy) pr. pass. pt., m. n. pl., P69 (mučim") pr. pass. pt., m. n. sg.

mučiti sja - to be tormented (vb.), impf. - Z2-71a (mučitsja) 3 sg. pr.; Z30 (mučitisja) inf., Z44 (mú-čitsja) 3 sg. pr., Z63 (múčitsja) 3 sg. pr., Z69 (mučitsja) 3 sg. pr., U30 (mučit$\widehat{\imath}$) inf., U44 (mu-čitsě) 3 sg. pr.!, U63 (mučitsja) 3 sg. pr., U69 (muči$\overset{t\widehat{s}}{e}$) 3 sg. pr.!; P30 (mučitisja) inf., P44 (mu-čitsja) 3 sg. pr., P63 (mučit'$^{\widehat{s}}$) 3 sg. pr.

m"nogoočit" - many-eyed (adj.) - V6,7 (mnogoočitaja) m. a. pl. lg.!

m"nog" - many (pronoun-adj.) - V29,30 (mnoga) ntr. a.

pl.; Z2-71a (mnóga) ntr. a. pl., Z2-73 (mnóga) ntr. a.

pl.; Z11 (mnógi) m. a. pl., Z30 (mnoga) ntr. a. pl.,

Z34 (mnóga) ntr. a. pl., Z35 (mnógi) m. a. pl., Z37

(mnóga) ntr. a. pl.,Z60(mnógimi)m.i.pl; U11 (mnozi) m. a.

pl., U30 (mnoga) ntr. a. pl., U34 (mnoga) ntr. a. pl.,

U35 (mnogi) m. a. pl., U37 (mnóga) ntr. a. pl., U60

(mnogimi) m. i. pl.; P11 (mnozi) m. a. pl., P30 (mno-

ga) ntr. a. pl., P34 (mnoga) ntr. a. pl., P35 (mno-

gy) m. a. pl., P37 (mnoga) ntr. a. pl., P60 (mno-

gymi) m. i. pl.

m"nož'stvo – multitude (noun) – Z2-88 (mnóžtvo) n. sg.,

Z2-98 (mnóžestvo) a. sg.

my – we (pronoun) – V14 (nam") s., V21 (nâs) g., V21

(ny) a., error for nyně, V22a (nâs) g., V22a (ny) a.,

error for nyně, V24 (nâs) g., V49 (nami) i., V52 (nami)

i., V100 (nâs) g.; Z2-14 (nam") d., Z2-21 (nas") g.,

Z2-21² (nás") a., Z2-24 (nâs) g., Z2-47 (námi) i., Z2-

49 (námi) i., Z2-52,53 (nami) i., Z2-59 (námi) i.,

Z2-71a (námi) i., Z2-74 (my) n., Z2-75 (ny) a.; Z14

(nám") d., Z19 (nás") a., Z24 (nás") g., Z25 (nás")

g., Z47 (námi) i., Z69 (námi) i., Z72 (nas") a., Z72

(nám") d., Z74 (mỳ) n., Z75 (nâs) a., Z76 (mỳ) n.;

U14 (nâ^m) d., U19 (nâs) a., U21 (nâs) g., U24 (nâs) g.,

U25 (nâs) g., U47 (nami) i., U63 (nami) i., U69 (nami)

i., U72 (nâs) a., U72 (nâ^m) d., U74 (my) n., U75 (nâs)

U76 (my) n.; P14 (nam") d., P19 (nâs) a., P21 (nâs) g.,

P24 (nã) g., P25 (nas") g., P47 (nami) i., P63 (nami)

i., P69 (nami) i., P72 (nã) a., P74 (my) n., P75 (nã)

a., P76 (my) n.

m'gla - mist (noun) - Z13 (mĺoju) i. sg.; U13 (m'gloju)

i. sg.; P13 (mgloju) i. sg.

m'ně - see az".

m'rtv" - dead (adj.) - Z2-80 (mertvyx") m. g. pl. lg.

mědjan" - bronze (adj.) - V22 (mědjana) ntr. n. pl.,

V103 (mědjanaja) ntr. n. pl. lg., V104 (medenaja) ntr.

a. pl. lg.; Z22 (mědjanaja) ntr. n. pl. lg.; U22 (me-

djanaâ) ntr. n. pl. lg.; P22 (medjanajà) ntr. n. pl.

lg.

mja - see az".

na - on, in (prep.), + a. or p. - V6,7 (na) + a., V10

(na) + p., V14 (na) + a., V14^2 (na) + a., V21 (na) +

a., error for nyně, V21^2 (na) + a., V22a (na) + a.,

error for nyně, V22a^2 (na) + a., V24 (na) + a., V25

(na) + a., V27 (na) + a., V29,30 (na) + a., V31 (na) +

a.!, V46 (na) + p., V48 (na) + a., V54 (na) + p., V57

(na) + p., V58 (na) + a., V82 (^{na}) + a., V97 (na) + a.,

V98 (na) + a., V107 (na) + a.; Z2 title (na) + a.,

Z2-5 (na) + a., Z2-6,7 (na) + a., Z2-10 (na) + p.,

Z2-14 (na) + a., Z2-21 (na) + a., Z2-27 (na) + a.,

Z2-29 (na) + a., Z2-29^2 (na) + a., Z2-46 (na) + p.,

Z2-48 (na) + a., Z2-54 (na) + p., Z2-71a (na) + a.,

Z2-71a^2 (na) + a., Z2-73 (na) + a., Z2-88 (ná) + a.,

Z2-91 (ná) + a., Z2-98 (na) + a.; Z7 (na) + a., Z10

(na) + p., Z14 (ná) + a., Z16 (ná) + a., Z19 (na) +

a., Z29 (na) + a., $Z29^2$ (na) + a., $Z29^3$ (na) + p.,

Z34 (na) + p., Z37 (na) + a., Z60 (na) + p., Z71 (na)

+ p.; U7 (na) + a., U10 (na) + p., U14 (na) + a.,

U16 (na) + a., U19 (na) + a., U29 (na) + a., $U29^2$ (na)

+ a., $U29^3$ (na) + p., U34 (na) + p., U37 (na) + a.,

U60 (na) + p., U71 (na) + p.; P7 (na) + a., P10 (na)

+ p., P14 (na) + a., P16 (na) + a., P19 (na) + a.,

P29 (na) + a., $P29^2$ (na) + a., $P29^3$ (na) + p., P34

(na) + p., P37 (na) + a., P60 (na) + p., P71 (na) +

p.

nad" - over (prep.), + i. - Z60 (nado); U60 (nã^{do}); P60

(nado).

nakladati - to place, lay on (vb.), impf. - V6,7 (na-

kladaja͡') pr. act. pt., m. n. sg.; Z2-6,7 (nakladaja)

pr. act. pt., m. n. sg.; Z7 (nakládaja) pr. act. pt.,

m. n. sg.; U7 (nakladaa͡) pr. act. pt., m. n. sg.; P7

(nakladaja͡) pr. act. pt., m. n. sg.

nami - see my.

nam" - see my.

naploditi - to fructify, replenish (vb.), pf. - V31

(napl$\overset{di}{o}$x") 1 sg. aor.; Z2-31 (naplódix") 1 sg. aor.

nap"lniti - to replenish (vb.), pf. - Z31 (napolnix")

1 sg. aor.; U31 (napolni͡) 1 sg. aor.; P31 (napolni^x)

1 sg. aor.

naroditi - to bear, give birth to (vb.), pf.- V29,30

(naro̧l") res. pt. m. sg.

narod" - people (noun) - Z2-88 (naróda) g. sg.

nastati - to come (vb.), pf. - V8 (nasta) 3 sg. aor.;
Z2-8 (nasta) 3 sg. aor.; Z8 (nastà) 3 sg. aor.; U8
(nasta) 3 sg. aor.; P8 (nasta) 3 sg. aor.

nas" - see my.

Natanail" - Nathanael (pro. noun) - V98 (Nafanail") n.

načati - to begin (vb.), pf. - Z26 (nača̧) 3 sg. aor.;
U26 (nač) for 3 sg. aor.; P26 (nača) 3 sg. aor.

naš' - our (pro.) - V6,7 (našim") m. i. sg., V73 (na-
šego) ntr. g. sg.; Z2-6,7 (našim") m. i. sg., Z2-19
(našem") m. p. sg., Z2-78 (naš") m. n. sg., Z2-83
(naš") m. n. sg.; Z72 (našix") m. g. pl.; U72 (naši)
m. g. pl.; P72 (naši^x) m. g. pl.

naju - see vě.

ne - not (particle) - V3 (ne), V4 (ne), V5 (ne), V38
(ne), V73 (ne), V83 (ne), V97 (ne); Z2-3 (ne), Z2-5
(ne), Z2-38 (ne), Z2-71a (ne), Z2-83 (ne), Z2-97 (ne);
Z37 (ne), Z37^2 (ne), Z38 (ne), Z45 (ne), Z72 (ne);
U37 (ne), U37^2 (ne), U38 (ne), U45 (ne), U72 (ne);
P37 (ne), P37^2 (ne), P38 (ne), P45 (ne), P72 (ne).

nebes'n" - heavenly (adj.) - V10 (nb^{s}nomu) m. d. sg.
lg., V98 (nb^{s}nyx") m. g. pl. lg.; Z2-10 (nb^{s}nomu) m.
d. sg. lg., Z2-98 (nb^{s}nyx") m. g. pl. lg.; Z10
(nbñomu) m. d. sg. lg., Z14 (nbnyi) m. n. sg. lg.;
U10 (nbñomu) m. d. sg. lg., U14 (nbny^i) m. n. sg. lg.;

P10 (nbn̂omu) m. d. sg. lg., P14 (nbn̂yi) m. n. sg. lg.

nebo - sky, heaven (noun) - V1 (nb̂o) n. sg., V15,12
(nb̂sa) a. pl., V15,12^2 (nb̂sa) n. pl., V48 (nb̂sa) a.
pl., V58 (nb̂sa) a. pl., V107 (nb̂a) a. pl.; Z2-1 (nbo)
n. sg., Z2-15,12 (nbo) n. sg., Z2-48 (nbsa) a. pl.,
Z2-91 (nbo) a. sg.; Z12 (nbo) n. sg., Z13 (nbo) a. sg.;
U12 (nbo) n. sg., U13 (nbo) a. sg.; P12 (nbo) n. sg.,
P13 (nbo) a. sg.

nemošč' - f., weakness (noun) - Z2-86 (nemošč") a. sg.

nemošč'n" - weak, powerless (adj.) - V21 (nemoščnyi) m.
n. sg. lg.; Z20 (nemošč'nei) f. d. sg. lg.; U20 (ne-
moščnoi̯) f. d. sg. lg.; P20 (nemoščnoi) f. d. sg. lg.;
Z2-20 (nemoščnei) f. d. sg. lg.

nemu - see on".

nesti - to carry (vb.), impf. - V10 (nesut') 3 pl. pr.;
Z2-10 (nesut") 3 pl. pr.; U10 (nesu̇) 3 pl. pr.; P10
(nesut') 3 pl. pr.

ni - nor, or (particle) - V73 (ni); Z2-73 (ni); Z37
(ni); U37 (ni); P37 (ni).

nim" - see on".

nišč' - poor (adj.) - V14 (niščim") m. d. pl. lg.;
Z2-14 (niščim") m. d. pl. lg.; Z14 (niščim") m. d. pl.
lg.; U14 (niščim) m. d. pl. lg.; P14 (niščim") m. d. pl.
lg.

noga - foot, leg (noun) - V82 (nozi) a. pl.; Z2-82
(nogámi) i. pl.; Z12 (nógu) g. du.; U10 (nô) g. pl.,
U12 (nogu) g. du.; P10 (nog") g. pl., P12 (nogu) g.

du.; Z2-82 (nozě) a. du.

Noe - Noah (pro. noun) - Z44 (Noi) n.; U44 (Noi) n.;
P44 (Noi) n.

nositi - to carry (vb.), impf. - V54 (nosivyi) past
act. pt., m. n. sg. lg.; Z2-54 (nosivyi) past act. pt.,
m. n. sg. lg.

nositi sja - to be carried (vb.), impf. - V58 (nosiv"-
šasja) past act. pt., m. n. du.

nuditi - to constrain (vb.), impf. - V86 (nudim") pr.
pass. pt., m. n. sg.; Z2-86 (nudim") pr. pass. pt., m. n.
sg.; Z39 (nudja) pr. act. pt., m. n. sg.; U39 (nudja)
pr. act. pt., m. n. sg.; P39 (nudja) pr. act. pt., m. n.
sg.

n" - but (conj.) - V5 (no), V18 (no), V38 (no), V73 (no);
Z2-5 (no), Z2-18 (no), Z2-38 (no), Z2-38^2 (no), Z2-59
(no), Z2-73 (no), Z2-74 (no), Z2-75 (no), Z2-80 (no);
Z38 (no), Z68 (no), Z70 (no), Z74 (no), Z75 (no); U38
(no), U68 (no), U70 (no), U72 (no), U74 (no), U75 (no);
P38 (no), P68 (no), P70 (no), P74 (no), P75 (no).

ny - see my.

nyně - now (adv.) - Z2-21 (nně); Z15 (nně), Z30 (nně),
Z35 (nně), Z39 (nně); U15 (nně), U32 (nné), U35 (nně),
U39 (nně), U76 (nně); P15 (nně), P32 (nně), P35 (nně),
P39 (nně).

o - oh (particle) - V14 (o), V21 (o), V22 (o), V39,40 (o),

V96 (ŏ), V103 (ö); Z2-14 (ŏ), Z2-21 (ŏ); Z14 (ŏ),

Z32 (ŏ); U14 (ŏ), U32 (ŏ); P14 (ŏ), P32 (ŏ).

o - about, on (prep.) + p. and a. - V title (o) + p.,

V96 (o) +p., V107 (o) +a.; Z2-19 (o) +p., Z2-96 (o) +p.;

Z27 (o) +p., U27 (o) +p.

obida - injury, wrong (noun) - Z34 (obidě) p. sg.; U34

(obidě) p. sg.; P34 (obide) p. sg.

oblak" - cloud (noun) - V15,12 (oblaky) a. pl.; Z2-15,

12 (oblaki) a. pl.; Z13 (oblaki) i. pl.; U13 (oblaky)

i. pl.; P13 (oblaky) a. pl.

oblačati - to wrap (vb.), impf. - Z2-15,12 (oblačaja)

pr. act. pt., m. n. sg.

obnoviti - to renew (vb.), pf. - Z2-71a (obnovl') res.

pt. m. sg.

obraz" - image, form (noun) - Z2-38 (obrazu) d. sg.;

Z38 (obrazu) d. sg.; U38 (obrazu) d. sg., U39 (obra-

zu) d. sg.; P38 (obraz^u) d. sg., P39 (obrazu) d. sg.

objazati - to wrap, bind (vb.), pf. - Z2-92 (obja-

zan") past pass. pt., m. n. sg.

od'ržati - to hold (vb.), impf. - Z2-73 (oderžimi)

pr. pass. pt., m. n. pl.

oděvati - to dress, clothe (vb.), impf. - V15,12

(odĕvaja) pr. act. pt., m. n. sg.

oko - eye (noun) - Z33 (oči) a. du.; U33 (ŏči) a. du.;

P33 (oči) a. du.

omyvati - to wash (vb.), impf. - Z2-71a (omyváxu) 3

pl. impf.; Z33 (omyváju^t) 3 pl. pr.; U33 (omyvajŭ) 3

pl. pr.; P33 (omyvajut') 3 pl. pr.

on" - he; that (pro.) - V2 (ja) m. a. pl., V4 (i) m.
a. sg., V6,7 (emu) m. d. sg., V10 (emu) m. d. sg.,
V13 (ego) m. g. sg., V13 (nemu) m. d. sg., V15,12
(ego) m. g. sg., V48 (nim") m. i. sg., V77 (ix") m. g.
pl., V106 (ja) m. a. pl., V108 (ego) m. g. sg.; Z2-13
(ego) m. g. sg., Z2-15,12 (ego) m. g. sg., Z2-20 (ego)
m. g. sg., Z2-75 (ix") m. g. pl., Z2-79 (nemu) m. d.
sg., Z2-81 (ego) m. a. sg., Z2-82 (ego) m. g. sg.,
Z2-84 (emu) m. d. sg., Z2-87 (ego) m. a. sg., Z2-93
(ego) m. a. sg., Z2-98 (nim") m. i. sg.; Z10 (emu) m.
d. sg., Z12 (ego) m. g. sg., Z13 (nemu) m. d. sg.,
Z15 (nix') f. p. pl., Z20 (ego) m. g. sg., Z23 (nim")
m. d. pl., Z25 (nemu) m. d. sg., Z35 (ego) m. g. sg.,
Z42 (emu) m. d. sg., Z60 (emu) m. d. sg.; Z9 (ix") m.
g. sg.; U9 (i) m. g. pl., U10 (emu) m. d. sg., U12
(ego) m. g. sg., U13 (nemu) m. d. sg., U15 (ni) f. p.
pl., U20 (e) m. g. sg., U23 (ni) m. d. pl., U25 (ně-
mu) m. d. sg., U35 (ego) m. g. sg., U42 (emu) m. d.
sg., U60 (emu) m. d. sg.; P9 (ix) m. g. pl., P10
(emu) m. d. sg., P12 (ego) m. g. sg., P13 (nemu) m.
d. sg., P15 (nix) f. p. pl., P20 (ego) m. g. sg., P23
(nim") m. d. pl., P25 (nemu) m. d. sg., P35 (ego) m.
g. sg., P42 (emu) m. d. sg., P60 (emu) m. d. sg.
/note that the g. forms express the 3 pers. poss. adj./
Z2-21 (on") m. a. sg., Z2-27 (on") m. a. sg., Z2-29

(on") m. a. sg., Z2-79 (oní) m. n. pl., Z2-84 (oní) f.
n. pl.!; Z19 (on") m. a. sg.; U19 (on") m. a. sg.; P19
(on") m. a. sg.

or'l" - eagle (noun) - V56 (orla) a. du.; V57 (orla)
a. du., V58 (orla) n. du.; Z2-56 (orla) a. du.

ostriti - to sharpen, whet (vb.), impf. - Z16 (ostrit") 3 sg. pr.; U16 (ostri) 3 sg. pr.; P16 (ostrit')
3 sg. pr.

osuditi - to condemn (vb.), pf. - Z30 (osudi) 2 sg.
aor.; U30 (osu ᵈ) 2 sg. aor.; P30 (osu ᵈ) 2 sg. aor.

os'l" - ass, donkey (noun) - V4 (osel") n. sg.; Z2-4
(osel") n. sg.

otřěti - to rub (vb.), pf. - Z2-82 (oterši) past act.
pt., f. n. du.

otrygnuti - to vomit (vb.), pf. - V86 (orygnuti) inf.;
Z2-86 (orynuti) inf.

ot" - from (prep.) + g. - V5 (oo), V21 (o), V22a (o),
V24 (o); Z2-5 (o), Z2-21 (o), Z2-24 (o), Z2-27 (o), Z2-
47 (o), Z2-59 (o), Z2-71a (o), Z2-80 (o), Z2-89 (o),
Z2-96 (o); Z title (o), Z10 (o), Z19 (o), Z24 (o), Z25
(o), Z32 (o), Z65 (o), Z66 (o), Z67 (o); U title (o),
U10 (o), U19 (o), U21 (o), U24 (o), U25 (o), U32 (o),
U44 (o), U65 (o), U66 (o), U67 (o); P title (o), P10
(o), P19 (o), P21 (o), P24 (o), P25 (o), P27 (o), P32
(o), P44 (o), P65 (o), P66 (o), P67 (o).

ot"valiti - to roll away (vb.), pf. - Z2-89 (ovaliti)
inf.

140

ot"vrěšči sja - to deny (vb.), pf. - V3 (ŏvergošašasja)

3 pl. aor.!; Z2-3 (sja...ŏvergoša) 3 pl. aor.!

ot"věščati - to answer (vb.), impf. - V20 (ŏvěščasta)

3 du. aor.

ot"ložiti - to lay aside, reject, refuse (vb.), pf. -

Z2-6,7 (ŏložim") 1 pl. pres./fut.; Z6 (ŏložim") 1 pl.

pres./fut.; U6 (ŏložim") 1 pl. pres./fut.; P6 (ŏloži^m)

1 pl. pres./fut.

ot"pustiti - to dismiss, let out of (vb.), pf. - V36

(ŏpustiti) inf.; Z2-86 (ŏpustiti) inf.

ot"selě - from now on (adv.) - Z21 (ŏselě); U21 (ŏselě);

P21 (ŏsele).

ot'c' - father (noun) - Vtitle (Ŏče) v. (sg.), V106

(Ŏca) g. sg., V107 (Ŏca) g. sg.; Z title (Ŏče) v. (sg.),

Z76 (Ŏca) a. sg.; U title (Ŏ) v. (sg.), U76 (Ŏca) a.

sg., P76 (Oca) a. sg.

oči - see oko.

paky - again (adv.) - Z2-48 ^P (páki); Z2-105 (páki).

pamjat' - f., memory (noun) - Z33 (pámjati) g. sg.; U33

(pamjati) g. sg.; P33 (pamjati) g. sg.

pasti - to fall (vb.), pf. - V82 (podosta) 3 du. aor.;

Z2-82 (pádši) past act. pt., f. n. du.

pastyr' - shepherd (noun) - Z9 (pástyri) n. pl.; U9

(pastyrja) a. pl.; P9 (pastyri) n. pl.

patriarx" - patriarch (noun) - V95 (potriârx") n. sg.;

Z41 (patriárx") n. sg.; U41 (patriárx") n. sg.; P41

(patriarx") n. sg.

pače - more, even more (comp. adv.) + g. - Z38 (páče),
Z71 (páče); U38 (pã), U71 (pã); P38 (pače), P71 (pače).

pelena - swaddling-clothes (noun) - V13 (pelenami) i.
pl., V15,12 (pelenami) i. pl., Z2-13 (pelenámi) i. pl.,
Z2-15,12 (pelenámi) i. pl.; Z13 (peleny) a. pl.; U13
(peleny) a. pl.; P13 (peleny) a. pl.

pers'sk" - Persian (adj.) - V10 (per'skyx") m. g. pl.
lg.; Z2-10 (pérskix") m. g. pl. lg.; Z10 (pér'skix")
m. g. pl. lg.; U10 (per'skÿ) m. g. pl. lg.; P10 (per-
sky^x) m. g. pl. lg.

peščera - cave, garden (noun) - V15,12 (peščery) g.
sg.; Z2-15,12 (peščery) g. sg.; Z15 (peščery) g. sg.;
U15 (peščery) g. sg.; P15 (peščery) g. sg.

plač' - f., lament (noun) - V6,7 (plač') a. sg., V77
(plač') a. sg.; Z2-6,7 (pláč') a. sg.; Z6 (plač') a.
sg.; U6 (plã) a. sg.; P6 (plã) a. sg.

plěn'nik" - prisoner (noun) - Z35 (polonjaník") n.
sg.; U35 (polonjaník") n. sg.; P35 (polonjanik") n.
sg.

po - for, after (prep.) + d. and + a. - V58 (po) + d.,
V106 (po) + d., V108 (po) + d.; Z2-38 (po) + d., Z2-
40 (po) + d.; Z26 (po) + d., Z38 (po) + d., Z38^2 (po)
+ d., Z75 (po) + a.; U26 (po) + d., U38 (po) + d.,
U38^2 (po) + d., U39 (po) + d., U 75 (po) + a.; P26
(po) + d., P38 (po) + d., P38^2 (po) + d., P39 (po) +
d., P75 (po) + a.

povelěti - to command (vb.), pf. - Z2-89 (povelě) 3 sg. aor.

povivati - to wrap (vb.), impf. - V13 (povivajušči) pr. act. pt., f. n. sg., V15,12 (povivaem") pr. pass. pt., m. n. sg.; Z2-13 (povivajušči) pr. act. pt., f. n. sg., Z2-15,12 (povivaem") pr. pass. pt., m. n. sg.; Z13 (povivajuščago) pr. act. pt., m. a. sg. lg.; U13 (povivajušče) for pr. act. pt., m. a. sg.; P13 (povivajušča) pr. act. pt., m. a. sg.

poviti - to wrap (vb.), pf. - Z13 (poviv'ši) past act. pt., f. n. sg.; U13 (povivši) past act. pt., f. n. sg.; P13 (povivši) past act. pt., f. n. sg.

povědati - to tell, inform, let know (vb.), pf. - Z27 (povědai) 2 sg. impv.; U27 (povědai) 2 sg. impv.; P27 (povědai) 2 sg. impv.

podobati - to become, be due, deserve (vb.), impf. - V108 (po^{do}bae^{t}) 3 sg. pr.

podob'n" - similar (adj.) - V56 (podobna) m. a. du.; Z2-56 (podobna) m. a. du.

pod"nožie - footstool (noun) - V15,12 (po^{d}nožie") n. sg.; Z2-15,12 (po^{d}nožie) n. sg.; Z12 (po^{d}nožie) n. sg.; U12 (po^{d}nožie) n. sg.; P12 (po^{d}nožie) n. sg.

požiti - to live (vb.), pf. - Z2-29 (požiti) inf.

poznati - to perceive, know, recognize (vb.), pf. - V3 (poznaša) 3 pl. aor., V4 (pozna) 3 sg. aor.; Z2-3 (poznaša) 3 pl. aor., Z2-4 (pozna) 3 sg. aor.

poiti - to go (vb.), pf. - Z24 (poídet") 3sg. pr./fut;
V24 (poidě) 3 sg. pr./fut.; P24 (poidet') 3 sg. pr./
fut.

poklanjati sja - to worship, greet (vb.), impf. - Z76
(poklanjáemsja) 1 pl. pr.

pokloniti sja - to worship, greet (vb.), pf. - U76
(poklonímsja) 1 pl. pr./fut.; P76 (polonim"ᔕ) for 1
pl. pr./fut.

poležati - to lie (vb.), pf. - V15,12 (poležati) inf.;
Z2-15,12 (poležáti) inf.

položiti - to lay (vb.), pf. - V6,7 (položim") 1 pl.
pr./fut.; Z2-87 (položíste) 3 du. aor.

pomazati - to anoint (vb.), pf. - Z2-71a (pomazávyi)
past act. pt., m. n. sg. lg.

pomilovati - to pardon, forgive, have mercy (vb.), pf.
- Z72 (pomílovati) inf.; U72 (pomilovati) inf.; P72
(pomilovati) inf.

poraziti - to strike, attack (vb.), pf. - V51 (poro-
ziᵛʸⁱ) past act. pt., m. n. sg. lg.; Z2-51 (poraziv")
past act. pt., m. n. sg.

poroda - paradise (noun) - Z40 (poródě) p. sg.; U40
(porodě) p. sg.; P40 (porědě) p. sg.

poroditi - to bear, give birth to (vb.), pf. - V2
(porodix") 1 sg. aor.; Z2-2 (porodíx") 1 sg. aor.

porugati - to abuse (vb.), pf. - Z2-59 (porugán")

past. pass. pt., m. n. sg.; Z67 (porugán") past pass.
pt., m. n. sg.; U67 (porugan") past pass. pt., m. n.
sg.; P67 (porugan") past pass. pt., m. n. sg.

porugati sja - to be abused (vb.), pf. - V39,40
(porugaet'sja) 3 sg. pr.; Z2-39 (porugáetsja) 3 sg. pr.

poslušati - to listen to (vb.), pf. + g. - V23a (poslušaite) 2 pl. impv.; Z2-23 (poslušaite) 2 pl. impv.

poslěd'n" - last (adj.) - Z2-84 (poslědnii) m. a. sg.
lg.

posmixati sja - to laugh (vb.), impf. - V39,40 (posmixaet'sja) 3 sg. pr.

pos"lati - to send (vb.), pf. - Z19 (pošlém") 1 pl.
pr./fut., U19 (poslem") 1 pl. pr./fut.; P19 (poslem")
1 pl. pr./fut.

potop" - flood (noun) - Z44 (potopa) g. sg.; U44 (potopa) g. sg.; P44 (potopa) g. sg.

prav'd'nik" - righteous man (noun) - V18 (pravednici) n.
pl.; Z2-18 (právednicy) n. pl., Z2-91a (právednicy) n.
pl., Z2-95 (právednicy) n. pl.; Z71 (právednik") g. pl.;
U71 (pravednĩk") g. pl.; P71 (pravednik") g. pl.

prav'd'n" - righteous (adj.) - Z18 (právednii) m. n.
pl. lg., Z44 (právednyi) m. n. pl. lg.; U18 (pravednii) m. n. pl. lg.; U44 (pravedn'i) m. n. pl. lg.!;
P18 (pravednii) m. n. pl. lg., P44 (pravědny) for m.
n. pl. lg.

priiti - to come, arrive (vb.), pf. - V18 (priidite)

2 sg. impv.!, V18 (priĭdete) 2 sg. impv.!, V81 (priĭdě) 3 sg. aor.; Z2-18 (priĭdete) 2 pl. impv. !, Z2-81 (priĭde) 3 sg. aor.; Z18 (priĭděte) 2 pl. impv., Z75 (priĭdi) 2 sg. impv.; U18 (priĭdetě) 2 pl. impv.!, U75 (priĭdi) 2 sg. impv.; P18 (priĭdete) 2 pl. impv.!, P75 (priĭdi) 2 sg. impv.

priklanjati sja - To bow, bend (vb.), impf. - V13 (priklanjajuščisja) pr. act. pt., f. n. sg.; Z2-13 (priklanjájuščisja) pr. act. pt., f. n. sg.

priniknuti - to bend, stoop (vb.), pf. - Z13 (prinĭkši) past act. pt., f. n. sg.; U13 (prinikši) past act. pt., f. n. sg.; P13 (prinikši) past act. pt., f. n. sg.

prinositi - to bring (vb.), impf. - Z10 (prinósjat") 3 pl. pr.

prisk"rb'n" - sorrowful (adj.) - V86 (priskorbna) f. n. sg.; Z2-86 (priskorbna) f. n. sg.

prisno - forever, eternally (adv.) - U76 (prŝno).

prispěti - to arrive (vb.), pf. - Z8 (prispě) 3 sg. aor.; U8 (prispe) 3 sg. aor.; P8 (prispě) 3 sg. aor.

pritešči - to come (vb.), pf. - Z2-82 (pritékši) past act. pt., f. n. du.

prixoditi - to come (vb.), impf. - Z9 (prixódit") 3 sg. pr.; U9 (prixodĭ) 3 sg. pr.; P9 (prixodit") 3 sg. pr.

provesti - to lead through (vb.), pf. - V46 (provedy)

for past act. pt., m. n. sg. lg.; Z2-46 (provel") res.
pt. m. sg.

proglasiti - to announce (vb.), pf. - Z2-19 (progĺím")
1 pl. pr./fut.

proobrazovati - to prefigure (vb.), impf. - V54 (proöb-
razova) 3 sg. aor.; Z2-54 (proöbrazovaše) 3 sg. impf.

propověděti - to preach (vb.), pf. - V106 (propovědite)
2 pl. impv.

prorok" - prophet (noun) - V title (prȓcě) p. pl., V18
(pr͡orci) n. pl.; V23a (pr rk") g. pl., V46 (pr͡ork") n.
sg., V51 (pr͡orky) n. sg.!, V51 (pr͡orka) g. sg., V55
(pr͡orci) n. pl., V95 (pr͡orcě) for n. pl., V101 (pr͡orky)
i. pl.; Z2-18 (pr͡orcy) n. pl., Z2-20 (pr͡ork") n. sg.,
Z2-46 (pr͡ork") n. sg., Z2-48 (pr͡ork") n. sg., Z2-51
(pr͡ork") n. sg., Z2-51 (pr͡orka) g. sg., Z2-71a (pr͡ork")
n. sg., Z2-95 (pr͡orcy) n. pl!; Z18 (pr͡orcy) n. pl.!,
Z46 (pr͡ork") n. sg., Z65 (pr͡orcěx") p. pl., Z70 (proro-
cy) n. pl.!; U 18 (pr͡orci) n. pl., U46 (pr͡ork") n. sg.,
U65 (pr͡orcě) p. sg. for p. pl.?, U70 (pr͡orci) n. pl.;
P18 (pr͡orci) n. pl., P46 (prorok") n. sg., P65 (pr͡orcěx)
p. pl., P70 (proroci) n. pl.

proslaviti - to praise (vb.), pf. - Z60 (prosĺávil")
res. pt., m. sg.; U60 (proslavi) res. pt. m. sg.; P60
(proslavil") res. pt. m. sg.

prosl'ziti sja - to weep, shed tears (vb.), pf. - Z2-91

(proslezisja) 3 sg. aor.

proxoditi - to go through, pass through (vb.), impf. -
Z9 (proxôdi^t) 3 sg. pr.; U9 (proxodja^t) 3 pl. pr.; P9
(proxo^{di}t") 3 sg. pr.

prědati sja - to be handed over, betrayed (vb.), pf. -
V97 (predavysja) for past act. pt., m. n. sg. lg.

pred" - before (prep.) + i. - Z2-38 (pr^{d}e); Z2-82 (pr^{d}e).

pred"stojati - to stand before, stand by (vb.), impf.
- Z2-88 (pr^{d}estojáxu) 3 pl. impf.

pred"teča - forerunner; (John) the Baptist (noun) -
Z65 (predoteča) n. sg.; U65 (prtč') for n. sg.; P65
(pr^{d}tčja) n. sg.!

preispod'n" - lowest (adj.) - V6,7 (preispodnem") m. p.
sg. lg., V41 (preispodnem") m. p. sg. lg.; Z2-6,7
(preispódnem") m. p. sg. lg., Z2-41 (preispódnem") m.
p. sg. lg., Z7 (preispodnem") m. p. sg.; U7 (preispódne^m)
m. p. sg.; P7 (preispodnem") m. p. sg.

presvět'l" - bright, radiant (adj.) - Z37 (presvětlago)
ntr. g. sg. lg.; U37 (presvětlago) ntr. g. sg. lg.; P37
(presvětlago) ntr. g. sg. lg.

prestol" - throne (noun) - V15,12 (pr^{s}tl") n. sg.; Z2-
15,12 (pr^{s}tl") n. sg.; Z12 (pr^{s}tl") n. sg.; U12 (pr^{s}tl")
n. sg.; P12 (pr^{s}tl") n. sg.

prestupiti - to transgress (vb.), pf.-Z40 (prestupíx")
1 sg. aor.; U40 (prestupi^x) 1 sg. aor.; P40 (prestu-

pix") 1 sg. aor.

prětvarjati sja - to change into, turn into (vb.), impf. - Z2-86 (pretvorjáetsja) 3 sg. pr.

prěčist" - immaculate (adj.) - V13 (prě͡staja) f. n. sg. lg.; Z2-13 (prě͡čtaja) f. n. s. lg.

psaltyr' - psalter (noun) - Z61 (psaltýr') a. sg.; U61 (pw͡ltr') a. sg.; P61 (pl͡tr').

pustiti - to allow, let, send (vb.), pf. - V5 (puščʹu) 1 sg. pr./fut.; Z2-5 (puščʹu) 1 sg. pr./fut.

pustynja - wilderness, desert (noun) - Z66 (pustýni) p. sg.; U66 (pustyni͡) p. sg.; P66 (pustyni) p. sg.

p"lk" - force, legion, host (noun) - V98 (polci) n. pl.

p'rvoz'dan" - first-created (adj.) - V26 (pervozdannyi̋) m. n. sg. lg., V95 (pervozdannyi̓) m. n. sg. lg.; Z2-26 (pr'vozdánnyi) m. n. sg. lg., Z2-95 (pr"vozdánnyi) m. n. sg. lg., Z26 (pervozdannyi͡) m. n. sg. lg., Z28 (pervozdánnyi) m. n. sg. lg.; U26 (pervoz͡dannyi͡) m. n. sg. lg., U28 (pervo͡z͡dannyi͡) m. n. sg. lg.; P26 (per͗vozdanny") m. n. sg. lg.!, P28 (pervoz͗dannyi͡) m. n. sg. lg.

p'rv" - first (adj.) - Z41 (pérvyi) m. n. sg. lg.; U41 (perv͡yi͡) m. n. sg. lg.; P41 (pervyi̓) m. n. sg. lg.

p'rsi - f. pl., breast (noun) - Z2-26 (pér̓si) a.

p'rst" - finger (noun) - V6,7 (per͡šty) a. pl.; Z2-6,7 (pérsty) a. pl.; Z7 (pérsty) a. pl.; U7 (per͡šty) a. pl.; P7 (persty) a. pl.

pěsn' - f., song (noun) - V6,7 (pě) for a. pl.; Z2-6,7
(pěsni) a. pl., Z6 (pěsn'mi) i. pl.; U6 (pěmi) i. pl.;
P6 (pěmi) i. pl.

rabota - work, labor (noun) - Z2-41 (rabotě) p. sg.

rab" - servant (noun) - V97 (raba) g. sg.; Z2-97
(rabà) g. sg.; Z35 (rab") n. sg.; U35 (rab") n. sg.;
P35 (rab") n. sg.

radi - for the sake of (postposition) + g. - Z2-31
(rádi); Z31 (rádi), Z38 (rádi), Z41 (radí), Z72 (rádi);
U31 (rá^{di}), U38 (rá^{di}), U41 (rá^{di}), U72 (rá^{di}); P31
(rá^{di}), P38 (rá^{di}), P41 (radi), P72 (rá^{di}).

razrěšiti - to free, let loose (vb.), pf. - Z2-93
(razrěšite) 2 pl. impv.

rai - paradise (noun) - Z2-105 (rái) a. sg.

ramo - shoulder (noun) - V54 (ramě) p. sg.; Z2-54
(rámě) p. sg.

raspjatie - crucifiction (noun) - V97 (rast'e) a. sg.

Rasuil" - (for) Raguel (pro. noun) - V98 (Rasuil") n.

rešči - to say (vb.), pf. - V23 (re) for 3 sg. aor.,
V94 (re) for 3 sg. aor., V102 (re) for 3 sg. aor.;
Z2-20 (rekoša) 3 pl. aor., Z2-23 (reče) 3 sg. aor.,
Z2-27 (re) for 3 sg. aor., Z2-78 (reče) 3 sg. aor.,
Z2-79 (rekoša) 3 pl. aor., Z2-80 (reče) 3 sg. aor.,
Z2-84 (rekoša) 3 pl. aor., Z2-87 (reče) 3 sg. aor.,
Z2-90 (reče) 3 sg. aor., Z2-91 (reče) 3 sg. aor.,
Z2-91^{2} (reče) 3 sg. aor., Z2-93 (reče) 3 sg. aor., Z2-
97 (reče) 3 sg. aor., Z2-105 (reče) 3 sg. aor.; Z7

(reče) 3 sg. aor., Z20 (rekósta) 3 du. aor., Z42
(rek") past act. pt., m. n. sg.; U7 (re$^{\widehat{c}}$) 3 sg. aor.,
U20 (rkosta) 3 du. aor., U23 (reče) 3 sg. aor., U42
(re$^{\widehat{c}}$) 3 sg. aor.; P7 (re$^{\widehat{c}}$) 3 sg. aor., P20 (rekosta)
3 du. aor., P23 (re$^{\widehat{c}}$) 3 sg. aor., P42 (reče) 3 sg.
aor.

rov" - pit (noun) - V51 (rov") a. sg.; Z2-51 (rov")
a. sg.

rog" - horn (noun) - Z2-71a (rógom") i. sg.!

roditi sja - to be born (vb.), pf. - V10 (rož^{d}ešusja)
past act. pt., m. d. sg.; Z2-10 (rõšusja) for past
act. pt., m. d. sg.; Z10 (rõšũ) for past act. pt., m.
d. sg., Z65 (rodisja) 3 sg. aor.; U10 (rož^{d}'šusja)
past act. pt., m. d. sg., U65 (rõ^{di}sja) 3 sg. aor.; P10
(rož^{d}'šusja) past act. pt., m. d. sg., P65 (rodisja)
3 sg. aor.

rugati sja - to abuse (vb.), impf. + d. - V20 (rugajuščesja) pr. act. pt., m. n. pl.; Z2-20 (rugajuščesja) pr. act. pt., m. n. pl.; Z20 (rugájuščesja) pr.
act. pt., m. n. pl., Z39 (rugâet...sja) 3 sg. pr.;
U20 (rugajuščisja) pr. act. pt., m. n. pl.!, U39
(rugâet'...sja) 3 sg. pr.; P20 (rugaju̅šči̅) for pr.
act. pt., m. n. pl., P39 (rugaèt'...sja) 3 sg. pr.

ruka - hand, arm (noun) - V26 (rukami) i. pl., V105
(rukoju) i. sg.; Z26 (ruka^{mi}) i. pl.; U26 (rukama)
i. du.; P26 (rukama) i. du.

r"p"t" - noise (noun) - V10 (ropot") a. sg.

Samuil" - Samuel (pro. noun) - V23a (Somoǐle) v.,
V98 (Semǐel") n.; Z2-71a (Samuǐl") n.

sam" - self (pro.) - V15,12 (sam") m. n. sg., V107
(sam") m. n. sg.; Z2-15,12 (sam') m. n. sg.; Z72
(sám") m. n. sg.; U72 (sam") m. n. sg., U72^2 (sa^m)
m. n. sg.; P72 (sam") m. n. sg.

svirjati - to pipe, play (vb.), impf. - Z9 (svirjá-
jut") 3 pl. pr.; U9 (svirjajǔ^t) 3 pl. pr.; P9 (svi-
rajût') 3 pl. pr.

svoi - my, his, her, its, our, your, their (pro.) -
V4 (svoégo) m. g. sg., V16 (svoimi) f. i. pl., V26
(svoě) ntr. a. sg., V38 (svoǐ) ntr. p. pl., V96
(svoém") m. p. sg.; Z2-4 (svoégò) m. g. sg., Z2-16
(svoimi) f. i. pl., Z2-26 (svojà) f. a. pl., Z2-38
(svoix") ntr. pr. pl., Z2-41 (svoim") m. i. sg.!,
Z2-71a (svoi) f. a. du., Z2-75 (svoè) ntr. a. sg.,
Z2-78 (svoim") m. d. pl., Z2-82 (svoimi) m. i. pl.,
Z2-95 (svoim") m. i. sg.!; Z7 (svojà) m. a. pl.,
Z10 (svoix") m. g. pl., Z26 (svoému) ntr. d. sg., Z33
(svoimi) f. i. pl., Z41 (svoégo) m. a. sg., Z72 (svoégo) ntr. g. sg.; U7 (svoja) m. a. pl., U10 (svoǐ) m.
g. pl., U26 (svoému) ntr. d. sg., U33 (svoimi) f. i.
pl., U41 (svoě) for m. a. sg., U72 (svoě) for ntr. g.
sg.; P7 (svoâ) m. a. pl., P10 (svoǐ) m. g. pl., P26

(svoíma) f. i. du., P26 (svoému) ntr. d. sg., P33

(svoimi) f. i. pl., P41 (svoě̇) m. a. sg., P72 (svoé-

go) ntr. g. sg.

<u>světozar'n"</u> - radiant (adj.) - V73 (světazarnago) ntr.g.

sg. lg.; Z2-73 (světozarnago) ntr. g. sg. lg.

<u>svět"</u> - world (noun) - V21 (svět") a. sg., V22a

(svět") a. sg., V24 (svět") a. sg., V25 (svět") a.

sg., V27 (svět") a. sg., V29,30 (světě) p. sg.; Z2-

21 (svět") a. sg., Z2-27 (svét") a. sg., Z2-29

(svéte) p. sg.; Z36 (svét") a. sg.; U36 (své̇) a.

sg.; P36 (svět") a. sg.

<u>svět'l"</u> - bright (adj.) - Z2-8 (svétlyi) m. n. sg. lg.;

Z27 (svétlyi) m. n. sg. lg.; U27 (světlyî) m. n. sg.

lg.; P27 (světlyî) m. n. sg. lg.

<u>Svjataja Svjatyx"</u> - Holy of Holies (noun phr.) - V56

(Stâa Stŷx") n.

<u>svjat"</u> - holy, saint (adj.) - V title (stŷ͡x) m. p. pl.

lg.; Z2 title (stgo) m. g. sg. lg.; Z title (stŷx) m.

g. pl. lg., Z76 (stomu) ntr. d. sg. lg., Z76 (stuju)

f. a. sg. lg.; U title (stŷx) m. g. pl. lg., U76 (stmu)

ntr. d. sg. lg., U76 (stuju) f. a. sg. lg.; P title

(stŷx) m. g. pl. lg., P76 (stomu) ntr. d. sg. lg., P76

(stuju) f. a. sg. lg. See also <u>Svjataja Svjatyx"</u> and

<u>Svjatyi Dux"</u>.

<u>Svjatyi Dux"</u> - Holy Ghost (noun phr.) - V57 (Dx" Stŷi)

n., V106 (Stgo Dxa) g.; Z2-48 (Stgo Dxa) g.; Z76 (Stgo

Dxa) a.; U76 (Stgo Dxa) a.

se - lo! (interjection) - V5 (se), V22 (se), V24 (se),
V41 (se), V46 (se), V51 (se), V56 (se); Z2-5 (se),
Z2-6,7 (se), Z2-24 (se), Z2-41 (se), Z2-46 (se), Z2-48
(se), Z2-51 (se), Z2-56 (se), Z2-71a (se), Z2-71a^2 (se);
Z8 (se), Z8^2 (se), Z16 (se), Z24 (se), Z26 (se), Z28
(se), Z30 (se), Z34 (se), Z34^2 (se), Z37 (se), Z41 (se),
Z46 (sè), Z65 (se); U8 (se), U8^2 (se), U16 (se), U24
(se), U26 (se), U28 (se), U29 (se), U30 (se), U32 (se),
U34 (se), U34^2 (se), U37 (se), U41 (se), U46 (se), U65
(se); P8 (se), P8^2 (se), P16 (se), P24 (se), P28 (se),
P30 (se), P32 (se), P34 (se), P34^2 (se), P37 (se), P41
(se), P46 (se), P65 (se).

serafim" - seraphim (noun) - V56 (serofěmu) d. sg.;
Z2-56 (serafimom") d. pl.

sestra - sister (noun) - V81 (sestrě) d. sg.; Z2-81
(sestrě) d. sg.

sila - strength (noun) - V86 (sily) n. pl.; Z2-20 (silě) d. sg., Z2-48 (siloju) i. sg., Z2-86 (sila) n. sg.;
Z20 (silě) d. sg.; U20 (silě) d. sg.; P20 (silě) d.
sg.

sil'n" - strong (adj.) - V101 (silen") m. n. sg.

Sinaiska Gora - Mount Sinai (noun phr.) - V46 (Sinai-
stěi Gorě) p.; Z2-46 (Sinaistei Gorě) p.

skvozě - through (prep.) + a. - Z2-46 (skvozě).

skoro - soon, quickly (adv.) - V82 (skoro); Z2-82
(skóro); Z16 (skóro); U16 (skoro); P16 (skoro).

skotii - cattle (adj.) - V15,12 (skotiix") f. p. pl.

skr'g"tati - to gnash (vb.), impf. - Z2-16 (skregtáše)
3 sg. impf.

skr'ž'tati - to gnash (vb.), impf. - V16 (skrež'taša)
3 sg. impf.!

sk"rb' - f., sorrow, woe (noun) - V6,7 (skorb') a.
sg.; Z2-6,7 (skórb") a. sg., Z33 (skórbiju) i. sg.; U33
(skorbiju) i. sg.; P33 (skórbiju) i. sg.

slava - glory, praise (noun) - V5 (slavy) g. sg., V99
(slavy) g. sg., V101 (slavy) g. sg., V108 (s^{1}ava) n.
sg., V108 (sľa: +) n. sg.; Z2-5 (slávy) g. sg., Z2-91
(slávu) a. sg.

slaviti - to glorify, praise (vb.), impf. - Z76 (slá-
vjašče) pres. act. pt., m. n. pl.; U76 (slavjašče) pres.
act. pt., m. n. pl.; P76 (slavjašče) pres. act. pt.,
m. n. pl.

slovo - word; tale (noun) - V title (slovo) n. sg.,V5 (slovo)
a.sg;Z2-title(slóvo)n.sg.,Z2-5(slóvo)a.sg.,Z2-19 (slóvo)
a. sg.; Z title (slóvo) n. sg.; U title (slo) n. sg.;
P title (slovo) n. sg.

slyšati - to hear (vb.), impf. - V1 (slyši) 2 sg. impv.,
V10 (slyšim") 1 pl. pr., V77 (slyša) 3 sg. aor., V82
(slyšavši) past act. pt., f. n. du.; Z2-1 (slýši) 2 sg.
impv., Z2-10 (slýšaxom") 1 pl. aor., Z2-26 (slýšav")
past act. pt., m. n. sg., Z2-86 (slýšu) 1 sg. pr.;
Z9 (slýšu) 1 sg. pr., Z10 (slýšu) 1 sg. pr., Z26 (slýšav") past act. pt., m. n. sg., Z37 (slyšu) 1 sg. pr.;
U9 (slyšu) 1 sg. pr., U10 (slyšju) 1 sg. pr., U26 (sly-

sav") past act. pt., m. n. sg., U37 (slysju) 1 sg. pr.; P9
(slyšju) 1 sg. pr., P10 (slyšju) 1 sg. pres., P37 (slyšu) 1 sg. pr.

sl'za - tear (noun) - Z2-71a (slezámi) i. pl.; Z19
(slezámi) i. pl., Z33 (slezámi) i. pl.; U19 (slezami)
i. pl., U33 (slezami) i. pl.; P19 (slezami) i. pl.,
P33 (slezami) i. pl.

sm'rděti - to stink (vb.), impf. - Z2-90 (smerdit")
3 sg. pr.

Solomon" - Solomon (pro. noun) - V23a (Solomon") n.,
V56 (Solomon") n., V96 (Solomoně) p., V97 (Solomona)
a.; Z2-56 (Solomon") n., Z2-96 (Solomoně) p., Z2-97
(Solomona) a.

Sotona - Satan (noun) - Z2-47 (Sotony) g., Z2-71a (Sotony) g.; Z32 (Sotony) g.; U32 (Sotony) g.; P32 (Sotony) g.

sotonin" - of Satan, Satan's (poss. adj.) - V5 (sotoniny) f. g. sg.; Z2-5 (sotoniny) f. g. sg.

stonati - to moan, groan (vb.), impf. - Z63 (stonja)
pr. act. pt., m. n. sg.; U63 (stonja) pr. act. pt., m.
n. sg.; P63 (stonja) pr. act. pt., m. n. sg.

strast' - f., passion (noun) - V54 (strāti) g. sg.;
Z2-54 (strti) g. sg.

straš'n" - fearful (adj.) - V101 (strašen") m. n. sg.;
Z2-14 (strašnyi) m. n. sg. lg.

struna - string (noun) - V6,7 (strupy!) a. pl.; Z2-6,7
(strúny) a. pl.; Z7 (strúny) a. pl.; U7 (struny) a. pl.;
P7 (struny) a. pl.

<u>Subota cvĕt'na</u> - the eve of Palm Sunday, Good Saturday (noun phr.) - Z2 - title (s[b]u cvĕtnuju) a. sg.

<u>sut'</u> - see <u>byti</u>.

<u>sušči</u> - see <u>byti</u>.

<u>s"</u> - with (prep.) + i. - V41 (s"), V41[2] (s"), V41 (so), V41[3] (s"), V46 (s), V48 (s), V49 (s), V52 (s), V95 (so), V95[2] (so), V98 (so), V101 (s"); Z2-39 (so), Z2-41 (s'), Z2-41 (so), Z2-46 (s), Z2-47 (s), Z2-49 (s), Z2-52,53 (s), Z2-71a (s), Z2-95 (s"), Z2-95 (so), Z2-98 (s); Z19 (so), Z47 (s), Z69 (s); U19 (s"), U47 (s), U63(s), U69 (s); P19 (s"), P47 (s), P63 (s), P69 (s).

<u>s"bljusti</u> - to observe (vb.), pf. - V106 (sobljusti) inf.

<u>s"vĕdĕti</u> - to know (vb.), impf. - Z72 (svĕdyi) pres. act. pt., m. n. sg. lg.; P72 (svĕsi) 2 sg. pr.

<u>s"vjazati</u> - to bind (vb.), pf. - Z2-75 (svjaži) 2 sg. impv.; Z75 (svjaži) 2 sg. impv.; U75 (svjaži) 2 sg. impv., P75 (svjaži) 2 sg. impv.

<u>s"grĕšiti</u> - to sin (vb.), pf. - V38 (sogrĕši[x]) 1 sg. aor., V39,40 (sogrĕši[x]) 1 sg. aor., V43 (sogrĕši) 3 sg. aor., V46 (sogrĕši) 3 sg. aor., V48 (sogrĕši) 3 sg. aor., V53 (sogrĕši) 3 sg. aor., V53a (sogrĕši) 3 sg. aor., V55 (sogrĕšiša) 3 pl. aor.; Z2-38 (sogrĕšix") 1 sg. aor., Z2-40 (sogrĕšil") res. pt., m. sg., Z2-43 (sogrĕši) 3 sg. aor., Z2-47 (sogrĕšil") res. pt., m. n. sg., Z2-50 (sogrĕšil") res. pt., m. sg., Z2-52,53 (sogrĕši) 3 sg. aor.; Z38 (sogrĕšix") 1 sg. aor., Z45 (sogrĕšil") res.

pt., m. sg., Z47 (sogrěšil") res. pt., m. sg., Z62

(sogrěšíl") res. pt. m. sg., Z64 (sogrěšíl") res. pt.,

m. sg., Z68 (sogrěšíl") res. pt., m. sg.; U38 (sogrěši^x)

1 sg. aor., U43 (sogrěši) 3 sg. aor., U45 (sogrěšili)

res. pt., m. pl., U47 (sogrěšil") res. pt., m. sg., U62

(s"grěši) res. pt., m. sg., U64 (s"grěši$^{l.}$) res. pt., m.

sg., U68 (sogrěšil") res. pt., m. sg.; P38 (s"grěši^x)

1 sg. aor., P43 (s"grěši) 3 sg. aor., P45 (s"grěšili)

res. pt., m. pl., P47 (s"grěšil") res. pt., m. sg.,

P62 (s"grěšil") res. pt., m. sg., P64 (s"grěšili) res.

pt., m. pl., P68 (s"grěšil") res. pt. m. sg.

s"z'danie - creation (noun) - Z2-39 (sozdaniem") i. sg.

!, Z2-75 (sozdánie) a. sg.

s"z'dati - to create (vb.), pf. - V56 (s"zdavy) for

past act. pt., m.n.sg., V105 (sozdal") res. pt., m.

sg.; Z2-29 (sózdal") res. pt., m. sg., Z2-56 (sozdà)

3 sg. aor., Z2-105 (sozdála) res. pt. f. sg.; Z29

(sozda^l) res. pt. m. sg.; U29 (soz^{d}al") res. pt. m.

sg.; P29 (s"z^{d}al") res. pt. m. sg.

s"kovati - to forge (vb.), pf. - V56 (skovavy) for

past act. pt., m. n. sg.; Z2-56 (skova) 3 sg. aor.

s"krušiti - to smash, crush, destroy (vb.), pf. - V104

(sokrušit") 3 sg. pr./fut.

s"krušiti sja - to be smashed, crushed, destroyed (vb.),

pf. - V103 (sokrušit"sja) 3 sg. pr./fut.!

s"lnce - sun (noun) - V73 (slnca) g. sg.; Z2-73 (slnca)

g. sg.; Z37 (slnca) g. sg.; U37 (slnca) g. sg.; P37

158

(slnca) g. sg.

s"niti - to descend, come down (vb.), pf. - V14 (sniti) inf., V42a (snidi) 2 sg. impv., V48 (snidi) for 3
sg. aor., V57 (snidet') 3 sg. pr./fut., V98 (snide) 3
sg. aor.; Z2-14 (sniti) inf., Z2-48 (snide) 3 sg. aor.,
Z2-98 (snide) 3 sg. aor.; Z14 (sniti) inf., Z72 (sniti)
inf.; U14 (sniti) inf., U72 (sniti) inf.; P14 (sniti)
inf.

s"něd' - f., food (noun) - Z2-51 (sněd') a. sg.

s"pasenie - salvation (noun)- Z8 (spsenia) g. sg.;
U8 (sp nija) g. sg.; P8 (spsenija) g. sg.

s"pasti - to save (vb.), pf. - V5 (spsu) 1 sg. pr./fut.;
Z2-5 (spasu) 1 sg. pr./fut., Z2-75 (spsi) 2 sg. impv.,
Z2-79 (spsetsja) 3 sg. pr./fut.

s"pas'n" - saving (adj.) - V54 (spsnyja) g. sg. f.
lg.; Z2-54 (spsenyja) g. sg. f. lg.

s"rěsti - to meet (vb.), pf. - Z2-81 (sretoša) 3 pl.
aor.

s"staviti - to compose (vb.), pf. - Z61 (sostavil")
res. pt., m. sg.; U61 (sostavi) res. pt. m. sg.; P61
(s"stavil") res. pt., m. sg.

s"tvoriti - to create (vb.), pf. - Z2-38 (sotvoren")
past pass. pt., m. n. sg.; Z38 (sotvoren") past pass.
pt., m. n. sg.; U38 (stvoren") past pass. pt., m. n.
sg., U39 (stvorena) past pass. pt., m. a. sg.; P38
(s"tvoren") past pass. pt., m. n. sg., P39 (s"tvorena)

past pass. pt., m. a. sg.

s"trĕti - to destroy, crush (vb.), pf. - V104 (sotre)
3 sg. aor.

s"trĕti sja - to be destroyed, crushed (vb.), pf. -
V103 (sotrèt" sja) 3 sg. pr./fut.!

s"tjažati - to acquire, get, possess (vb.), pf.- V4
(stežavšago) past pass. pt., m. a. sg. lg.

syn" - son (noun) - V2 (sn̂y) a. pl., V41 (sn̂om") i.
sg.! V51 (sn̂") n. sg., V95 (sn̂om") i. sg.!, V96 (sn̂u)
p. sg., V106 (Ŝna) g. sg.; Z2-2 (sǹy) a. pl., Z2-41
(sǹom") i. sg.!, Z2-51 (sǹ") n. sg., Z2-56 (s̀n") n.
sg., Z2-95 (sǹom") i. sg.!, Z2-96 (sn̂u) p. sg.; Z41
(sǹa) a. sg., Z76 (s̀na) a. sg.; U41 (s̀na) a. sg., U76
(s̀na) a. sg.; P41 (ŝna) a. sg., P76 (s") for a. sg.?

s' - this (pro.) - V23a (sem") m. p. sg., V29,30 (se)
ntr. a. sg., V29,30 (sem") m. p. sg., V31 (sego) ntr.
g. sg., V57 (si) for m. a. du. or m. a. pl. correctly,
V105 (si) f. n. sg., V105^2 (si) f. n. sg.; Z2-21 (segò) m. g. sg., Z2-29 (se) ntr. a. sg., Z2-31 (sego)
m. g. sg., Z2-38 (sego) ntr. g. sg., Z2-40 (siju) f.
a. sg., Z2-75 (segò) m. g. sg., Z2-105 (sia) f. n.
sg.!, Z2-105^2 (sia) f. n. sg.!; Z15 (siá) for f. g.
sg., Z15 (síx") f. g. pl., Z19 (seja) f. g. sg., Z29
(se) ntr. a. sg., Z29 (séĭ) f. p. sg., Z34 (sei) f.
p. sg., Z38 (siju) f. a. sg., Z38 (segò) ntr. g. sg.,
Z44 (sêm") m. p. sg., Z45 (séĭ) m. n. sg.!, Z69 (sém")

160

m. p. sg., Z70 (sego̍) ntr. g. sg.; U15 (sia) f. g.

sg.!, U15 (si͓) f. g. pl., U19 (sia) for f. g. sg.,

U29 (sei͡) f. p. sg., U34 (sei͡) f. p. sg., U34^2 (sei͡)

f. p. sg., U38 (siju͡) f. a. sg., U38 (sego) ntr. g.

sg., U44 (sem') m. p. sg., U45 (sii͡) m. n. pl., U63

(se͏ᵐ) m. p. sg., U69 (sem') m. p. sg., U70 (sego) ntr.

g. sg.; P15 (sija̍) f. g. sg., P15 (si͓) f. g. pl., P19

(sea̍) f. g. sg., P26 (se̍) ntr. a. sg., P29 (se) ntr.

a. sg., P29 (sei̍) f. p. sg., P34 (sei) f. p. sg.,

P34^2 (sei̍) f. p. sg., P38 (siju̍) f. a. sg., P38 (sego)

ntr. g. sg., P45 (sii̍) m. n. pl., P63 (sem") m. p.

sg., P69 (sem") m. p. sg., P70 (sego) ntr. g. sg.

s'de - here (adv.) - Z2-83 (zdě); Z44 (zdě), Z47

(zdě), Z63 (zdě), Z69 (zdě); U47 (zdě), U63 (zdě),

U69 (zdě); P44 (zde), P47 (zdě), P63 (zᵈě), P69 (zdě).

s'rd'ce - heart (noun) - Z33 (srᵈce) a. sg.; U33

(srᵈce) a. sg.; P33 (srᵈce) a. sg.

sěděti - to sit, be sitting (vb.), impf. - V6,7 (sědja)

pr. act. pt., m. n. sg., V41 (sědja) pr. act. pt., m.

n. sg., V107 (sěde) 3 sg. aor.; Z2-6,7 (sědjai) pr.

act. pt., m. n. sg. lg., Z2-41 (sedja) pr. act. pt.,

m. n. sg.; Z7 (sědja̍) pr. act. pt., m. n. sg., Z32

(sedját") 3 pl. pr., Z47 (sedít") 3 sg. pr.; U7 (sed-

ja) pr. act. pt., m. n. sg., U32 (sedjaᵗ) 3 pl. pr.,

U47 (sedit') 3 sg. pr.; P7 (sedja) pr. act. pt., m.

n. sg., P32 (sedjat') 3 pl. pr., P47 (sedit') 3 sg. pr.

takože - thus, in the same way (adv.) - Z64 (takože);
U64 (tako^ž); P64 (tako^ž).

tamo - there (adv.) - Z21 (támo); U21 (tamo); P21
(tamo).

Tartail" - Tartael, error for Tartarus? (pro. noun) -
V98 (Tartail") n.

tvar' - f., creature, creation (noun) - V39,40 (tva-
r'ju) i. sg.; Z35 (tvárem") d. pl.; U35 (tvare^m) d.
pl.; P35 (tvarem") d. pl.

tvoi - your, 2 sg. (poss. adj.) - V39,40 (tvoéju) f.
i. sg., V41 (tvoi) m. n. pl., V46 (tvoi) m. n. sg.,
V51 (tvoi) m. n. sg., V54 (tvoéjá) f. g. sg., V73
(tvoégo) ntr. g. sg., V73^2 (tvoégo) m. g. sg.; Z2-29
(tvoém") m. p. sg.!, Z2-38 (tvoému) m. d. sg., Z2-39
(tvoim") ntr. i. sg.!, Z2-41 (tvoí) m. n. sg., Z2-46
(tvoi) m. n. sg., Z2-46 (tvoéjû) f. i. sg., Z2-48 (tvói)
m. n. sg., Z2-51 (tvoi) m. n. sg., Z2-54 (tvojà) f. g.
sg.!, Z2-71a (tvoi) m. n. sg., Z2-73 (tvoégò) ntr. g.
sg., Z28 (tvoí) m. a. sg., Z32 (tvoì) m. n. pl.,
Z36 (tvoí) m. a. sg., Z37 (tvoégò) ntr. g. sg., Z38
(tvoému) m. d. sg., Z40 (tvoju) f. a. sg., Z41 (tvoí)
m. n. sg., Z70 (tvoì) m. n. pl., Z76 (tvoému) ntr. d.
sg.; U28 (tvoî) m. n. sg., U32 (tvoî) m. n. pl., U36
(tvoî) m. a. sg., U37 (tvoe) ntr. g. sg., U38 (tvoému) m. d. sg., U39 (tvoému) m. d. sg., U40 (tvoju)
f. a. sg., U41 (tvoî) m. n. sg., U70 (tvoi) m. n. pl.,
U76 (tvoé^m) for ntr. d. sg.; P28 (tvoi) m. n. sg., P32

(tvoⁿ) for m. n. pl., P36 (tvoĭ) m. n. sg., P37 (tvoê)

for ntr. g. sg., P38 (tvoêmu) m. d. sg., P39 (tvoêmu)

m. d. sg., P40 (tvoju) f. a. sg., P41 (tvoĭ) m. n. sg.,

P70 (tvoĭ) m. n. pl., P76 (tvoêmu) ntr. d. sg.

tv'rdo - tightly (adv.) - V22 (tverdo); Z22 (tvérdo);

U22 (tverdo); P22 (tverdo).

tebě - see ty.

tešči - to run, flow (vb.), impf. - V82 (tekosta)
3 du. aor.

ti - see ty.

tix" - quiet (adj.) - V6,7 (tixia) f. a. pl. lg.;

Z2-6,7 (tixi) f. a. pl.

to - then, but (conj.) - V57 (to), V101 (to); Z2-40

(to), Z2-47 (to), Z2-49 (to), Z2-79 (to), Z2-83 (to), Z2-83² (to),

Z2-91 (to); Z38 (to), Z43 (to), Z45 (to), Z45² (to), Z62

(to), Z72 (to); U38 (to), U43 (to), U45 (to), U45²

(to), U47 (to), U62 (to), U67 (tŏ), U72 (to); P38 (to),

P43 (to), P45 (to), P47 (to), P62 (to), P72 (to).

tobě - see ty.

toliko - only (adv.) - Z34 (tólko); Z34 (tolky); P34

(tol'ko).

Troica - Trinity (noun) - Z76 (Tr͡ocu) a.; U76 (Tr͡oju)

a.; P76 (Tr͡ocu) a.

tu - there (adv.) - Z2-88 (tu).

tuga - sorrow, woe, anguish (noun) - V73 (tugoju) i.

sg.; Z2-73 (tugóju) i. sg.; Z33 (tugóju) i. sg.; U33

(tugoju) i. sg., U34 (tuze) p. sg.; P33 (tugoju) i. sg.,

P34 (tuze) p. sg.

t" - this (pronoun) - V25 (tot") m. n. sg., doubled
form, V38 (togo) m. g. sg., V47 (tot) m. n. sg., dbld.
fm., V49 (tot') m. n. sg., dbld. fm., V52 (tot) m. n.
sg., dbld. fm., V55 (tĭ) m. n. pl., V58 (toĭ) m. a.
sg. lg., V105 (taja) f. g. sg.?, V108 (tomu) m. d.
sg.; Z2-43 (toi) m. n. sg. lg., Z2-47 (t̆oi) m. n. sg.
lg., Z2-47^2 (tói) m. n. sg. lg., Z2-49 (tói) m. n.
sg. lg., Z2-50 (tŏi) m. n. sg. lg., Z2-52,53 (tŏi) m.
n. sg. lg., Z2-52,53^2 (tói) m. n. sg. lg., Z2-71a
(tói) m. n. sg. lg.; Z11 (togŏ) m. g. sg., Z12 (tomu)
m. d. sg., Z13 (togŏ) m. g. sg., Z25 (tói) m. n. sg.
lg., Z43 (tói) m. n. sg. lg., Z47 (toi) m. n. sg. lg.,
Z47^2 (toi) m. n. sg. lg., Z61 (tŏi) m. n. sg. lg.,
Z62 (t̂oi) m. n. sg. lg., Z67 (tói) m. n. sg. lg., Z68
(tói) m. n. sg. lg., Z69 (toi) m. n. sg. lg.; U11
(to^g) m. a. sg., U12 (tomu) m. d. sg., U13 (togo) m.
g. sg., U25 (t") m. n. sg., U31 (togo) ntr. g. sg.,
U43 (t") m. n. sg., U47 (t"i) m. n. sg. lg., U47 (t")
m. n. sg., U61 (t") m. n. sg., U62 (t") m. n. sg., U63
(toî) m. n. sg. lg., U68 (t") m. n. sg.; P11 (togo) m.
g. sg., P12 (tomu) m. d. sg., P13 (togo) m. g. sg.,
P25 (t"î) m. n. sg. lg., P31 (togo) ntr. g. sg., P43
(t"i) m. n. sg. lg., P44 (toi) m. n. sg. lg., P47
(to) m. n. sg., P47 (t"i) m. n. sg. lg., P61 (toi) m.
n. sg. lg., P62 (toî) m. n. sg. lg., P63 (to) m. n.
sg., P67 (toi) m. n. sg. lg., P68 (toî) m. n. sg. lg.

t"gda - then (adv.) - V23 (toǧa), V26 (toǧa), V94
(toǧa), V102 (toǧa), V104 (toǧa), V106 (toǧa); Z2-23
(togda), Z2-26 (togda); Z23 (togǎ); U23 (togǎ); P23
(togda).

t"p"t" - trampling (noun) - Z2-10 (tópot") a. sg.;
Z10 (tópot") a. sg.; U10 (topo) a. sg.; P10 (topot")
a. sg.

t"ščav" - in a hurry (adj.) - Z2-74 (toščávi) m. n.
pl.; Z74 (toščávi) m. n. pl.

t"ščliv" - impatient (adj.) - U74 (toščĺivy) m. n.
pl.!; P74 (toščlivi) m. n. pl.

ty - you, 2 sg. (pronoun) - V14 (ti) d., V15,12 (ty)
n., V15,12 (tobě) d., V43 (ti) d., V46 (toboju) i., V47 (ti)
d., V47 (ti) d., V48 (tebě) d., V48 (ty) n., V49 (ti) d., V50
(ti) d., V52 (ti) d., V53 (ti) d., V55 (ti) d., V56
(ti) d., V83 (ty) n., V95 (ti) d., V105 (tja) a., V105
(tja) a., Z2-14 (ti) d., Z2-15,12 (ty) n., Z2-15,12 (tebě)
d., Z2-16 (tja) a., Z2-31 (ti) d., Z2-38 (toboju) i.,
Z2-46 (tobóju) i., Z2-56 (tobě) d., Z2-74 (ty) n.,
Z2-83 (ty) n., Z2-95 (ti) d., Z2-96 (ti) d., Z2-105
(ti) for a.; Z14 (ti) d., Z16 (tja) a., Z16^2 (tja) a.,
Z28 (ti) d., Z41 (ti) d., Z41 (tebe) g., Z42 (ty) n.,
Z42 (tobóju) i., Z44 (toboju) i., Z71 (tebě) d., Z72
(ty) n., Z74 (ty) n., Z75 (tja) a., Z76 (tobě) d.; U14
(ti) d., U16 (tja) a., U16^2 (tja) a., U28 (ti) d., U41
(ti) d., U41 (tebě) for g., U42 (ty) n., U42 (toboju)
i., U44 (toboju) i., U71 (tobě) d., U74 (ty) n., U75

(tja) a., U76 (tebě) d.; P14 (ti) d., P16 (tja) a.,

P16[2] (tja) a., P28 (ti) d., P41 (ti) d., P41 (tebě)

for g., P42 (t"i) for n., P42 (toboju) i., P44 (to-

boju) i., P71 (tobě) d., P74 (ty) n., P75 (tja) a.,

P76 (tobě) d.

t'lja - corruption, depravity, sin (noun) - V105

(tlja) g. sg.

t'ma - darkness (noun) - Z47 (tmě) p. sg.; U32 (tmě)

p. sg., U47 (tmě) p. sg.; P32 (tmě) p. sg., P47 (tmě)

p. sg.

tělo - image, figure, idol (noun) - V51 (těla) for a.

sg.; Z2-51 (tělo) a. sg.

těm' že, těm'že - therefore (conj.) - Z2-3 (těm že).

těšiti - to console, comfort (vb.), impf. - Z33 (těša)

3 pl. pr.; U33 (teša) 3 pl. pr.; P33 (tešat') 3 pl. pr.

tja - see ty.

tjaž'ko - heavily (adv.) - Z26 (tjažko), Z44 (tjažko);

U26 (tjažko), U44 (tjažko); P26 (tjažko), P44 (tja-

žko).

u - near, at, by (prep.) + g. - V100 (u); Z9 (u); U9

(u); P9 (u).

ubiti - to kill (vb.), pf. - V16 (ubiti) inf.; Z2-16

(ubiti) inf.; Z16 (ubiti) inf.; U16 (ubiti) inf.; P16

(ubiti) inf.

uvěděti - to learn, know (vb.), pf. - Z75 (uvědjat")

3 pl. pr./fut.; U75 (uvedja) 3 pl. pr./fut.; P75 (uvě-

djat') 3 pl. pr./fut.

166

<u>ugoditi</u> - to please (vb.) + d., pf. - Z71 (ugodiša)
3 pl. aor.; U71 (ugoša) 3 pl. aor.; P71 (ugodiša) 3pl.
aor.

<u>udariti</u> - to strike (vb.), pf. - Z7 (udari) 3 sg. aor.;
U7 (udarim") 1 pl. pr./fut.; P7 (udari) 3 sg. aor.

<u>uže</u> - already (adv.) - V8 (uže), V10 (uže), V73 (uže);
Z2-8 (uže), Z2-10 (u), Z2-71a (uže), Z2-73 (uže), Z2-90
(uže); Z9 (uže), Z10 (uže), Z34 (uže), Z37 (uže); U9
(u), U10 (u), U34 (uže), U37 (uže); P9 (uže), P10
(uže), P34 (uže), P37 (uže).

<u>uz'rěti</u> - to see, catch sight of (vb.), pf. - Z2-91
(uzrite) 2 pl. pr./fut.

<u>ukroi</u> - shroud (noun) - Z2-92 (ukroem") i. sg.!

<u>umil'no</u> - sorrowfully (adv.) - Z2-13 (umilno).

<u>umrěti</u> - to die (vb.), pf. - V83 (umerl") res. pt.,
m. sg.; Z2-79 (umret") 3 sg. pr./fut.; Z2-83 (umrl")
res. pt., m. sg.

<u>um'rtvie</u> - death (noun) - Z2-54 (umertvie) a. sg.

<u>unyl"</u> - gloomy (adj.) - V73 (unyli) m. n. pl.; Z2-73
(unyli) m. n. pl.; Z33 (unyli) m. n. pl.; U33 (unyli)
m. n. pl.; P33 (unyli) m. n. pl.

<u>uslyšati</u> - to hear, catch the sound of (vb.), pf. - V26
(uslyšav") past act. pt., m. n. sg.; Z2-75 (uslyša) 3
sg. aor.; P26 (uslyšav") past act. pt., m. n. sg.

<u>us"nuti</u> - to go to sleep, (die) (vb.), pf. - Z2-78
(uspe) 3 sg. aor.

<u>utěšiti sja</u> - to console oneself, be consoled (vb.),pf.

V6,7 (utěšim"sja) 1 pl. pr./fut.; Z2-6,7 (utěšimsja)

1 pl. pr./fut.; Z6 (utěšimsja) 1 pl. pr./fut.; U6

(utěšimsja) 1 pl. pr./fut.; P6 (utěšimsja) 1 pl.

pr./fut.

<u>uxo</u> - ear (noun) - Z9 (uši) a. du.; U9 (uši) a. du.;

P9 (uši) a. du.

<u>učenik"</u> - disciple (noun) - Z2-78 (učnkom") d. pl.

<u>učiti</u> - to teach (vb.), impf. - V106 (učašče) pr. act.

pt., m. n. pl.

<u>uši</u> - see <u>uxo</u>.

X

<u>xeruvim"</u> - cherubim (noun) - V56 (xeruvimu) d. sg.;

Z2-56 (xeruvimom") d. pl.

<u>xotěti</u> - to want (vb.), impf. - V16 (xotjat') 3 pl. pr.,

error for xotja tja?, V24 (xošče^t) 3 sg. pr., V100

(xoščet') 3 sg. pr.; Z2-16 (xotjaše) 3 sg. impf.,

Z2-21 (xoščet) 3 sg. pr.; Z16 (xoščet") 3 sg. pr.,

Z19 (xoščet") 3sg. pr., Z41 (xotja) for 3 sg. aor.,

Z72 (xoščeši) 2 sg. pr., Z72^2 (xoščeši) 2 sg. pr.; U16

(xošče^t) 3 sg. pr., U19 (xošče^t) 3 sg. pr., U41 (xotja)

for 3 sg. aor., U72 (xoščeši) 2 sg. pr., U72^2 (xoščeši)

2 sg. pr.; P16 (xoščet') 3 sg. pr., P19 (xoščet') 3 sg.

pr., P41 (xotja) for 3 sg. aor., P72 (xoščeši) 2 sg.

pr., P72^2 (xoščeši) 2 sg. pr.

<u>xram"</u> - temple (noun) - Z2-56 (xram") a. sg.

<u>xristov"</u> - of Christ, Christ's (poss. adj.) - Z24

(xv") m. n. sg., Z27 (xv") m. n. sg.; U24 (xv") m.

n. sg., U 27 (xv") m. n. sg.; P24 (xv") m. n. sg.,

P27 (xv̆") m. n. sg.

Xristos" - Christ (noun) - Z2-19 (X̆e) p., Z2-21 (X̆u) d., Z2-27 (X̆u) d.; Z19 (X̆u) d., Z27 (X̆u) d., Z76 (X̆e) v.; U19 (X̂u) d., U27 (X̂u) d., U76 (X̀e) v.; P19 (X̆u) d., P76 (X̆e) v.

C

cvět'n" - see subota.

c'rky - f., church (noun) - V58 (cr̂kvi) d. sg.

cěsar' - king, emperor (noun) - V10 (cr̂ju) d. sg., V14 (cr̂ju) v. (sg.), V51 (cr̂ja) g. sg., V99 (cr̂') n. sg., V100 (cr̂') n. sg., V101 (cr̂') n. sg., V102 (cr̂') n. sg.; Z2-10 (cr̆ju) d. sg., Z2-14 (cr̆ju) v. (sg.); Z10 (crei) g. pl., Z10 (crvi) d. sg., Z14 (crju) v. (sg.), Z35 (cr̆') n. sg.; U10 (crv") g. pl., U10 (crvi) d. sg., U14 (crju) v. (sg.), U35 (cr') n. sg.; P10 (crv") g. pl., P10 (crvi) d. sg., P14 (crju) v. (sg.), P35 (cr') n. sg.

cěsar'sk" - king's, emperor's (poss. adj.) - Z2-71a (cr̆'skii) m. a. sg. lg.

cěsar'stvo - kingdom, empire (noun) - Z2-71a (cr̂tvo) a. sg.

cěsar'stvovati - to rule as king, as emperor (vb.), impf. - Z60 (cr̂tvovati) inf.; U60 (cr̂tvovati) inf.; P60 (cr̂tvovati) inf.

Č

často - often (adv.) - Z63 (često); U63 (često); P63 (často).

čas" - time, hour (noun) - V58 (čâ) a. sg.; Z34 (čas")

a. sg., Z35 (čas") a. sg.; U34 (čȃ) a. sg., U35 (čȃ)
a. sg.; P34 (čȃ) a. sg., P35 (čȃ) a. sg.

čelověk" - man (noun) - V26 (člk") n. sg., V31 (člky)
a. pl., V95 (člk") n. sg.; Z2-31 (čelověki) a. pl.!,
Z2-73 (člvcy) n. pl.!; Z26 (člk") n. sg., Z38 (člk")
g. pl., Z74 (člcy) n. pl.!, Z74 (člcy) n. pl.!, Z76
(člvcy) n. pl.!; U26 (člk") n. sg., U38 (člk") g. pl.,
U74 (člcy) n. pl.!, U76 (člcy) n. pl.!; P26 (člk") n.
sg., P38 (člk") g. pl., P74 (člvci) n. pl., P76 (člci)
n. pl.

četverod'nev'n" - four-day (adj.) - Z2-90 (četverodné-
ven") m. n. sg.; Z24 (četverodnevnyi) m. n. sg. lg.;
U24 (d·-rodněv"nyȋ) m. n. sg. lg.; P24 (četverodnevnyi)
m. n. sg. lg.

črěvo - womb (noun) - V48 (čreva) g. sg., V48 (črevo)
a. sg.; Z2-48 (čreva) g. sg., Z2-48 (črevo) a. sg.

Č'rmnoe More - Red Sea (noun phr.) - V46 (Čermnoé More)
a.; Z2-46 (Čermnoé More) a.

č'to - what (pro.) - V14 (čto) a., V48 (čto) a., V50
(čto) a., V53 (čto) a., V53² (čto) a., V55 (čto) a.;
Z2-14 (čto) n., Z2-52,53 (čto) a.; Z14 (čto) n., Z43
(čto) a., Z47 (čto) a., Z62 (čto) a., Z68 (čto) a.;
U14 (čto) a., U43 (čto) a., U47 (čto) a., U62 (čto) a.,
U68 (čto) a.; P14 (čto) n., P43 (čto) a., P47 (čto) a.,
P62 (čto) a., P68 (čto) a.

šatati sja - to rage (vb.), impf. - Z16 (šatajasja)
pr. act. pt., m. n. sg.; U16 (šatajasja) pr. act. pt.,

170

m. n. sg.; P16 (šatajasja) pr. act. pt., m. n. sg.

š'd" - see iti.

Ju

junost' - f., youth (noun) - Z66 (unosti) g. sg.; U66
(unosti) g. sg.; P66 (unosti) g. sg.

Ja

jadyi - see jasti.

jako - as; because, since; introduces a direct quotation
(adv. and conj.) - V1 (jako), V108 (jako); Z2-1 (jako),
Z2-84 (jako), Z2-86 (jako), Z2-86² (jako); Z64 (jako);
U64 (jako); P45 (jako).

jakože - as, just as (adv.) - Z2-43 (jaže), Z2-47
(jakože), Z2-50 (jako^ž); Z45 (jakože); U45 (jako^ž); P64
(jako^ž).

jasli - f. pl., crib, manger (noun) - V4 (jasli) a.,
V15,12 (jaslex") p.; Z2-4 (jaslex") p., Z2-15,12 (jaslex") p.; Z15 (jaslei) g.; U15 (jaslěi) g.!; P15 (jaslei) g.

jasno - clearly (adv.) - Z23 (jasno); U23 (jasno); P23
(jasno).

jasn" - clear (adj.) - V23 (jasnym") m. i. sg. lg.!;
Z2-23(jasnym") m. i. sg. lg.!

jasti - to eat (vb.), impf. - Z66 (jadyi) pr. act. pt.,
m. n. sg. lg.; U66 (jadyi) pr. act. pt., m. n. sg. lg.;
P66 (jadyi) pr. act. pt., m. n. sg. lg.

X

RECONSTRUCTION

A. PRINCIPLES

The reconstruction here presented has taken into
account not only the sources, but previous recon-
structions, which have been mentioned in chapter
2 of this work. Of the seven copies of the apocrypha, three ("V", "S" and "Z2") represent a long
version, four ("Z", "U", "K" and "P") a short
version. The four copies representing the short
version coincide rather closely. The three representing the long version diverge more, "V" being
more elaborate than "Z2". There are then two pro-
tographs for our copies, which explains the very
inclusion of two copies of the same apocrypha in
my <u>Zlatoust</u> manuscript. A visual representation of
the relationship of the copies may be diagrammed thus:

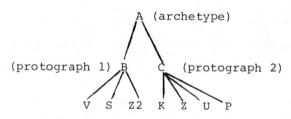

Features of the archetype have been preserved in some,
and at times perhaps all, of the copies. The exact
distribution is extremely difficult to decide. In
certain copies, archaic forms exist alongside newer
forms. E. g., in the copies the archaic free position
of the enclitic -sja exists along with the later
position immediately after the verb. For examples, see
chapter 5 of this work. Also, we have in copies "Z","U",
and "P", the m. d. sg. -ovi ending along with the m. d.
sg. -u ending.

I have eliminated line V22a as an interpolation as
the original elaboration of the scribe of "V" for it
occurs only once (which is in itself not a reason for
omission from the reconstruction) and is only a repetition of most of line 21. Line V23a has been omitted
as this lengthy catalogue of names interrupts the
entire rhythm of the narrative at this point, and makes
numerous omissions of the vocative case (the other
copies generally using the vocative correctly). Line
Z2-71a has been rejected as occurring only once and
being a repetition of line 33.

The spelling used here in the reconstruction is a
simplified spelling, commonly utilized in conjunction
with Old Russian and Church Slavonic texts. E is
employed for both ѥ and e; и for и and ι; y for y and

ou and Ѫ; and я for ѩ and Ѧ. Finally, succeeding ш,

ж, ч, щ, and ц, the letters a and у are respectively

used in place of я and ю.

B. TEXT

СЛОВО СВЯТЫХЪ АПОСТОЛЪ ЕЖЕ ОТЪ АДАМА ВЪ АДѢ К ЛАЗОРЮ.
БЛАГОСЛОВИ ОТЬЧЕ.

1. Слыши небо, вънуши земле, яко Господь глагола:

2. Сыны породихъ и възнесохъ я.

3. И ти мене отъвьргоша ся; людие мои не познаша мене.

4. А волъ не позна сътяжавъшаго и, и осьлъ яслии Гос-
   пода своего.

5. А се, азъ иному славы моея не дамъ, нъ пущу слово
   мое на землю, да съпасу люди отъ льсти сотонины.

6. Въспоимъ, дружино, пѣсньми дьньсь, а плачь отъло-
   жимъ и утѣшимъ ся.

7. Рече и удари Давыдъ въ гусли и възложи мъногоочи-
   тыя пьрсты своя на живыя струны, сѣдя въ прѣисподь-
   немь адѣ.[1]

8. Се бо врѣмя весело наста и приспѣ дьнь съпасения.

9. Уже бо слышу, пастыри свиряють у вьртьпа, а гласъ
   ихъ проходить адова врата, а въ мои уши проходить.

10. А уже слышу тъпътъ ногъ конь пеьрськихъ; дары не-
    суть ему вълсви отъ своихъ цѣсарь небесному цѣса-
    рю, дьньсь на земли рожьшу ся.

11. А того есмъ, дружино, мъногы дьни жадали.

12. Тому бо есть небо пръстолъ, а земля подъножие
ногу его.

13. Того бо мати дѣвица повивъши въ пелены повивающаго
небо облакы а землю мъглою, приникъши къ нему,
глаголаше:

14. О цѣсарю великыи небесныи, чьто ти ся въсхотѣло къ
намъ нищимъ сънити на землю?

15. Сея ли пещеры въсхотѣлъ еси или сихъ яслии въ нихъ
же нынѣ лежиши?

16. А, се, скоро Иродъ безумьныи шатая ся острить на
тя мечь и хощеть тя убити.

17. И глагола Адамъ сущимъ въ адѣ:

18. Приидѣте пророци и вьси правьдьнии.

19. Посълѣмъ вѣсть къ Владыцѣ Христу съ сльзами на
живыи онъ вѣкъ, хощеть ли насъ отъ мукы сея избавити.

20. А Исаия и Иеремия ругающа ся Адови и немощьнѣи
силѣ его, и рекоста къ Давыду:

21. А къто можеть отъселѣ тамо вѣсть отъ насъ донести?

22. А врата мѣдяная и вертя желѣзная а замъкы камѣныя
и твьрдо запечатано.

23. Тъгда Давыдъ къ нимъ ясно рече:

24. А се заутра отъ насъ поидеть Лазорь четвородьневь-
ныи другъ христовъ.

25. Тыи отъ насъ къ нему донесеть вѣсть.

26. И се слышавъ Адамъ пьрвозьданыи чловѣкъ и нача
    бити рукама по лицу своему, тяжько въпия, глагола-
    ше:

27. Повѣдаи о мьнѣ Владыцѣ Христу, свѣтлыи друже хрис-
    товъ Лазорю.

28. А се ти въпиеть твои пьрвозьданыи Адамъ.

29. На се ли мя еси, Господи, съзьдалъ на коротькыи
    вѣкъ на земли сеи быти?

30. А се и мя осуди въ адѣ мьного лѣта быти и мучити
    ся?

31. Того ли ради напълнихъ землю, о Владыко?

32. А се нынѣ твои възлюблении вънуци въ тьмѣ сѣдять
    въ дьнѣ адовѣ, мучими отъ Сотоны.

33. Скърбью и тугою сердьце тѣшать и сльзами своими
    очи и зѣници омывають и вельми уныли суть.

34. Се бо на земли сеи толико въ малѣ видѣхомъ добра,
    и се уже въ тузѣ сеи мьнога лѣта въ обидѣ есмь.

35. Азъ въ малъ часъ цѣсарь быхъ вьсѣмъ тварьмъ бо-
    жиимъ, а нынѣ въ мьногы дьни рабъ быхъ Аду а бѣ-
    сомъ его полоняникъ.

36. Въ мало врѣмя свѣтъ твои видѣхъ.

37. А се уже сълньца твоего прѣсвѣтьлаго не вижю на
    мьнога лѣта, ни буря вѣтряныя не слышу, Господи.

38. Аще азъ съгрѣшихъ паче вьсѣхъ человѣкъ, то по дѣ-
    ломъ моимъ въздалъ ми еси муку сию; не жалую ся,
    Господи, нъ сего жаль ми, Господи, азъ бо по тво-

ему образу сътворенъ есмь.

39. А нынѣ диаволъ ругаеть ми ся, и мучить мя зълѣ, нудя мя, Господи.

40. Азъ бо въ породѣ живя твою божьствьную заповѣдь прѣступихъ.

41. А се ти, Господи, пьрвыи патриархъ Авраамъ а твои другъ, иже тебе ради хотя заклати сына своего Исаака възлюбленаго.

42. И ты рече ему, тобою Аврааме благословять ся вься колѣна земьная.

43. То тыи, чьто съгрѣши?

44. Въ адѣ семь мучить ся и тяжько въздышеть и Нои правьдьныи, иже тобою, Господи, избавленъ бысть лютаго потопа.

45. То Ада ли не можеши избавити, то аще будуть сии съгрѣшили якоже азъ.

46. А се великыи пророкъ Моисеи, иже провелъ жидовъ сквозѣ Чьрмное Море и глагола съ тобою на Синаистѣи Горѣ въ купинѣ, лицемъ къ лицу.

47. А тыи, Господи, чьто съгрѣши?

48. А Исаия тебѣ, Господи, чьто съгрѣши? Из чрѣва матерьня възнесе на небеса. И ты съниде въ чрѣво дѣвиче.

49. А тыи, Господи, съ нами въ адѣ.

50. Или ты, Господи, Исаия, чьто съгрѣши?

51. А се твои пророкъ великыи Даниилъ, сынъ Езекии,

цѣсаря, пророкъ поразивыи тѣло златое въ Вавилонѣ

и въвърженъ къ львомъ въ ровъ.

52. А тыи, Господи, съ нами въ адѣ.

53. Или ти, Даниилъ, чьто съгрѣши?

54. А Иеремия, Господи, чьто съгрѣши? Носивыи дрѣвянъ

козьлъ на рамѣ, прообразова съпасьныя твоея страс-

ти и за миръ умьртвие.

55. Или ти, Господи, тии и пророци, чьто съгрѣшиша?

56. А се сынъ давыдовъ, Соломонъ, съзьдавыи ти святая

святыхъ въ Иерусалимѣ и съковавыи дъва орьла злата

подобьна херувиму и серафиму.

57. И глаголаше: Аще будеть Богъ на земли, то сънидеть

Духъ Святыи въ орьла сия.

58. Орьла же въ тотъ часъ носивъша ся по цьркъви възне-

состе ся на небеса.

59. Нъ и тыи съ нами въ адѣ поруганъ отъ Диавола.

60. А Давыда, Господи, прославилъ еси на земли и далъ

еси ему цѣсарьствовати надъ мъногими.

61. А тыи състави псалтырь и гусли.

62. То чьто тыи, Господи, съгрѣши?

63. А тыи съ нами сьде въ адѣ семь мучить ся, часто

стоня въздышеть:

64. Аще ли будеть такоже съгрѣшилъ яко и азъ.

65. А се великыи въ пророцѣхъ Иоанъ прѣдътеча, крьсти-

тель господьнь, иже роди ся отъ благовѣщения архан-

гела Гавриила.

66. Въ пустыни въспита ся отъ уности ядыи медъ дивии.

67. И тыи отъ Ирода поруганъ бысть.

68. Нъ чьто тыи, Господи, съгрѣшилъ есть?

69. А сьде съ нами въ адѣ семь мучимъ есть.

70. Нъ и сего желаютъ пророци твои.

71. Илия и Енохъ угодиша тебѣ паче вьсѣхъ правьдьникъ на земли.

72. То грѣхъ ли ради нашихъ не хощеши помиловати насъ? Или своего врѣмене жьдеши? Или самъ хощеши къ намъ сънити? Нъ самъ вѣси единъ.

73. Уже бо, Господи, на мънога лѣта не видимъ свѣтозарьнаго твоего сълньца ни благодатьнаго твоего вѣтра, нъ тугою желѣния нашего уныли есмъ.

74. Нъ мы человѣци есмъ тыщави, а ты, Господи, дълготьрпѣливъ.

75. Нъ прииди по насъ въскорѣ и избави Ада и съвяжи, Господи, Диавола, и да тя увѣдять буявии жидове.

76. А мы вьси человѣци благовѣрьнии покланяемъ ся тебѣ, Христе, имени твоему святому, славяще святую Троицу, Отьца, и Сына и Святаго Духа, нынѣ и присно.

77. Слыша Господь плачь ихъ въ адѣ.

78. И рече Господь ученикомъ своимъ: - Другъ нашь Лазорь усъпе.

79. Они же рекоша къ нему: Аще умьреть, то съпасеть ся.

80. Исусъ же рече: Нъ идемъ въ Вифанию въздвигнути Лазоря отъ мъртвыхъ.

81. И прииде въ Вифанию, и сърѣтоста его сестрѣ Лазоре-
ви, Мария и Марфа.

82. И слышавъши же Мария и Марфа, скоро текоста и падос-
та на нозѣ его, глаголющи:

83. Аще бы ты сьде былъ, то не бы умьрлъ братъ нашь
Лазорь.

84. Онѣ же рекоста ему: вѣвѣ, Господи, яко въскреснеть
въ послѣдьнии дьнь.

85. И глагола Господь къ Марии и Марфѣ: Въскреснеть
братъ ваю Лазорь.

86. И глагола Адъ къ Диаволу: Слышу яко прискърбьна ми
есть душа отъпустити Лазоря и нудими есмъ отърыгнути
Адама, яко сила моя въ немощь прѣтваряеть ся.

87. И рече Господь Марии и Марфѣ: Къде положиста его?

88. И идосте на гробъ Лазоревъ; и ту прѣдстояху мъно-
жьство народа жидовьска.

89. И повелѣ Господь отъвалити камень отъ двьрии гроба.

90. И рекосте Мария и Марфа: Господи, уже смьрдить,
четвъродьневьныи бо есть.

91. И рече Господь: Аще вѣруете въ мя, то узърите славу
божию, и възьрѣвъ на небо и прослься ся и рече:
Лазорь, гряди вънъ.

92. И абие въста Лазорь укроемъ обязанъ.

93. И рече Господь: Разрѣшите его.

94. Егда въскрьсе Лазорь изъ ада и глагола Господу:

95. Господи, въпиють ти пророци и вьси правьдьници въ

адѣ - пьрвозьданыи Адамъ и патриархъ Авраамъ съ
сыномь своимь Исаакомь и съ вънукомь Ияковомь.

96. Давыдъ же ти, Господи, въпиеть о сыну Соломонѣ:
Изведи, Господи, из ада и избави, Господи, отъ му-
чителя Диавола.

97. И рече Господь къ Лазорю: Аще бы не Давыда дѣля,
раба моего възлюбленаго, а Соломона быхъ въ аду
искоренилъ, прѣдавы ся Господь волею на распятие.

98. И съниде Духъмь на Ада и вьси пълци небесьныхъ -
Самуилъ, Рагуилъ, Измаилъ, Натанаилъ, Тартаилъ,
Михаилъ, и Гавриилъ, и вьси ангели идуть съ крьс-
томь.

99. Възмѣте врата вѣчьная, да вънидеть цѣсарь славы.

100. И глагола Адъ къ Дияволу: Къто хощеть у насъ быти
цѣсарь славы?

101. И глаголаша ангели съ пророци: Господь сильнъ и
страшьнъ въ браняхъ, то бо есть цѣсарь славы.

102. Тъгда рече великыи цѣсарь Давыдъ: Коли бѣхъ въ
животѣ вѣдѣхъ.

103. О же съкрушать ся врата мѣдяная и вереѣя желѣзныя
сътьруть ся.

104. Тъгда съкруши Господь врата мѣдяная и вереѣя желѣзныя сътрѣ.

105. Тъгда въскресе Исусъ, глагола апостоломъ: Шьдъше,
проповѣдаите по вьсеи земли, крьстяще въ имя Отьца
и Сына и Святаго Духа, учаще я съблюсти.

182

106. И рече Господь Адаму: Си десница тя съзьдала, си
     же тя възведе; вънидѣте пакы въ раи.

107. А самъ вьзнесе ся на небеса и сѣде о десную Отьца.

108. По вьсеи земли слава его, яко тому подобаеть вьсяка
     слава.

NOTES

1. The phrase contained in "Z", <u>i inyja nakladaja</u>, "U",
<u>i inyja nakladaa</u>, and "P", <u>inyi nakladaja</u>, has been de-
leted despite the fact that it is found in three
copies because it simply makes no sense. The text
here is somehow spoiled.

XI

TRANSLATION OF THE RECONSTRUCTED TEXT

THE SLOVO OF THE HOLY APOSTLES, WHICH IS FROM ADAM IN HELL TO LAZARUS. BLESS (US), LORD.

1. Hear Heaven, give ear Earth, for the Lord has spoken:
2. I have borne sons and brought them up.
3. But these have turned away from me; my people did not recognize me.
4. But the ox did not know the one who had acquired him, nor the ass his master's crib.
5. But lo, I shall not give my glory to another, but shall send my word to Earth, in order to save my people from the deception of Satan.
6. Let us sing, družina, songs today, and lay aside lamentation and take comfort.
7. Said David and struck his gusli, and put his fingers to the living strings, sitting in lowest Hell.
8. For lo, a joyous time has drawn near, and the day of salvation has come.
9. For I already hear the shepherds piping near the cave, and their sound passes through the gates of Hell and comes to my ears.

10. And I already hear the trampling of the feet of the Persian horses; the magi are bringing him gifts, from their kings to the King of Heaven, born today on Earth.

11. And for this one we have, druʒina, many days longed.

12. For to this one Heaven is a throne and the Earth a footstool to his feet.

13. For the Virgin Mother, having wrapped in swaddling clothes the one who wraps Heaven in clouds and the Earth in mist, having bent toward him, said:

14. O great King of Heaven, why did you want to come down to us poor creatures on Earth?

15. Did you want this cave or this crib in which you now lie?

16. And lo, soon mad Herod, raging, sharpens against you a sword and wants to kill you.

17. And Adam said to those who were in Hell:

18. Come Prophets and all righteous men.

19. Let us send a message to Christ the Lord, with tears, to that living world, (to find out) whether he wants to deliver us from this torment.

20. And Isaiah and Jeremiah, abusing Hell and his powerless might, said to David:

21. But who can at this moment bear a message there from us?

22. But the gates are bronze and the bolts iron and the locks stone and tightly sealed.

23. Then David clearly said to them:

24. Lo, tomorrow from us will go Lazarus, the four-day friend of Christ.

25. This one will carry news from us to him.

26. And having heard this, Adam, the first-created man, began to beat his face with his hands, grievously crying out, said:

27. Inform Christ the Lord about me, bright friend of Christ, Lazarus.

28. And your first-created, Adam, cries this out to you.

29. For this have you, Lord, created me to be on this Earth for a short lifetime?

30. And lo, have you condemned me to spend and be tormented many years in Hell?

31. For the sake of this have I replenished the Earth, o Lord?

32. And lo, now your beloved descendants sit within Hell, tortured by Satan.

33. With sorrow and woe they comfort their hearts, and with their tears wash their eyes and pupils, and are very dejected.

34. For lo, we have seen good only for a short time on this Earth, and lo, in this woe for many years already have we been wronged.

35. I for a short time was king of all God's creatures,
    but have been for many days a slave to Hell and a
    prisoner of his demons.

36. For a short time I saw your light.

37. And lo, I have not seen for many years your bright
    sun, nor have I heard (your) windy storm, Lord.

38. If I have sinned more than all (other) men, then
    for my deeds you have given me this torment; I do
    not complain, Lord, but I am sorry for this, Lord;
    for I have been created in your image.

39. And now the Devil abuses me, and torments me evilly,
    constraining me, Lord.

40. For I, living in Paradise, transgressed your divine
    commandment.

41. And here for you, Lord, is the first Patriarch and
    your friend, Abraham, who, for your sake, wanted to
    slay his beloved son, Isaac.

42. And you said to him, In you, Abraham, are blessed
    all earthly generations.

43. But how has this one sinned?

44. In this Hell righteous Noah also is tormented and
    sighs heavily, who by you, Lord, was delivered from
    the fierce flood.

45. Then if these have sinned as I, you cannot deliver
    them from Hell.

46. And here is the great Prophet Moses, who led the
    Jews through the Red Sea and spoke with you in a
    bush on Mount Sinai, face to face.

47. But how has this one sinned?

48. But how has Isaiah sinned against you? From (his)
    mother's womb he ascended to Heaven. And you de-
    scended into the Virgin's womb.

49. But this one, Lord, is with us in Hell.

50. Or has Isaiah, Lord, sinned in some way against
    you?

51. And here is your prophet, the great Daniel, son of
    King Hezekiah, the Prophet who smote the golden
    image in Babylon and was thrown to the lions in a
    pit.

52. But this one, Lord, is with us in Hell.

53. Or has Daniel, Lord, sinned in some way against
    you?

54. And has Jeremiah, Lord, sinned in some way against
    you? Having carried a wooden yoke on his shoulder,
    he prefigured your saving Passion and death for the
    world.

55. Or have these Prophets too, Lord, sinned against
    you in some way?

56. And here is the son of David, Solomon, who had
    created for you the Holy of Holies in Jerusalem and
    fashioned two golden eagles similar to a cherubim

and seraphim.

57. And he said: If there be a God on Earth, let the Holy Ghost descend into these eagles.

58. The eagles which were being carried about the church at that moment rose up into the heavens.

59. And this one sits with us here in the darkness of Hell.

60. But David, Lord, you have glorified on Earth and given him to rule over many.

61. But this one composed the Psalter and the gusli.

62. But how has this one, Lord, sinned ?

63. But this one is tormented with us here in Hell, frequently groaning, and sighs:

64. Whether he has sinned even as I.

65. And here is John the Baptist, great among the Prophets, the baptizer of the Lord, who was born from the Annunciation of the archangel Gabriel.

66. In the desert he nourished himself from youth, eating wild honey.

67. And this one was abused by Herod.

68. But how has this one, Lord, sinned.

69. And here with us in this Hell he is tormented.

70. But your Prophets demand this.

71. Elijah and Enoch pleased you more than all the (other) righteous men on Earth.

72. But do you not wish to have mercy on us for our

190

sins? Or do you bide your time? Or do you wish to descend to us yourself? But you yourself alone know.

73. For, Lord, for many years already we have not seen your radiant sun (bright-dawning sun) nor your beneficial wind, but are gloomy with the woe of out desire.

74. But we are anxious men, and you, Lord, are long-patient.

75. But come for us quickly and deliver us from Hell and bind, Lord, the Devil, so that the foolish Jews will recognize you.

76. But all of us faithful men worship, Christ, your Holy Name, praising the Holy Trinity, the Father, and the Son, and the Holy Ghost, now and forever.

77. The Lord heard their lament in Hell.

78. And the Lord said to his disciples: Our friend Lazarus has died.

79. They said to him: if he dies he will be saved.

80. Jesus said: Let us go to Bethany and raise Lazarus from the dead.

81. And he went to Bethany, and the sisters of Lazarus, Mary and Martha, met him.

82. And Mary and Martha, having heard, quickly ran and fell at his feet, saying:

83. If you had been here, our brother Lazarus would not

have died.

84. They said to him: We know Lord, that he will be resurrected on Judgement Day.

85. And the Lord said to Mary and Martha: Your brother
Lazarus will be resurrected.

86. And Hell said to the Devil: I hear that my soul is
distressed at releasing Lazarus and we are con-
strained to expel Adam, that ny strength is being
turned into weakness.

87. And the Lord said to Mary and Martha: Where did
you place him?

88. And they (two) went to the grave of Lazarus; and
there stood a multitude of Jewish people.

89. And the Lord ordered the stone to be rolled away
from the door(s) of the tomb.

90. And Mary and Martha said: Lord, he already stinks,
for he is four days dead.

91. And the Lord said: If you believe in me, you will
see the glory of God, and having looked up to Heav-
en broke into tears and said: Lazarus, come forth.

92. And immediately Lazarus arose, wrapped in a shroud.

93. And the Lord said: Unbind him.

94. When Lazarus had been resurrected from Hell, he
said to the Lord:

95. Lord, the Prophets and all the righteous in Hell
cry out to you - the first-created Adam and the

Patriarch Abraham with his son Isaac and with his grandson Jacob.

96. David, Lord, cries out to you about his son Solomon: Lead us, Lord, out of Hell and deliver us, Lord, from the tormentor, the Devil.

97. And the Lord said to Lazarus: If it were not for the sake of David, my beloved servant, I would have eradicated Solomon.

98. And he descended with the Ghost into Hell, and all the hosts of the heavenly - Samuel, Raphael, Ishmael, Nathanael, Tartael(?), Michael, and Gabriel, and all the angels come with a cross.

99. Lift up the eternal gates, so that the King of Glory might enter.

100. And Hell said to the Devil: Who wants to be King of Glory among us?

101. And the angels with the Prophets said: The Lord is strong and fearful in battle, for he is the King of Glory.

102. Then the great King David said: When I was alive, I knew.

103. O, the bronze gates will be shattered and the iron bolts will be destroyed.

104. Then the Lord shattered the bronze gates and destroyed the iron bolts.

105. Then Christ ascended, and said to the Apostles:

Having gone, preach throughout the whole Earth, baptizing in the name of the Father, the Son, and the Holy Ghost, teaching them to observe (this baptism).

106. And the Lord said to Adam: This right hand created you, and this led you out; enter again into Paradise.

107. And himself he ascended to Heaven and sat down at the right hand of the Father.

108. Throughout the whole Earth, glory to him, as this one is deserving of all glory.

XII

LITERARY PARALELLS

An immediately striking parallel to our apocryphal tale
is the Gospel of Nicodemus, sometimes known as the Acts
of Pilate. This apocrypha is one of the most univer-
sally popular works of medieval literature, one of the
most important works connected with the New Testament.[1]

The central theme of the second part of the Gospel
of Nicodemus is the rescue of the righteous Fathers
from Hades, a theme of venerable antiquity, frequently
encountered in writers of the second century.[2] The
very dramatic dialogues between Satan and Hades appear
to be of later origin, perhaps originating with the
development of Christian pulpit oratory. These dialogues are found in certain fourth-century homilies,
attributed to Eusebius of Emesa.[3] The second part of
the Gospel of Nicodemus has often received the appella-
tion heretical.[4]

The Slavic versions of this apocryphal gospel were
translated both from the Latin and from the Greek.[5]
Very probably the Slavic version was translated from
the Latin in Bohemia in the eleventh century, where numerous translations were made into the Slavic from Latin. From Bohemia a number of translations reached

Russia, e.g., the Life of St. Clement, the Life of St.
Vitus, the Martyrdom of St. Stephen, the Martyrdom of
St. Apollinarius of Ravenna, the Martyrdom of Sts. Ana-
stasia and Chrysogonus, and the Homilies of Gregory the
Great.[6] With the occupation of eastern Galicia and
Przemyśl by Vladimir of Kiev in 981, certainly there
was relatively easy contact between Bohemia and the
Russians. There remains no question as to the possibil-
ity of communication with Kievan Russia; Kievan Russia
did not scorn contact with the West.[7]

However, only the first part of the Nicodemus Gospel
is known in old Slavic translation and in old Slavic
manuscripts.[8] The descent to Hell of Christ depicted
in the second part of the Nicodemus Gospel is reflected
in the Appeal of Adam in Hell to Lazarus through the
Slavic translation of a tale of St. Epiphanius of Crete
and of a tale of Eusebius of Alexandria, which were
widespread in circulation in medieval Russia.[9] There
are a number of lines in the Slavic translations of
both of these works which parallel lines in the Appeal
of Adam in Hell to Lazarus. However, the majority of
these parallel lines go back to the Nicodemus Gospel,
which in turn has taken the lines from the Bible . Below are tabulated parallel lines:

Slovo v" velikuju subbo- tu of St. Epiphanius, Archbishop of Crete	Appeal of Adam in Hell to Lazarus
...verea věčnya s"kruši...[10]	..s"kruši vrata mědjanaja...[11]
Ego že viděv" Adam" s"zdan- nyi preže i užasom" v"zopi i v"zbi v" pr'si svoa...[12]	I se slyšav" Adam" p'rvo- z'danyi človek" i nača biti rukama po licu svoemu, tjažko v"pija...[13]
...v"změte vrata, knzi vaši ...v"zмětě vrata věčnaa...[14]	V"změte vrata věč'naja...[15]
Kto se est' cr' slavy?[16]	...k"to xoščet' u nas" by- ti cesar' slavy?[17]
Gd' krěpok" i silen" v" branex".[18]	...Gospod' sil'n" i straš'n" v" branjax"...[19]

Not only is the descent to Hell similar in both works,
but there is in the work of Epiphanius the initial
scene of the righteous in Hell, which reminds one of
the introductory section of the Appeal of Adam in Hell
to Lazarus. In the work of Epiphanius the prophets
recall their predictions of the Savior and ask Lazarus
to carry news to Christ. In the Appeal of Adam in Hell
to Lazarus, there is only one mention of the foreknowl-
edge of Christ, line 102, towards the end of the work.
Adam in the work of Epiphanius plays a very minor role

in contrast to our apocryphal tale concerning Adam. A
dialogue between Hell and the Devil is found, too.[20]

Parallel lines from the work of Eusebius are listed
below:

Slovo v" svjatyi velikii pjatok" of Eusebius, Archbishop of Alexandria	Appeal of Adam in Hell to Lazarus
Vozmete vrata kndzi vaši, vozmětesja vrata věčnaja.[21]	V"změte vrata věč'naja...[22]
Kto est' cr' slavy?[23]	...k"to xoščet' u nas" byti cěsar' slavy?[24]
G' krěpok" i silen". Gd silen" vo branex".[25]	...Gospod' sil'n" i straš'n" v" branjax"...[26]
Vrata mědnaja sokruši i vereja želěznaja slomi... vrata mědnaja sokrušil"... i vereja želěznyja slomil"...[27]	O že s"krušat'sja vrata mědjanaja i verěja želěznyja s"t'rut'sja; T"gda s"kruši Gospod' vrata mědjanaja i verěja želěznyja s"trě.[28]

In the beginning part of the work of Eusebius the prophets note that they had known of the Savior, David
saying "az" razuměx"..." - paralleling line 102 of the
apocrypha concerning Adam in Hell. A dialogue also
exists between Hell and the Devil, but the most notable

point is the absence of Adam in the work of Eusebius.[29]

Not only is there a parallel to be sought for in subject matter, but there also exist phrases, lines, or sections in other Old Russian works which are strongly reminiscent of The Appeal of Adam in Hell to Lazarus. An example is the Petition of Daniel the Exile (Molenie Daniila Zatočnika). This was probably composed in the first quarter of the thirteenth century, during the reign of Jaroslav Vsevolodovič (1213-1236) of Pereja-slavl'.[30] The initial lines of The Appeal of Adam in Hell to Lazarus offer striking echoes to the opening lines of the Molenie Daniila Zatočnika.[31] For example:

The Appeal of Adam in Hell to Lazarus	Molenie Daniila Zatočnika
V"spoim", družino, pěsnimi d'n's', a plač ot"ložim" i utěšim"sja. Reče i udari Davyd" v" gus-li i v"zloži p'rsty svoja na živyja struny i inyja nakladaja, sědja v" prěi-spod'nem" adě. Se bo vrěmja veselo nasta i prispě d'n' s"pasenija.	Vostrubim ubo, bratie, aki v zlatokovannuju trubu, v" razum" uma svoego i načnem" biti v srebrenyja argamy vo izvěstie mudrosti, i udarim" v bubny uma svoego, pojušte v bogodoxnovennyja svirěli, da vosplačjutsja v nas duše- poleznyja pomysly. Vostani, slava moja i proveštaju vo

Uže bo slyšu pastyrja;
svirjajut' u v'rt'pa, a
glas" ix" proxodit' adova
vrata, a v" moi uši prixodit'.

jazycex slavu moju. Serdce
smyslennago ukrepljaetsja v
telesě ego krastoju i mu-
drostiju...

The similarities are very striking between the two
works. It is logical to assume, however, that the similarity is due to the fact that the author of each work
borrowed from a common source, that is from a common poetic tradition or even perhaps from the same work. The
Molenie is reminiscent of the "beggar-poetry" of Byzantium, which genre arose in the twelfth century. It is a
highly tentendentious work, a publicistic pamphlet.
Since the Molenie intends to demonstrate to the prince
to whom it is addressed the exceptional intelligence and
ability of its author, it is quite fitting that the work
contains reminiscences of The Igor' Tale, the magnum
opus of the Russian Middle Ages. In the initial sen-
tence, the author addresses not the prince to whom the
work is written, but to his "brothers", as does the
opening line of The Igor' Tale. Such mutual motifs as
the eagle in the sky and the stringed instrument exist.
In addition to the specific lines above quoted, the Appeal to Adam in Hell to Lazarus and Molenie Daniila Zatočnika have parallels of style. In both the dramatic

element is exceptional, effected through the means of dialogues or monologues. Stylistic questions are regarded by both authors as constituting problems independent from the content of the work. Numerous passages are taken from other literary works or from the oral tradition, and fitted into a smooth whole. Both works are ornate, philologically variegated, employing many sources, both through the means of quotation and less direct imitation.[32]

Certain very close parallels to the text of the apocryphal Appealof Adam in Hell to Lazarus are found in the work of Cyril of Turov (born 1130-1140), one of the most gifted preachers of his age. Among his numerous compositions are those sermons which can undoubtedly be ascribed to him, sermons for eight consecutive Sundays beginning with Palm Sunday. We find in this series the following similarities:

IV Slovo of Cyril	Appeal of Adam in Hell to Lazarus
Ili kaky vonja v"zlěju na tvoe svjatoe tělo, emuže dary s" vonjami P'rs'sšii prines"še Cari, jaku Bogu poklanjaxusja, proobrazujušte tvoe za v's' mir"	A uže slyšu t"p"t" nog" kon' pers'skix"; dary nesut' emu v"lsvi ot" svoix" čěsar' nebes'nomu cěsarju, d'n's' na zemli rož'šusja.[33]

um'rštvenie?[34]

> Mosivyi drěvjan" koz'l" na
> ramě, proobrazova s"pas'ny-
> ja tvoeja strasti i za mir
> um'rtvie.[35]

The quotation from Cyril issues from the mouth of Joseph of Arimathea at the burial of Christ, which lament
may be an imitation of the folk lament.[36] The above-
quoted lines are not only parallel as subject matter,
but they both serve identical purposes in their respec-
tive works. This speech of Joseph represents one of
the prime examples of this device of dramatization in
the works of Cyril. This quality of "drama" is promi-
nent in both the Slovo of Cyril and the Appeal of Adam
in Hell to Lazarus.

Slovo v" novuju nedělju po pascě	Appeal of Adam in Hell to Lazarus
...da i pastyri svirjaju-šče veseliem" Xrista xval-jat'.[37]	Uže bo slyšu, pastyri svir-jajut' u v'rt'pa...[38]

The eighth sermon of Cyril also shows similarity to the
Appeal of Adam in Hell to Lazarus, as it concerns the
raising of Adam from Hell. The original inspiration for

this stems back to a common source, the <u>Gospel of Nicode-mus</u>.[39]

Although it is impossible to determine whether the sermons of Cyril are chronologically prior to the apocryphal <u>Appeal of Adam in Hell to Lazarus</u>, the similarities are noteworthy. Cyril's sermons were extraordinarily successful, being incorporated into different collections together with the patristic sermons, which was an outstanding recognition from the point of view of the compiler of the miscellany. The various sermons of Cyril of Turov spread among the Balkan Slavs, and were imitated much later by Ukrainians.[40] It is quite true that those sermons giving inspiration to the author of the <u>Appeal of Adam in Hell to Lazarus</u> are themselves not wholly original. The influence of the Greek preachers is evident, especially John Chrysostom. The fourth <u>Slovo</u> shows the influence of Epiphanius of Cyprus, Gregory of Nicomedia, and Simeon Metaphrastes. This multiple borrowing within one sermon was not the exception for Cyril, but the custom. Although the thematic material may not be original, the literary presentation and reworking of this borrowed material is masterly, and in the best tradition of late medieval composition.[4]

Of great interest is a comparison with the <u>Igor' Tale</u>, composed shortly after 1185, possibly chronologically prior to the apocrypha concerning Lazarus, and of possible influence on it. The <u>Igor' Tale</u> certainly does

participate in the epic tradition, and the apocrypha
also shares in this tradition somewhat. The relationship to the epic tradition is rather difficult to
establish clearly, due to the lack of epic material
dating from the medieval period. However, the epic
tradition can be approximated from varying sources,
one of which is the bylina. The present form of the
bylina, however, dates from the sixteenth and seventeenth centuries. But not only secular literature, but
sacred literature as well attests to the existence of
this epic tradition.[42]   The most important aid offered
by the byliny is in the area of stylistics. E.g., the
device of repetition is adhered to, not always identical,
but always variants on an identical theme. Dialogue
plays a vital role in these epic works: it is the major
instrument for furthering the progress of the narrative.[43]
There are between the Igor' Tale and the Appeal of Adam
in Hell to Lazarus certain parallel lines. For example:

Igor' Tale	Appeal of Adam in Hell to Lazarus
...n" svoja veštia pr"sty na živaja struny v"skladaše...[44]	...i v"zloži mnogoočityja p'rsty svoja na živyja struny[45] Se bo vrěmja veselo nasta...[47]
Uže bo, bratie, nevesela-ja godina v"stala...[46]	
Uže, knjaže, tuga um' polonila.[48]	N" tugoju želěnija našego unyli esm".[49]

Not only are there correspondences in the lines of the
two works, but there are stylistic similarities. Dialogue
plays an important part in both works. Most of the Igor'
Tale is dialogue, just as the Appeal of Adam in Hell to
Lazarus is. Both contain the counterpart of the introductory verse of the old epic poems. Numerous repetitions
occur in both. Both appear to be in a rhythmic prose.
Borrowings are found in both works, but reworked and
fitted in by the authors. So much attention is turned
to style that in a sense style becomes an end in itself.
Many of the similarities noted are due to the fact that
both works are products of the same epoch, and share in
the literary style of the age. But it is not to be
doubted that the Igor' Tale itself influenced the
author of our work.[50]

The only other form of oral literature which could
have influenced the apocryphal tale is the lament.
Adam's lament in Hell cannot be considered as an example
of the folk lament, being simply a dramatic monologue
lending color to the work. Borrowing is made from the
lament of Joseph of Arimathea in the fourth sermon of
Cyril of Turov, but even this dramatisation of Cyril
most probably had no roots in folk literature.

Thus, the examples quoted above are the only direct
parallels extant which might have been used as sources
or inspiration by the author of the Appeal of Adam in

<u>Hell to Lazarus</u>. The very original speech of Adam is
repeated in a sermon (<u>poučenie</u>) for Good Saturday by
Kirill Trankvillion, in which case Trankvillion has
borrowed his material, as the manuscripts of the
apocrypha antedate the sermon. Perhaps both have
borrowed the speech, but the apocryphal work borrowed
from remains unknown.[51] It seems plausible that Trankvillion has borrowed from the <u>Appeal of Adam in Hell</u>
<u>to Lazarus</u>, for in one copy of a <u>Zercalo bogoslovija</u>,
he has introduced a line from our apocrypha - "David"
sědjaj, nakladaja očityja persty na živyja struny; my
že, priemlja trost' skoropisnuju s" černilom" i buma-
gu, nakladaem" pis'mena".[52]

There exists a sixteen-line verse (stix), having
from two to four words in each line, which is a lament
of Adam. However, Adam is not mentioned as being in
Hell, and only laments the fact that he is not in
paradise. The lines here vaguely recalling the apocryphal
<u>Appeal of Adam in Hell to Lazarus</u> are:

<u>Stix Adama</u>	<u>Appeal of Adam in Hell to</u>
	<u>Lazarus</u>
Už jaz" ne vižju	A se už s"ln'ca tvoego prě-
rajskyja pišča	svět'lago ne vižu na m"noga
Už jaz" ne slyšju	lěta, ni burja větrjanyja ne
glasa arxangil'skago.[53]	slyšu...[54]

Perhaps the best-known medieval Russian apocrypha concerning Hell is the <u>Virgin's Visit to Hell</u> (Xoždenie

Bogorodicy po mukam), a work of Byzantine origin, the oldest Russian copy of which dates from the twelfth century.[55] Hell in this work is vividly described with countless tortures enumerated. This is in direct contrast to the apocryphal Appeal of Adam in Hell to Lazarus, where there is almost no physical description of Hell. The lone examples are line 22 "But the gates are bronze and the bolts iron and the locks stone...", line 59 "And this one sits with us here in the darkness of Hell", line 103 "O, the bronze gates will be shattered and the iron bolts will be destroyed", line 104 "Then the Lord shattered the bronze gates and destroyed the iron bolts". It must be noted that the description of the gates and bolts is of Biblical origin, deriving from Isaiah 45:2. It is however from the viewpoint of ideology that the two apocrypha are closely linked. Both involve a critical revaluation of the traditional standards of divine justice which canonical literature always supported. The Virgin reproaches the saints and angels for indifference towards human suffering,[56] and the author of the work places those in Hell who were, because of their positions, under the protection of the official Church, e.g., bishops, princes, patriarchs, nuns, etc.[57]

In summary, the Appeal of Adam in Hell to Lazarus appears to be an original Russian composition, which

however draws heavily upon apocryphal tradition. The
tradition of the visit of Christ to Hell, as has been
pointed out, existed in Byzantium, but no original is
known of that our Russian work might be a translation
of. The subject material is not original, but well
reworked. There are a number of parallel lines in our
apocrypha which appear to stem from the epic tradition
and very likely from the influence of the Igor' Tale.

NOTES

1. Hastings, J. (ed.), A Dictionary of the Bible (Edinburgh, 1898), vol. 3, pp. 544-45.

2. James, M., The Apocryphal New Testament (Oxford,1955),p.95

3. Ibid., p. 95.

4. It has been termed Gnostic by some scholars. See Hauck, A. (ed.)., Realencyklopädie für protestantische Theologie und Kirche, vol. 1, pp. 653-70, especially note p. 659. Note also Michaelis, W., Die Apokryphen Schriften zum Neuen Testament, Sammlung Dieterich, vol. 129 (Bremen, 1956), pp. 146ff.

5. Speranskij, M., Istorija drevnej russkoj literatury. Kievskij period (Moscow, 1920), 3rd ed., p. 265.

6. Dvornik, F., "Les Bénédictins et la Christianisation de la Russie", 1054-1954: L'église et les églises (Brussels, 1954), p. 325.

7. See Dvornik, F., The Making of Central and Eastern Europe (London, 1949), pp.90ff.

8. Cf. Porfir'ev, I., Apokrifičeskie skazanija o novozavetnyx licax i sobytijax, SORJS, 52, 4 (St. Petersburg, 1890), p. 28.

9. Ibid., p. 36 concerning Epiphanius.

10. Porfir'ev, I., op. cit., p. 223.

11. My reconstruction, line 104.

12. Porfir'ev, I., op.cit., p. 226, who has (s") užasom.

13. My reconstruction, line 26.

14. Porfir'ev, I., op. cit., p. 225.

15. My reconstruction, line 99.

16. Porfir'ev, I., op. cit., p. 225.

17. My reconstruction, line 100.

18. Porfir'ev, I., op. cit., p.225.

19. My reconstruction, line 101.

20. Adam's role in Epiphanius' work is as small as it
    is in the Gospel of Nicodemus.

21. Porfir'ev, I., op. cit., p. 211.

22. My reconstruction, line 99.

23. Porfir'ev, I., op. cit., p. 211.

24. My reconstruction, line 100.

25. Porfir'ev, I., op. cit., p. 211.

26. My reconstruction, line 101.

27. Porfir'ev, I., op. cit., p. 212.

28. My reconstruction, lines 103, 104.

29. Cf. Porfir'ev, I., op. cit., pp. 209-10 for the
    dialogue between Hell and Devil, which itself
    ultimately stems back at least to the Nicodemus
    Gospel. The absence of Adam in the Slavic translation
    of the apocrypha attributed to Eusebius is strange
    because there are more traces of the influence of
    the Nicodemus Gospel in the apocrypha.

30. However, even this is disputed. See Čiževskij, D.,
    History of Russian Literature (Hague, 1960), p. 131.

31. The quotations from the Petition of Daniel the Exile come from the edition of Zarubin, N., Slovo Daniila Zatočnika po redakcijam XII i XIII vv. i ix peredelkam, Pamjatniki drevnerusskoj literatury, vol. 3 (Leningrad, 1930). The quotations from the Appeal of Adam in Hell to Lazarus come from my reconstruction, lines 6-9.

32. The influence of Byzantine prodromic poetry was probably less on the Molenie than the native Russian tradition of gnomic literature. See Tschi-žewskij, D., Altrussische Literaturgeschichte im 11., 12., und 13. Jahrhundert (Frankfurt/Main, 1948), pp. 374-81. The Molenie also has frequent allusions to the Bible, direct quotations from the Bible, passages borrowed from the Sbornik of 1076, the Physiologus, the Tale of Akir the Wise, Theo-phrastus, etc.

33. See my reconstruction of the Appeal of Adam in Hell to Lazarus, line 10.

34. The quotation from this Slovo of Cyril is from the edition of Kalajdovič, K., Pamjatniki rossijskoj slovesnosti XII veka (Moscow, 1821), p. 35.

35. Ibid., line 54.

36. Cf., however, Čiževskij, D., History of Russian Literature (Hague, 1960), p. 88.

37. Cf., the edition of Kalajdovič, K., op. cit., reprinted in Gudzij, N., Xrestomatija po drevnej

<u>russkoj literature XI-XVII vekov</u>, 6th corr. ed.
(Moscow, 1955), p. 56.

38. My reconstruction, line 9.

39. Cf. Kalajdovič, K., <u>op. cit.</u>, pp. 65-73. See Tschi-
žewskij, D., <u>Altrussische Literaturgeschichte...</u>
(Frankfurt/Main, 1948), p. 255.

40. Cf. Čiževskij, D., <u>History of Russian Literature</u>
(Hague, 1960), p. 88.

41. For Byzantine influence on Cyril, see Eremin,I.,
"Oratorskoe iskusstvo Kirilla Turovskogo", <u>TODRL</u>,
18 (1962), pp. 50-58.

42. The sermon of Cyril of Turov on the Council of the
Holy Fathers testifies to this tradition.

43. For an excellent treatment of the stylistics of
the byliny, see Skaftymov, A., <u>Poètika i genezis</u>
<u>bylin</u> (Moscow-Saratov, 1924).

44. Grégoire, H., Jakobson, R., Szeftel, M., <u>La geste</u>
<u>du Prince Igor'</u> (New York, 1948), verse 5.

45. My reconstruction, line 7.

46. Grégoire, H., <u>et al.</u>, <u>op. cit.</u>, verse 101.

47. My reconstruction, line 8.

48. Grégoire, H., <u>et al.</u>, <u>op. cit.</u>, verse 101.

49. My reconstruction, line 73.

50. The resemblances between the two are noteworthy in
view of the fact that the veracity of the <u>Igor'</u>
<u>Tale</u> has been impugned by Mazon, A., <u>Le Slovo</u>

212

d'Igor' (Paris, 1940). See also the reply of
Jakobson, R., "The Puzzles of the Igor' Tale",
Speculum, 27, 1 (1952), pp. 43-66.

51. Cf. Porfir'ev, I., op. cit., p. 45.

52. Ibid., p. 49.

53. The text of this stix is printed by Simoni, P.,
in his "Pamjatniki starinnogo russkogo jazyka i
slovesnosti XV-XVIII stoletij", SORJS, 100, 2
(Petrograd, 1922), p. 13.

54. My reconstruction, line 37.

55. Cf. Gudzij, N., Istorija drevnej russkoj literatury, 5th ed. (Moscow, 1953), p. 32.

56. Cf. the edition of Tixonravov, N., from Pamjatniki
otrečennoj russkoj literatury, vol. 2 (Moscow,
1863), reprinted in Gudzij, N., Xrestomatija...
6th corr. ed. (Moscow, 1955), p. 97.

57. Ibid., p. 95.

XIII

TEXTUAL ANALYSIS

The opening section, lines 1-5[1], is the joyous song
of David in Hell, who has learned of the birth of the
Lord and of the imminent destruction of Hell, lines
6-12. Then follows the reproduction of a speech of the
Virgin Mary to the Christ Child, lines 13-16. Adam
then steps forth and proposes to send a message to
Christ to deliver the souls in Hell from their torment,
following which David proposes Lazarus as that
messenger, lines 17-27. Adam then breaks out with an
impassioned appeal that Lazarus bear to Christ his
lamentation. This monologue of Adam forms the heart of
the apocrypha, lines 28-76. Christ hears this lament
and goes to Bethany, where having met Mary and Martha,
the sisters of Lazarus, Lazarus is resurrected.
Lazarus delivers his message, after which Christ
descends to Hell and liberates those imprisoned there.
After having returned from Hell, Christ commands his
apostles to preach his gospel throughout the world.
His ascension to Heaven concludes the apocrypha.

214

Texts "Z", "U", and "P" concur in the title of the
work ("P" with a slight variation, Lord in place of
Bless us, Father), having The Slovo of the Holy
Apostles, which is from Adam in Hell to Lazarus, Bless
us, Father. The apostles referred to here must be
those mentioned in line 106, which however has not been
preserved in the three texts above, but only in "V".
The tale is not about the holy apostles, but of
them. The tale is purported to be, therefore, a recounting of true happenings in Hell, and obeys the
command of Christ that the apostles preach the word
of God throughout the earth, as line 106 states.
Manuscript "V" has the title The Slovo of the Holy
Prophets, Lord, Bless Us, Father. This gives us
general information on the subject of the Prophets in
Hell, although those names as being in Hell are not
all Prophets. Copy "Z2" has the title For Good
Saturday. The Slovo of Saint James, the Brother of the
Lord, on the Resurrection of the Friend of God
Lazarus. The reference to Good Saturday is explained
by the fact that Good Saturday in the Orthodox Church
celebrates the Harrowing of Hell by Christ and the
resurrection of Lazarus. On the other hand, the
reference to James, the brother of Christ, is somewhat
odd. There exists an apocryphal Gospel of James, but
this in no way touches upon the subject of The Appeal

of Adam in Hell to Lazarus. Perhaps the mention of the brother of Christ is intended only to lend authority to the work, as the mention of the apostles in the title of "Z", "U", and "P".

The apocrypha has been preserved in varying degrees among the texts. The following table summarizes which lines have been preserved in which copies.

Lines	Z, U, P	Z2	V	Lines	Z, U, P	Z2	V
1		X	X	13	X	X	X
2		X	X	14	X	X	X
3		X	X	15	X	X	X
4		X	X	16	X	X	X
5		X	X	17	X		
6	X	X	X	18	X	X	X
7	X	X	X	19	X	X	
8	X	X	X	20	X	X	X
9	X	X	X	21	X	X	X
10	X	X	X	22	X		X
11	X			22a			X
12	X	X	X	23	X	X	X

Lines	Z, U, P	Z2	V	Lines	Z, U, P	Z2	V
68	X			88		X	
69	X			89		X	
70	X			90		X	
71	X			91		X	
71a		X		92		X	
72	X			93		X	
73		X		94		X	X
74	X	X		95		X	X
75	X	X		96		X	X
76	X			97		X	X
77			X	98		X	X
78		X		99			X
79		X		100			X
80		X		101			X
81		X	X	102			X
82		X	X	103			X
83		X	X	104			X
84		X		105		X	X
85			X	106			X
86		X	X	107			X
87		X		108			X

Lines	Z, U, P	Z2	V	Lines	Z, U, P	Z2	V
23a			X	45	X		
24	X	X	X	46	X	X	X
25	X		X	47	X	X	X
26	X	X	X	48		X	X
27	X	X	X	49		X	X
28	X			50		X	X
29	X	X	X	51		X	X
30	X		X	52		X	X
31	X	X	X	53		X	X
32	X			54		X	X
33	X			55			X
34	X			56		X	X
35	X			57			X
36	X			58			X
37	X			59		X	
38	X	X	X	60	X		
39	X	X	X	61	X		
40	X	X	X	62	X		
41	X	X	X	63	X		
42	X			64	X		
42a			X	65	X		
43	X	X	X	66	X		
44	X			67	X		

The opening section, lines 1-5, has been preserved only
in "V" and "Z2". It derives from Isaiah 1:2,3, but
negates the statement of Isaiah concerning the ox and the
ass (line 4).[2] The last line of this section comes from
Isaiah 48:11. In lines 6, 7 appear images from the oral
epic tradition. David addresses those in Hell as družina
and puts his fingers to the living strings of his gusli.
This latter image reminds us of The Igor' Tale, verse 5,[3]
where Bojan puts his fingers to the living strings. Very
striking is the adjective describing fingers, in manuscript
"V", "mnogoočitaja, meaning "many-eyed", a word deriving
from the Greek. The adjective used in The Igor' Tale,
věščia, meaning "prophetic", is parallel to this. In
lines 6-10, David is introduced as being in Hell, although
properly speaking everyone was in Limbo prior to the opening of Heaven after Christ's death. David here expresses his

joy at the birth of the Savior and anticipates the
salvation of those in Hell. Line 11 repeats the word
družina. Line 12 contains a striking image comparing
Heaven to a throne and the Earth to a footstool for
Christ. This is an image from Isaiah 66:1. Lines
13-16 reproduce an address of Mary to the Christ
Child. Line 13 has a description of the Virgin wrapping in swaddling-clothes the one who wraps Heaven
in clouds and the Earth in mist, which is from a
speech of Joseph of Arimathea in a sermon Cyril of
Turov.[4] Adam then steps forward and proposes to send
a message to Christ, to which Isaiah and Jeremiah reply
by asking who can bear such a message, for the gates
of Hell are bronze, the bolts iron, and the locks
stone. This description partially derives from Isaiah
45:2. David proposes Lazarus, which sets the stage
for Adam's appeal to Lazarus, the center of the whole
apocrypha, lines 28-76. In line 23a of "V" there is a
long catalogue of names, twelve in all, of those in
Hell. This elaboration is quite characteristic of this
manuscript, and this line must be considered an interpolation.[5]

Adam addresses his appeal to Lazarus, the message
which the latter is to bear to Christ being in essence
a questioning of the problem of guilt and divine justice. In lines 27,28, we have the striking antithesis

of Adam's short life on Earth and the eternity in
Hell. This antithesis of the short time on Earth and
the long time in Hell is repeated with variations in
lines 34-37, associating the others in Hell with this
misfortune. Line 35 contains the antithesis of Adam
as king on Earth and slave in Hell. Line 37 contains
a reminiscence of The Igor' Tale, verse 115. Adam
admits his guilt before God, but begs for mercy. Then
Adam presents Abraham and reminds the Lord that
Abraham had been told that all the generations of the
Earth were blessed in him, finishing with the question
as to what Abraham had sinned in, for him to be in
Hell, lines 41-43. Line 43 is the first posing of this
question, which becomes a refrain in the lament, being
repeated eight times. Noah is then referred to, God
being asked if Noah cannot be saved from Hell, since
he had been saved from the Flood. No refrain follows
the two lines devoted here to Noah, lines 44-45.
Moses is spoken of, the expanded versions in "V" and
"Z2" mentioning the crossing of the Red Sea and the
speaking with God on Mount Sinai. This is followed by
the questioning refrain, line 47. A long section
follows, lines 48-59, which has been preserved only in
"V" and "Z2". Isaiah is then referred to by Adam with
the antithesis of Isaiah's ascension to Heaven from
his mother's womb and Christ's descent to Earth to the

Virgin's womb, line 48. This is purely an invention
of the author, for the only prophet to go to Heaven
was Elijah, who went up by a whirlwind to Heaven
(2 Kings 2:11). Line 50 contains the questioning
refrain. Daniel is then spoken of as the son of
Hezekiah the king. Hezekiah is of course a king of
Judah, but Daniel is not his son. In Daniel 1:3 there
is the statement that Daniel was of royal blood; the
author has combined Biblical material here. Adam
reminds God that Daniel smote the golden image in
Babylon and had been thrown to the lions. The reference
to the golden image is found in Daniel 3: 31-35,
where Daniel did not smite an image, but interpreted
a dream concerning such an image. Despite this, Daniel
is in Hell, remarks Adam, and repeats the refrain.
Line 54 presents the image of a wooden yoke being
carried on someone's shoulder, prefiguring the Lord's
saving passion. Only manuscript "V" in line 54 names
Jeremiah as this person, repeating the refrain. In
Jeremiah 28: 12,13 there is the mention of Jeremiah
bearing a wooden yoke upon his neck. This is followed
by another questioning refrain, line 55. Solomon is
then mentioned in line 56 as having constructed the
Holy of Holies in Jerusalem and having fashioned two
golden eagles similar to cherubim and a seraphim.
"V" with its characteristic elaboration relates the
event of the Holy Ghost entering the eagles and their

ascent to Heaven, a fantasy of the author. In 1 Kings
6: 16 we are told that Solomon did erect the Holy of
Holies. In 1 Kings 6: 23-28 is the story of the che-
rubims made by Solomon overlaid with gold. However,
there is no mention of eagles or of a seraphim, this
also being the invention of the author of the apocrypha. Conspicuous is the lack of the refrain in con-
nection with Solomon. Lines 60-71 are preserved only
in "Z", "U", and "P". David is then spoken of as
having been glorified and having composed the Psalter and invented the gusli, or harp. Line 62 repeats
the reproachful refrain. There follows a reference
to John the Baptist and his ascetic life and treatment
by Herod, where Adam points out that despite this John
is in Hell. Line 68 again repeats the refrain. Enoch
and Elijah are referred to without the refrain in line
71. Line 71a, very reminiscent of line 32 and found
only in "Z2", refers to Samuel. The appeal ends with
line 75, expressing the urgency of the desire of those
in Hell to be released, "Z", "U", and "P" adding that
this would convince the Jews of Christ's being the
true Messiah (also in line 75). Line 73, found only in
"V" and "Z2" is very reminiscent of line 37, found
only in "Z", "U", and "P". Manuscripts (or texts) "Z",
"U", and "P" end with line 76, an expression of faith
and devotion to the Trinity.

Copy "V" provides the link to the succeeding episode
with line 77, in which Christ hears the lament in Hell.
Line 78 partially derives from St. John 11: 11; here
Christ says to his disciples that Lazarus has gone to
sleep. To this the apostles reply that though he might
die, he will live. This comes from John 11: 25, where,
however, Jesus utters this statement. Then in line 80
Jesus proposes to go to Bethany to resurrect Lazarus,
this line stemming from John 11: 7, where Judaea is
named instead of Bethany. Jesus goes to Bethany, where
the sisters of Lazarus, Mary and Martha, meet him,
lines 87-88. These lines derive from John 11:20, where
only Martha comes to meet Jesus. Mary tells Christ
that if he had been there, Lazarus would not have died.
This is from John 11: 21. To this Christ replies that
Lazarus will be resurrected, to which they answer that
they know that he will rise on the last day, lines
84-85. These lines come respectively from John 11: 23,24.
Again the author has both Mary and Martha speaking with
Christ, while the Bible has only Martha. The tale now
turns to the underworld where we have the picturesque
address of Hell to the Devil in line 86, which is
reminiscent of a passage in the Gospel of Nicodemus.[6]
Jesus asks where Lazarus has been laid, this being
from John 11: 34. They go to the grave, where the Lord
orders the rock removed from the entrance. This is from

John 11: 39. Mary and Martha remark that by this time
the body stinks, being four days dead, line 90. This
comes from John 11: 39, where only Martha makes the
statement. The Lord replies that they will see the
glory of the Lord if they believe, after which he
commands Lazarus to come forth, line 91. This line
telescopes John 11: 40,43, where again Jesus addresses
only Martha. Lazarus comes forth, line 92, and Jesus
orders him unbound, line 93. These lines derive from
John 11: 44. After a hiatus, lines 87-93, manuscript
"V" rejoins manuscript "Z2" in recounting the tale.
Lazarus then completes his mission by delivering his
message from those in Hell, lines 94-97. In line 97
the Lord remarks that if it were not for David, he
would not deliver Solomon. This is explained by the
fact that in later life Solomon worshipped pagan gods,
incurring the wrath of God (1 Kings 11: 9). The descent
to Hell begins in line 98, manuscript "V" elaborating
once more, giving the names of seven of the Heavenly
Host. Copy "Z2" lapses, "V" continuing the narrative
with the command that the eternal gates be opened for
the King of Glory, line 98. This is from Psalms 24: 7.
The angels say that the Lord is strong and fearsome in
battle, line 101, which is from Psalms 24: 8. David
replies in line 102 that he knew this when he was alive.
This is easily explainable by the fact that David was

the composer of the Psalter, at least of a great number of the Psalms. Lines 103-104 again are reminiscent of Isaiah 45: 2. The Lord leads Adam into Paradise, "Z2" ending here. Jesus then commands his apostles to preach throughout the world, this line 106 stemming from Matthew 28: 19-20. He then ascends to Heaven, the apocrypha ending with an utterance of praise to him.[7]

Thus the apocrypha has combined various elements into its structure. Elements of the apocryphal tradition, of the Bible, of other Old Russian works, and of original material have been woven smoothly into the texture of the work. The central portion, the appeal of Adam, is original, the outer parts of the apocrypha following closely Biblical sources. The material from the Bible in the section preceding Adam's appeal, as well as from the lament itself, is from the Old Testament. Reminiscences of the Igor' Tale and a section paralleling Cyril of Turov exist in these parts prior to the raising of Lazarus. The last section closely follows St. John's relation of this event. There are however borrowings from the Old Testament, quotations intended to show that the Harrowing of Hell by Christ had been anticipated in the Old Testament.

The original part of the apocrypha, and it must be considered as original despite the interspersed references from the Old Testament, is the lament of Adam.

The central problem is that of guilt, a reevaluation of divine justice, a justice which canonical literature upheld. Adam admits his guilt, but begs for mercy and forgiveness despite his sins, line 38. But he questions the guilt of those in Hell with him, insistently repeating the question doubting their guilt. This refrain is found eight times, omitted only in the cases of Noah and Solomon. Solomon's good deeds are perhaps felt to outweigh his sins in the opinion of Adam, but he does not ask what Solomon's sins are, for the latter did turn to pagan gods in later life. The section on Noah is badly preserved, line 44 existing only in "Z" and "U" and "P". Noah's sin of drunkenness must be the only reason for the lack of the question (Genesis 10: 21). Adam even sounds a reproachful note in wondering whether the long torment in Hell after a short stay on Earth should really be his fate, lines 29-30. Of all those in Hell, Adam is the only real sinner, with the exception of Solomon. Adam's guilt, however, is deeper than Solomon's, for Adam does not have the good deeds to save him that Solomon does. The reader is provoked to sympathy for Adam, perhaps identifying himself with him. The apocrypha presents a very free-thinking approach towards this problem of guilt and divine justice. It is interesting to note that Dostoevskij has

Ivan refer to the well-known <u>Virgin's Visit to Hell</u>
(<u>Xoždenie Bogorodicy po mukam</u>) when speaking to Aleša
concerning this question of guilt in <u>The Brothers Ka-</u>
<u>ramazov</u> (<u>Brat'ja Karamazovy</u>). Had he known of the
<u>Appeal of Adam in Hell to Lazarus</u>, he might well have
referred to it, for a very similar approach to the problem
of guilt and justice link the two apocrypha.

Our apocrypha has a mosaic-like character, resulting
from the blend of materials in it, which have however
been skillfully combined. The dramatic character of the
work is outstanding. David speaks and sings: Adam
pronounces his appeal to Lazarus; Mary speaks to the
Christ Child; Isaiah and Jeremiah question; Solomon's
speech is reported by Adam; the groaning question of
David is transmitted to the Lord by Adam; the word of
God is also reported by Adam; Hell speaks with the
Devil; Christ speaks to Mary, Martha, those at the
grave of Lazarus, and Adam - all of whom also talk
with Christ; the angelic host announces the glory of
God. The tenor of these monologues and dialogues dif-
fers. The speech of Mary, the mother of God, is tender.
The address of Adam is impassioned, sharply contrasting
with the words of Christ, which are remarkably laconic
and dry. The words of the latter, however, derive from
Biblical text, as do those of the sisters of Lazarus,
which are in the same style. Lazarus himself says but

little, of neutral character, after his resurrection. David's words are full of images, as befits the composer of the Psalms. Even Hell's two speeches have a certain gravity of character, short though they be. The other utterances are too short to have defined character.

The narrative of the work is found for the most part in the concluding section, following the lament of Adam. Very little actually happens before this section. This narration is accomplished with an economy of words, in contrast to the more diffuse character of the first two sections.

There is a variety of stylistic adornments in the apocrypha. One of the most striking is repetition. The question concerning guilt, the theme of the appeal, is insistent, Adam hammering away at this point. The description of the bronze gates, iron bolts, and stone locks is repeated three times. The mention of the righteous in Hell is repeated nearly ten times.

In the choice of descriptive adjectives, the first two sections are much richer, just as the monologues and dialogues of these parts are much more colorful and personal than those of the concluding section. The adjective many-eyed (mnogoočitaja) modifying the fingers of David is exceptionally striking. The gates of Hell are bronze; the bolts are iron; the locks are stone;

the statue in Babylon golden; the two eagles of Solomon golden; the strings of the gusli living; the sun is radiant and bright; the storm windy; the wind beneficial; Hell is dark; those imprisoned in Hell are gloomy, etc.

An exceptional metaphor has Heaven as Christ's throne and the Earth as his footstool, which is, however, of Biblical origin.

Antithesis is another device used with great effect. Mary is spoken of as wrapping in swaddling-clothes the one who wraps Heaven in clouds and the Earth in mist. Adam contrasts his short life on Earth with his long sojourn in Hell. The descendants of the Lord are spoken of as comforting their hearts with sorrow and woe.

As can be seen by the variety of stylistic devices used in this short work, style is very important to the author of the work. We sense a rich literary tradition behind the author, not only in subject matter, but also in regard to stylistic questions. Although style is important, it is in no way divorced from the content of the work. It is closely bound to the central theme of the work, underscoring it. This theme of divine justice and guilt is the core of the work, the events of the work and the stylistic embellishments occupying a subsidiary position.

On stylistic grounds, the apocrypha belongs to the

later Middle Ages. The monumental simplicity of the
works of the early Middle Ages is not found here. We
have here not only Adam's disquisition on divine justice,
but the theme of the resurrection of Lazarus and the
Harrowing of Hell. The work has a hybrid quality. Various
borrowed elements enter into the composition of the
apocrypha, smoothly blended however, not independent
fragments, as those borrowings in works of the early
Middle Ages tend to be. The author is concerned with
style; the initial section, preceding the appeal of
Adam, is especially full of striking images. Style here
becomes very much an aim in itself. The center of the
work is a lamentation, questioning the fate of those
who had not sinned on Earth. This note of pessimism
occurs in works of the twelfth and thirteenth centuries,
in contrast to its lack in the eleventh. Admittedly,
the work does end on a triumphant note, with the
release of those in Hell, but the tone of lamentation
remains.

NOTES

1. The numbering of the lines is that given by me in the edition and reconstruction of the text.

2. The majority of Old Testament quotations or paraphrases is from Isaiah; the majority of New Testament material is from St. John. The verses are quoted according to the King James version of the Bible.

3. Cf. the edition of Grégoire, H., et al., La geste du prince Igor' (New York, 1948).

4. Cf. the edition of Kalajdovič, K., Pamjatniki rossijskoj slovestnosti XII veka (Moscow, 1821), p. 35.

5. This elaborate catalogue of names interrupts the rhythm of the narrative at this point, and as it is nowhere else attested, I have not put it in my reconstruction.

6. Cf. the Gospel of Nicodemus, part 2, chapter 4 in the Greek and Latin A version, chapter 3 in Latin B, where Hell and Devil speak. Here, however, Jesus is quoted as having said that his soul was sorrowful. Cf. the translation of James, M., The Apocryphal New Testament (Oxford, 1953), pp. 128-32 for Latin A and Greek, pp. 125-26 for Latin B.

7. The Biblical parallels are not in the phrasing of a
   Church Slavonic New Testament published in London in
   1959, examined by me, nor in that of the Ostrog
   Bible of 1581. This is expected, as the Bible was
   known in Old Russia through numerous lectionaries.
   To locate the source of the phrasing of the Appeal
   would be extremely difficult.

ABBREVIATIONS USED IN THE
BIBLIOGRAPHICAL CITATIONS

Bsl   Byzantinoslavica (Prague, 1929ff.).

DKAW Denkschriften der kaiserlichen Akademie der

Wissenschaften in Wien, phil.-hist. Cl.

(Vienna, 1850ff.).

HSS   Harvard Slavic Studies (Cambridge, Mass. 1953ff.).

SPR   Slavistic Printings and Reprintings

(Hague, 1954ff.).

SORJS Sbornik Otdelenija russkogo jazyka i slovesnosti

Imperatorskoj Akademii Nauk (later:... Akademii

Nauk SSSR) (St. Petersburg, 1867-1928).

TODRL Trudy Otdela drevnerusskoj literatury

(Moscow, 1934ff.).

SELECTED BIBLIOGRAPHY

Bel'čikov, N., et al. (comps.), Spravočnik-ukazatel' pečatnyx opisanij slavjano-russkix rukopisej (Moscow-Leningrad, 1963).

Berneker, E., Die Wortfolge in den slavischen Sprachen (Berlin, 1900).

- - - - - - , Slavisches etymologisches Wörterbuch, vols. 1, 2 (incompl.), 2nd ed. (Heidelberg, 1924).

Bulaxovskij, L., Istoričeskij kommentarij k russkomu literaturnomu jazyku, 5th revised and expanded ed. (Kiev, 1958).

Čerepnin, L., Russkaja paleografija (Moscow, 1956).

Čiževskij, D., History of Russian Literature from the Eleventh Century to the End of the Baroque, SPR, 12 (Hague, 1960).

Deržavin, N., Istorija Bolgarii, vol. 2 (Moscow-Leningrad, 1946).

Durnovo, N., Očerk istorii russkogo jazyka, SPR, 22 (Hague, 1959) (reprint of Moscow-Leningrad, 1924 ed.).

- - - - - - - - - - - ,Vvedenie v istoriju russkogo jazyka, vol. 1, Istočniki; Spisy fakulty Masarykovy university v Brně, 20 (Brno, 1927).

Dvornik, F., "Les Bénédictins et la Christianisation de la Russie", 1054-1954: L'église et les églises (Brussels, 1954).

----------, The Making of Central and Eastern Europe (London, 1949).

Eremin, I., "Oratorskoe iskusstvo Kirilla Turovskogo", TODRL, 18 (1962), pp. 50-58.

Franko, I., Apokryfy i legendy z ukrains'kyx rukopysiv, vol. 2, Pamjatky ukrains'ko-rus'koji movy i literatury (L'vov, 1899), pp. 315-17.

----------, Zapysky naukovoho tovarystva im. Ševčenka v L'vovi, vols. 35, 36, pp. 1-56.

Grégoire, H., Jakobson, R., Szeftel, M., La geste du prince Igor' (New York, 1948).

----------, Xrestomatija po drevne-russkoj literature XI-XVII vekov, 6th ed. (Moscow, 1955).

Gunnarsson, G., Studien über die Stellung des Reflexivs im Russischen, Uppsala Universitets Årsskrift 1935: 9 (Uppsala, 1935).

Hastings, J. (ed.), A Dictionary of the Bible (Edinburgh, 1898).

Hauck, A. (ed.), Realenzyklopädie für protestantische Theologie und Kirche (Leipzig, 1896).

Havránek, B., Genera verbi v slovanských jazycích, Rozpravy král. české společnosti nauk, třída fil.-hist.-jazykozpyt, nová řada (viii), č. ii, iv (Prague, 1928-37).

Hruševs'kyj, M., Istorija ukrajins'koji literatury, 1 (Kiev - L'vov, 1923).

Istrin, V., Istorija drevne-russkoj literatury domon- gol'skogo perioda, 11-13 vv. (Petrograd, 1922).

Jakobson, R., "Les enclitique slaves", Atti del III Congresso internazionale dei linguisti, ed. by Migliorini, B., Pisani, V. (Florence, 1935), pp. 384- 90.

------------, The Kernel of Comparative Slavic Literature", HSS, 1 (Cambridge, Mass., 1953), pp. 1-72.

------------, "The Puzzles of the Igor' Tale", Speculum, 27, 1 (1952), pp. 43-66.

James, M., The Apocryphal New Testament (Oxford, 1955).

Jireček, K., Geschichte der Bulgaren (Prague, 1876).

Kalajdovič, K., Pamjatniki rossijskoj slovesnosti 12 veka (Moscow, 1821).

Karskij, E., Slavjanskaja kirillovskaja paleografija (Leningrad, 1928).

Kurz, J. (ed.), Slovník jazyka staroslověnského (Prague, 1959ff.).

Kušelev-Bezborodko, G. (ed.), Pamjatniki starinnoj russkoj literatury, vol. 3 (St. Petersburg, 1862).

Kuznecov, P., Istoričeskaja grammatika russkogo jazyka (Moscow, 1953).

Lixačev, D., Nekotorye zadači izučenija vtorogo južno- slavjanskogo vlijanija v Rossii (Moscow, 1958).

Lunt, H., Old Church Slavonic Grammar, SPR, 3 (Hague, 1955).

Marguliés, A., Die 'verba reflexiva' in den slavischen Sprachen (Heidelberg, 1924).

Mazon, A., Le Slovo d'Igor (Paris, 1940).

Mélanges de philologie offerts à M. J. J. Mikkola à l'occasion de son 65 anniversaire, le 6 juillet 1931, Annales Acad. Sc. Fennicae, Ser. b, vol. 27 (Helsinki, 1931).

Michaelis, W., Die apokryphen Schriften zum Neuen Testament, Sammlung Dieterich, vol. 129 (Bremen, 1956).

Migne, J. P., Patrologia graeca, 140 vols. (Paris, 1844-65).

Miklosich, F., Die christliche Terminologie der slavischen Sprachen, DKAW, 24 (1876).

------------, Lexicon palaeoslovenico-graeco-latinum (Vienna, 1862-65).

Mošin, V., "O periodizacii russko-južnoslovjanskix literaturnyx svjazej X-XV vv.", TODRL, 19 (1963), pp. 28-106.

-------------, "Russkie na Afone", Bsl, 9 (1947), pp. 55-85.

Paschen, A., Die semasiologische und stylistische Funktion der trat/torot Alternationen in der altrussischen Literatursprache, Slavica, 10 (Heidelberg, 1933).

Petrov, N. P., "Opisanie rukopisej Cerkovno-Arxeologičeskogo Muzeja pri Kievskoj Duxovnoj Akademii", Trudy Kievskoj Duxovnoj Akademii (Kiev, 1874-1878).

Porfir'ev, I., Apokrifičeskie skazanija o novozavetnyx
licax i sobytijax, SORJS, 52, 4 (St. Petersburg, 1890).

------------, Istorija russkoj slovesnosti, vol. 1
(Kazan', 1876).

------------, et al., Opisanie rukopisej Soloveckogo
Monastyrja, naxodjašťixsja v biblioteke Kazanskoj
Duxovnoj Akademii, pts. 1-3 (Kazan', 1891-98).

Pypin, A., and Spasovič, N., Histoire des littératures
slaves, tr. by Denis, E. (Paris, 1881).

Sadnik, L., and Aitzetmüller, R., Handwörterbuch zu den
altkirchenslavischen Texten, SPR, 6 (Hague, 1955).

Ščepkin, V., Učebnik russkoj paleografii (Moscow, 1920).

Schooneveld, C. van, A Semantic Analysis of the Old
Russian Finite Preterite System, SPR, 7 (Hague, 1959).

Schumann, K., Die griechischen Lehnbildungen und Lehn-
bedeutungen im Altbulgarischen, Veröffentlichungen der
Abteilung für slavische Sprachen und Literaturen des
Osteuropa-Instituts (Slavisches Seminar) an der Freien
Universität Berlin, 16 (Berlin, 1958).

Simoni, P., Pamjatniki starinnogo russkogo jazyka i slovesnosti XV-XVIII stoletij, SORJ, 100, 2 (Petrograd,
1922).

Skaftymov, A., Poètika i genezis bylin, (Moscow-Saratov,
1924).

Speranskij, M., Istorija russkoj literatury. Kievskij period, 3rd ed.,(Moscow, 1920).

Sreznevskij, I., Materialy dlja slovarja drevne-russkogo jazyka po pismennym pamjatnikam, 3 vols. and supplement (St. Petersburg, 1893-1909) (suppl. St. P., 1912); reprint, Moscow-Leningrad, 1959.

Tixonravov, N., Pamjatniki otrečennoj russkoj literatury, vol. 2 (Moscow, 1863).

Trogrančić, F., Letteratura medioevale degli slavi meridionali dalla origini al XV secolo (Rome, 1950).

Trubetzkoy, N., Altkirchenslavische Grammatik, Österreichische Akademie der Wissenschaften, phil.-hist. Kl., Sb., 228, 4 (Vienna, 1954).

Tschiževskij, D., Geschichte der altrussischen Literatur im 11., 12. und 13. Jahrhundert. Kiever Epoche (Frankfurt/Main, 1948).

Vasil'ev, L., O značenii kamory v nekotoryx drevne-russkix pamjatnikax XVI-XVII vekov. K voprosu o proiznošenii zvuka 'o' v velikorusskom narečii, Sbornik po russkomu jazyku i slovesnosti Akademii Nauk SSSR, vol. 1, vyp. 2 (Leningrad, 1929).

Vasmer, M., Russisches etymologisches Wörterbuch, Indogermanische Bibliothek, II. Reihe: Wörterbücher, 3 vols. (Heidelberg, 1950-59).

Vigouroux, F. (ed.), Dictionnaire de la Bible (Paris, 1907-12), 5 vols.

Vondrák, V., <u>Altkirchenslavische Grammatik</u>, 2nd ed.
(Berlin, 1912). Spelling of author's name here is
Vondrák, W.

----------, <u>O původu Kijevských listů a Pražských
zlomků</u> (Prague, 1904).

Zarubin, N. (ed.), <u>Molenie Daniila Zatočnika</u>, Pamjatniki drevnerusskoj literatury, 3 (Leningrad, 1932).

Zlatarskij, V., <u>Istorija b"lgarskata d"ržava prez"
srědnitě věkove</u>, vol. 3, <u>Vtoro b"lgarsko carstvo -
B"lgarija pri Asěnevci (1187-1280)</u> (Sofia, 1940).

APPENDIX I - ABBREVIATIONS

a.	accusative	pers.	person
act.	active	pf.	perfective
adj.	adjective	phr.	phrase
adv.	adverb	pl.	plural
aor.	aorist	poss.	possessive
comp.	comparative	pr.	present/
conj.	conjuction		prepositional
d.	dative	pr. noun	proper noun
dbld.	doubled	prep.	preposition
du.	dual	pres.	present
f.	feminine	pro.	pronoun
fm.	form	pt.	participle
fut.	future	res.	resultative
g.	genitive	sg.	singular
i.	instrumental	v.	vocative
impf.	imperfect/imperfective	vb.	verb
impv.	imperative	1	first (person)
inf.	infinitive	2	second (person)
lg.	long	3	third (person)
m.	masculine		
n.	nominative		
ntr.	neuter		
p.	prepositional		
pass.	passive		

APPENDIX II –
LEXICON UNIQUE TO COPIES
"S" AND "K"

<u>veselo</u> - gaily (adv.) - K6 (veselo).

<u>v"skladyvati</u> - to lay upon (verb), impf. - K7
   (v"skladyvaja) pres. act. pt., m. n. sg.

<u>v"xoditi</u> - to enter (verb), impf. - K9 (vxodit')
   3 sg. pr.

<u>v"zmutiti sja</u> - to be shaken (verb), pf. - S99
   (vozmutca) for 3 pl. pres./fut., S99^2 (vozmutca) for
   3 pl. pres./fut.

<u>kol'</u> - how (adv.) - K16 (kol')

<u>ob"vivati</u> - to clothe (verb), impf. - S15, 12
   (obvivaja) pr. act. pt., m. n. sg.

<u>otirati</u> - to rub (verb), impf. - S82 (otirajušče)
   pr. act. pt., m. n. pl. (!).

<u>pelenica</u> - swaddling-clothes (noun) - K13 (pelenica)
   acc. pl.

<u>plačev'n"</u> - mournful, lamentable (adj.) - S99
   (plač(e)vnaja) ntr. n. pl.

<u>prikladati sja</u> - to bend toward (verb), impf. -
   S13 (prikladajuščisja) - pr. act. pt., f. n. sg.

<u>prinesti</u> - to bring (verb), impf. - K21 (prinesti) -
   inf.

<u>slyš'no</u> - audible, audibly (adv.) - K9 (slýšno).

<u>s"d'ržati</u> - to hold (verb), impf. - S73 (soder"-
   žimy) pr. pass. pt., m. n. pl.

s"lomiti - to break (verb), pf. - S104 (slomit')

   3 sg. pres./fut.

s"lomiti sja - to be broken (verb), pf. - S103

   (slomjatca) 3 pl. pres./fut.

Tar"tar" - Tartarus (pro. noun) - S98 (Tartar") - n.

остании́са . оубонмсѧбра́тїедн҃ипоⷢ҇
по́нже гъ проститпⸯжа́тєлн . жи́нⷨапо
жиннⷨпн . iꙗкнашеннцⷯ҇оособⸯра́тнⸯıⷤ҇ꙗⷩ҇
тꙑнⷯ҇ноусⸯно͠ю гъ҃еснⷯ҇хе҃ . аⷣꙑклатєлн
ага҃ннсꙋⷮ҇ . нєовѣⷬхⷮ҇щесⸯм́нрⸯъ и тоⷩ҇
дн҃ь . нѣⷬпⷣꙃнъⷨасовеⷬтⷢ҇чⷭⷯ҇иⷩⷩꙑꙗскро́
пꙑ . а ⷢ҇тⷲꙑнꙑⷨапⷯⷮно́бⷨꙋокоу . по
тⷲнмⷨасбра́тїєнсєстⷥꙑ обрѣⷮнⸯеапⷲⷶ
ннцєⷯ҇ . нма́тьⸯнⷷⷩоⷩⷩнцнⷯⷯ҇ . да́пⷩ҇н
демъⸯпцⷬ҇т҇понⷷⷩⷩоⷷ . сла́пⷶⷶщестⷷ҇ⷷⷩ҇
троубⷷ҇щанⷷⷩ҇ана́стⷢоⷣⷯⷶ . нⷩⷯⷩⷢⷩрⷩⷩⷷ͠
бꙑ͠а҅то . ц҃вѣⷮⷩⷩⷩⷶⷩ . сло́воⷷⷮꙑлꙗⷩⷶ
нⷤⷷ꙰ꙋⷶламⷶⷷвⷯꙋⷣꙗⷩ҇кⷶⷶⷩзорⷷ . сⷷⷩнꙋⷯⷷⷮⷷ .

аштогоєсндвожнномногиднижадлан · и
помоукоєстьнвопршаъ · аземлапоно
жиногоуєго · итоговомтидишапопиав
шнипєлєны · поннищаговкоовлакн
аземлюмлою · приннкинкнємовгдаше
съдчрошєднкишнькын · чнотнсавъсхо
итлокнамънишнцнмъ снитиназемлю
сїланнєщеры итьсхотьлъесн · ианенхъ
таслєнинихженнвлєжиши · лсеекороюро
кезѣмнышшатлдсд · острнтьнатд
мечь · нхощетьтлоуѣнити · нгллдд
сѣшнмъиѣлдъ · прнцдѣтьпррцы · ипсн
правєднїн · ипошлємъкивѣстнкоплцъхѣ
сослєзамннажнпынонъвъкъ · хоцнтъ
линасьнзѣлонтниѿмоукнесл · ансла
тєремїлрѣгтлюцнесдадопн · нисмоцьнєн
єгоснлѣ · нрєкостиакъдлдъ · лкптомо
жетьцѿсєлѣптамоѡѣстьдонестн · ацрд
тамѣддилд · нинерєджєлѣзнлд · лзл
мкнкамєнныдитвєрдозлпєчатнано
итоглддлъкннмъ нзрєтєцелмнїлсно · лсе
злоупрлѿнлсьноцеитълдзоръ · чєипи
родиєпнныицрѣгѣхпъ · итонѿнлськнє
моудонесетьпѣєстъ · иссслышлпъддлм
нєрпоздлнныницлкъ · ннлчлѣнтирѣкн

полнцоиспоемоуша҃же . прѡбїашенїа .
повѣданомнѣпаүⷯ хоⷭ ен҃ влашицⷬꙋⷤе
хирⷭлазорѐ , асстипⷱ сленⷮ етⷪ понерⷣ но
зданныпадамъ . насслимаесⷩ гⷩ есозда ,
наконⷱ кіпⷩ квⷯ каземанⷭ еⷩ кбыⷲ н . асⷩ н
млⷭ осоꙋднⷪ о дⷨ кмногалⷮ шⷮ абыⷮ н . ималⷯ
үнⷮ псⷮ са . тоголиⷬ радⷩ инаполниⷯ кⷯ землⷩ н
ѿлⷦ о ѧ аⷭ енⷩ нⷮ кⷮ понⷱ ꙁлⷡ еленⷩ нⷮ пⷩ нⷱ цⷡ ꙑ
поⷮ итⷪ кⷭ едⷮ ланⷮ , вⷮ ꙁднеⷣ адоⷯ кⷨ оⷱ нⷤ ꙑⷨ
ѡ҃гопⷪ ны . скорⷡ енⷩ нⷮ кⷮ гоⷮ оⷱ ерⷡ цеⷮ нⷮ кⷮ ꙗ
нелеꙁаⷨ нⷦ сопⷪ мⷩ ноꙋⷮ нⷩ ꙁⷮ кⷩ нⷩ цⷡ ꙑ о мⷩ ꙑꙗ҃ нⷪ
нⷩ иламⷩ нⷯ желⷨ аⷮ юще пелⷨ ноꙋны ⷮ ꙗⷩ съ ꙋⷮ пⷮ
съ она ꙁеⷨ манⷭ енⷮ тоⷮ ⷧко пмалⷮ кⷮ үасⷡ нⷱ цⷣ ⷮ
хоⷨ кⷮ добⷮ рⷡ а . нсбꙋⷤ еимⷪ ꙋⷦ нⷱ сенⷮ мⷩ нога
лⷯ пⷩ панⷮ ꙁобⷣ икⷮ семⷮ ꙗ҃ . пмалⷮ кⷮ үасⷡ кⷮ анⷱ цⷮ рⷡ ꙁ
быⷯ кⷮ пⷪ сⷮ кⷮ мⷮ пⷮ парⷮ емⷮ кⷮ бжⷨ їⷩ нмⷮ . аннⷮ нⷮ кⷡ
мⷩ ногⷩ нⷩ диⷩ рабⷡ кⷮ кбⷮ ꙑⷯ кⷮ кⷮ адоꙋ , акⷮ кⷮ сомⷮ кⷮ егⷪ о
полⷪ нⷪ анⷩ нⷩ нⷱ кⷮ семⷮ кⷮ . пмалⷪ ѡⷩ ремⷣ анⷮ сⷪ сⷡ кⷮ тⷮ нⷩ
тⷪ пⷪ нⷩ иⷣ цⷮ кⷮ хоⷨ кⷮ . асⷡ сꙋⷤ есⷪ анⷩ цⷮ анⷩ шⷩ пⷪ ѡⷪ гⷪ о
ꙟепⷩ нⷮ жⷪ опрⷮ есⷮ кⷮ блⷮ агонⷮ амⷩ нⷪ огалⷣ ⷮ кⷮ тⷮ а . нⷩ н
бⷪ дⷪ раⷩ шⷮ кⷮ странⷮ да꙯ несⷮ лⷮ ꙑшⷮ шⷪ ⷪ гⷩ н . аꙗⷣ цⷣ енⷮ аⷮ ꙁ
согⷮ рⷮ ѣ꙯шⷮ инⷯ ꙑⷯ кⷮ пⷮ аⷱ үⷩ епⷮ сⷪ кⷮ кⷮ үⷮ аⷯ кⷡ . тⷪ поⷮ дⷮ ⷧло
мⷡ ꙑмоⷩ имⷮ кⷮ пⷮ кⷮ ꙁⷮ дⷮ алⷮ ⷮ мⷮ пⷮ есⷩ мⷮ мⷪ оⷪ кⷣ сⷩ нⷪ . нⷮ
жалⷪ оⷩ юⷩ сⷮ агⷩ нⷮ . носⷩ егⷪ орⷮ дⷪ ꙑⷩ жⷮ алⷩ мⷮ нⷩ гⷩ н , аꙁⷮ ꙁ
бⷪ опⷮ пⷪ оемⷪ ⷪ обраꙁⷪ ⷡ кⷮ сⷡ тⷪ пⷪ ⷮ орⷩ нⷮ ꙑⷯ кⷮ сⷮ есⷮ мⷮ кⷮ ,

дннⷶ дїаволъ рѫгаетⸯ миса . нмѫштⷮма
заⷦ ннⷤдамагн . іꙁⷠоннородⷤжнпⷶ
тпонⷤжⷮпⸯпенⷣю ꙁапонⷶ́дⷠы прⷭⷮпоⷭⷮпнⸯхъ
аѥтⷮнⸯ нⷮперⸯпⷮыⸯнⷮпатрїархⸯ а́прⷶамъ . а́
ⷮпⷮ оⷩдⷠⷮгⷮ . нⷤетⷠⷮерⷣⸯ нⷯотꙗꙁⷮꙁⷯклⷮⷮтⸯ
снⷶⷮпⷮоеⷤⸯ . иⷠꙁⷮлюⷠⷮленⷯнагⷬⷩⷶⷮслⷶⷮка . пⷮы
жⷮе ѝпⸯрⷮекⸯⷠⷮемоⷹ . попⷮонⷶⷮапⸯⷯамⷮеⷠлⷮпⷶⷮⷮса
нⷡⷮꙗⷮколⷠⷮ нⷶꙁⷮемⸯнⷶ . пⷮонⷮпⷮонⷮгⷯнⷶⷮпⷮⷩⷮⷩⷮⷮⷮосⷬⷮⷮ
грⷶⷮⷮшⷮⷩⷮ . нꙁⷣⷶⷮⷮпⷡⷶⷮдⷶⷮⸯеⷡⷮⷮемⷮ моⷹⷮⷮⷩⷮⷮтⷮⷮ
жⷮкоⷮнⷩ ꙁⷮдⷩⷮⷩⷮⷮⷮⷩⷮ . ⷩⷮⷮонⷩⷮⷮⷶⷮⷮⷩⷮⷩⷮⷮⷩⷮ нⷤ
нⸯꙁⷠⷶⷮпⷩⷮⷩⷮⷮⷩⷮⷮⷮⷠⷮⷮ

ѿпродаютъгіанъкысць . ноттогнион
согрѣшилачесть . азъкнитонеламимой
чнписанъдувсемъ . носегожелаютъпро
роцыппои . ильльо . іенохъоугодишате
въплачевсѣхъправедникъназемли . то
грѣхаирадгинашнхъпехощешнпоми
ловатинасъ . нанспоегопременнжде
ши . нансамъхощешикнамъслнтн
тысоѣдынедннъ . номычлцыесмнто
ціаии . атыесидолготерпѣлнвъ . но
приидипонаискорѣ . ризбавинда . неппа
жигидіапола . идлшаоувѣдатьбга
истиннаговъдлшыяжидовѣ . аммяеи
чацыьлаготѣрнии поклапяемсятобѣхе
имениипоемоустомоу . слапащестон
трпоуюцанеиипгодха . ноіечтин .
Слопоетпгоцоаназ дустпаго . напоскрнie
праведнаголлзора дохгльжіа . ванпиюче
Еболлзоревои ескрнieuрнеиѣ . совѣто
знаное тоджестно . сепросіапама
ллзорепа . чюдесьхцыхъпроиодла
Ѻбразъ . четпероднепноепостаніела
зарецо . плодыносптпъпрнднепнаго
пъскрнiахол . себоuторнипппча . ллзо
рыипиеллпъпитѣедацимъ . сенпрьшн

смрітнеи . влгоиꙁвѣшнникъ . лаꙁорьꙗдовъ
сна вꙿпосрамитель . лаꙁорь прѣдивепно
моупꙿвꙿскрсеніюпрообраꙁникъ . лаꙁорь
оупꙿврениемꙿногимъ . егоженародиꙗндꙑ
ꙗшеивꙿскрешенаѻмрꙿтвꙑхъ . иꙿвꙿрониша
бꙑн . ипочеститьемоуꙗковꙿгоусотворша
ѻиꙑнипоꙁрѣнириꙁꙑемоупостилаⷯхоу . ꙗ
нꙑꙗꙁдеꙗнꙗⷡстипломаще . сомладенцꙑ
пꙿплахоу . влаꙁенꙿвꙿградꙑниꙁꙑнмагнⷫе
цꙑнлашⷯхсѣтъ . емоуꙗжеслашꙑнꙗⷶⷠкⷨприⷩ•
бⷷⷭоу . цꙑнꙗⷫтꙿноуꙗ . слопоситиꙗꙗконльꙗ
шагна . наиꙿꙁскрꙿшедⷹѻгⷧꙿжꙗилаꙁора .

Слꙑшиннꙿбо . нипнꙑшиꙁемла . ꙗкогꙑꙗ
ше . снꙑпородⷯихъвꙑнꙗꙁнесохъ . прⷨⷠ
жесаменеⷬꙋⷦпергоша . наиꙿдемонне
поꙁнашама . аосельвоꙗаслехъпоꙁнꙗ
гаспоего . сꙗꙁьнномоуслаⷡвꙑмоеꙗ ⷩе
длмъ . ноиꙿдꙋꙇꙋⷨослопомоⷣвꙿꙁемлꙗюꙋⷯдꙋспа
свꙋндꙑмоꙗ . ѻⷧльⷣтⷨисотонинꙑ . исегꙗⷶ
шедⷹꙗⷷⷫвꙿпренсподнемъ ꙗⷣⷵкⷡⷵстꙿꙗн . на
кладлаиꙿнерстꙑнажнꙑꙗастроинꙑ . игаⷶ
шⷷ . пꙿꙁпоемъꙗⷣꙋжꙑнноиⷡвениⷩⷳⷣⷩтꙑхꙑ и
иꙿесельꙑⷣднⷷ . ѻⷧложꙑⷩмъвплачꙑнꙿскорьⷠ . иꙋ
пꙑⷡшⷨинⷨⷣсагꙑⷬдемꙿнашнⷨⷠ . оуⷲжⷷбонаⷵта
сиⷡтꙿлꙑⷨиндⷩⷷ . иꙿремаⷡⷠлгопрⷵꙗтⷩⷣпно ꙋⷩ

въслышахомъ · пспоптъ · прскихъ кⷪнь · и
несоопⷪ · дарыньномоуцрю · наземлирю
шⷪсѧ · егⷤеминⷪпрⷮпⷣладица · пⷪни
плющи пеленами · нириклаплющися
кнемⷪꙋ · оумнаноглаше · сⷪвысоки нбⷭⷭⷷ
пⷩынⷷбесмерⷮнⷿыⷯцрю · упⷪсланⷲⷮ · ксхⷪ
пⷩѣ кнамъ · нⷳⷰⷩ · снⷯшна землю · не
щрⷿланⷮъсхⷪпⷩѣ · ннⷿлⷣѣсⷷⷯъпⷪлѧжа
спн · пеленами пⷪпинаемъ · аⷲⷿгⷿⷷсам
облⷿкнⷪблⷿчⷿⷺ · трⷰⷷгⷩⷩⷪпрⷮлⷿ · лзⷷ
млⷿпⷪнⷪжⷷ · егⷤⷷйрⷪдⷿⷷбезⷨⷿⷷⷩⷿⷿⷿⷰⷷⷷ
гⷩлⷿⷲⷷзⷪⷷбⷿⷷⷷⷷⷪⷩⷿⷿⷩⷿ · кⷪⷷлⷿⷲⷷⷷⷿⷷⷪⷷⷿⷷⷷⷷ
снⷿⷷⷷⷷ · нⷪⷷⷷⷷⷷⷷⷷⷷⷷⷷⷷ · нⷿⷷⷷⷷⷷⷷⷷⷷⷷ
дⷿⷷⷷⷷ · лⷿⷷⷷⷷⷷⷿⷷⷷⷷⷷⷷⷷⷷⷷⷷⷷⷷⷷⷷ
нⷷⷷⷷ · нⷷⷷⷷⷷⷷⷷ · нⷷⷷⷷⷷⷷⷷⷷⷷⷷⷷⷷⷷⷷ
нⷷⷷⷷⷷⷷⷷⷷⷷⷷⷷⷷ · рⷷⷷⷷⷷⷷⷷⷷⷷⷷⷷⷷ
сⷪⷷⷷⷷⷷ · кⷷⷷⷷⷷⷷⷷⷷⷷⷷⷷⷷⷷⷷ
снⷷⷷ · нⷷⷷⷷⷷⷷⷷⷷⷷⷷⷷⷷⷷⷷⷷⷷⷷ
хⷷⷷⷷⷷⷷⷷⷷⷷⷷⷷⷷⷷⷷⷷⷷ · пⷷⷷ
гⷷⷷⷷⷷⷷⷷⷷⷷⷷⷷⷷⷷⷷ · пⷪслⷷⷷⷷⷷ
шⷷⷷⷷⷷⷷ · лⷷⷷⷷⷷⷷⷷⷷⷷⷷⷷⷷⷷ
лазорⷷⷷⷷⷷⷷⷷ · нⷷⷷⷷⷷⷷⷷⷷⷷⷷⷷⷷⷷ
нⷷⷷⷷⷷⷷⷷⷷ · нⷷⷷⷷⷷⷷⷷⷷⷷⷷⷷⷷⷷ
снⷷⷷⷷⷷⷷ · лазарⷷⷷⷷⷷⷷ · нⷷⷷⷷⷷ
рⷷⷷⷷⷷⷷⷷⷷⷷⷷⷷⷷⷷⷷⷷⷷⷷ

пишєдѹ насѣимаєнгисоздальнакоро
ткпончѣнкѣ посѣвшиппоємъножи
пп неєголнппрдизѣмлєнападнхъчи
лошѣкн помєжллоюєлгн агѣосогрѣ
шнхъѣцѵклєхъепонхъпрєтокою носєто
жльмн ижєпотпоємоюкразѣсопно
рєнчѣсмь нтппоймъсоздднимъадъсодл
поломъпорхѵаєнса ацєазѣгнсогрѣшн
лѣ, попоѵѣломъмонмъвпѣздалъмпсп
люокоѵєю фсєнпонизпоаныппдрогъ
апралмь сєномъєпоначьнсааком ́ нєо
пноокємъакопомъ прѣвопрѣседлппє
исподнєлючадѣ наигнпппонсогрѣшиш
жєазѣ асєппонпрркъмоусєн ижєпро
цѣлѣжидонъєкпозѣтєрмноєморєдєсни
цєнопноєю нгаапъєпповєонасинанѣєп
горѣвпкоопинѣвлнцємъвклнцоуѿпонпон
гнснамнпвадѣмоѹтнмъѿсоппоы нан
ипппонсогрѣшнлаакожѣазѣ асєгнпппон
пррккисаа нзчрєпамппрнапѣзнєсєнѣ
нанѣса нпакнєннлдєпоѵрєвомпрпнвъ да
нєтппомъпснлоютгодѵа пппонпонгнєна
мнпнъадѣ, наигппонсогрѣшнлъаколзч
асєппонпєлнкінпрркъданнлъснѣєзєкіа
пррка, порлзнпѵпптѣло златтопплпнлонѣ

ннпержень бысть колом посн(ъ)дапронъ .
апонгнчтосогр(ъ)шнн . нтоснамнноадъ .
нженоснпындрепань козелънарамъ . про
образоmашесены апполастрнн . нза
мнр(ь)оумершнн . асегнснъдадн(ь)ъсоломо
нъсоздн юкъ храмъ вочераимъ . нскопа
днаорла златаподобнахеропнмомъ . нсе
рафнмолъ . нонтоснамнн(ъ)ддудъпороу
ганюднапола . асегнпррктпонсамоу
нльнженомазакшнрогомъннацтпо . то
кнопамурвекнппенецъ . нтоснамннъ
дудмоучнтса . нсеоужегнснправеднццы
намногапременапъдудъмоучнмы(н)осогоны
нслезамнзеннцыомышахоусвон . оуже
воннамногалатпаненнднмысовтозарна
готпоегослнца . ннлгодарнаготпоего
нвтра . нотоугоноодержнмнесмаоуныцн
номьнгнчлвцытоцрапн . апыгндолгоге
рпблнпъ нако . носпенеоесозданне . тн
знеднныгннзолдасего . нспажнднапола
роуслышагь млтвоунхъ нпъздыхание . н
речетьоучнкомъснонмъ . дроугънашнъ
лазароусен . оннжерекошакнемоуаще
оумрепъ тоспсетса . нс(ъ)жереце . нонде
мъ попнфанюпъздпнгноутнлазора

ѿмерïпыхъ . ипрïидеьпнфанїю . нере
шоаегосесирькаазореиы . марїа . ıима
рфа . скоропрнишсхин . ипаддипреноса
мнïошыми . наласыпонмиотершино
зькıего . игаюши . гиашебытыздѣьаıъ
тонекыıоумрѣьрапѣнашькаазорь . нгаа
гъмарфенмарïн . ащеимаешеиврх̑ . то
иѣскрнетъьрапѣьпашькаазорь . онже
рекошлемоу . вѣмыгнıакоьѣскрнетъ
ппослѣднïндиь . нгааддıакъдıаполоу
слышıдıакопнекоркнаесипадша . ѿпои
спïнипиааазорѧ . инхдımѣѣмпюрнн̑
ипиаадма . ıакоснаамофпнемощьпрı
ипорѧеишса . нречегъ марïнимарфıъ
гдѣположисиегго . ипдосиапагрокı
ааазорепъ . нтхıрестоахоимносиоо
народажıцоаьска . иповедѣгьшпаинин
кааменьѿдıлерïнгрока . нречемарïанмарфа
гноужесмердипьчеıппероднепепькоесип .
нречегъ . ащеоѣроуешенма . тооузри
пıеслапоуьжïю . ипъзрвⱶⱶнамⱶонпросе
знса . нрече . лазорьградипопъ . ıакıе
пⱶсипааазорьоукроемькоказапъ . нречⱶ
гъразрѣшнинегго . ıегдапⱶскрⱶлаазорь
нзогда . нгаакгоу . гишⱶпïотⱶчнпрры

нисправедницыпадѣ прьвозданныи
адамъ ипатриархъ авраамъ . съсномъ
споимъ исаакомъ исопнукомъ ииаковъ
мъ . дадѣ женигиюшетчосниусоло
монѣ . извединизоада . ивзбанги
ѿмоучителадиапола . иречегькалазорю .
ацѣ бы недѣдракамоегопъзлюбленнаго .
исоломонавыхъ искоренилъ поадѣ . исни
дѣдхомьнаадама . имножестпонекъныхъ
понснимъ . иречегь адамоу . ѣаппдѣ
сницасоздала . ѣадѥетапьзиеде . иници
тепакипран • ⹂ссчпии . Слопоюпьскре
сенипришедшагоолазора . поучениесппго
июаназлаустаго . влгослопишюте . ∴

риидѣпцепразнолюбцы ипьзлюбленни
пачесоофегоавинин христолюбцы . на
сладипшеса дненеизреченныа радостии
себопьсианамьпрестьбшла радостьпре
ипсюоцпи препрапедныхъ сапцемъ . и
параюципипьскресениехпо . наслажаюцип
ипрныхъсрца . снмнчюдесапьзпода пюе
нанерховныистьпень , престагопостиа
набнчаюципе ꙩожаюципеасапподнизкадо
инѣмъ ипрочихъдоврыхъдѣлехъ сево
радостьсеть . пообразъпритпапоскресениюхпу

римсѧ идокрадиела
втѧжемь · соманцн
кетнїєвземьшедл
срацвсїшла · слака
щеблаиьградьиио
иилагиь · бгъгьиаи
паємослаєоѱемь ·
исотьиль · · · єчиш
гаосиьиаиьиве
шидала · виьадїв
каворю · · ·

Б̃ьсоєдрджинноиь
мидиь · аплашоло
жинль · оуптешимсѧ
предкьоударимтьвго
сли · кьзлоимьиь
отьисоаиажикьи
стрдиьи нинвьаиа
кладла асфдактре
исподиеадів сєбовре
макеселоиаста · ге
прїшедиьсннѧ оу
вослышшовастьрл
свираю оу вєртела
агаипроходмадо
какра дь поиоушн

прїшдн доуслышю
топомококомьтерькьи
ниведарыиесоуедько
скисовон вьмьно
моурки · диьиаземи
ромьшодсѧ · аитосьи
дрджиномноидни
кадали · томдбоє
ивортиль · аємлѧ
попожїєиогдєго ·
могомтидвцєповї
вшиивтелемы · лови
ваюциєивоѡвлаись
аємлюомьглою при
никшикиемдгаши ·
ѡрювеликьиииемы
чтотиисавьсхотив
ло · кипаииицииснити
иаземлю сїалипеци
рывьсхотельєси ·
илисилиаслвйвни
жениителеавьши ·
ієскоройдобьдмны
шатаиасашстрина
тамечь ирощета
оукинти · иглаада

сѡщимъвъадшлтрі
идетивъсрѹщиивси
праведнїи · послемъ
вестысвъдцрⷭ҇ость
слезами, паꙗнивыи
ѿпꙋⷭ҇въсихꙋщели
насⷮѡтвⷦ҇сиаⷩ҇га
вити · англа пⷣеⷬемъа
рⷪгаюⷳ҇нсⷶ адови,
инемощнонсилаѣ̈
ирⷦостакодвꙑꙗкто
може ѿселѣтамо
ѿнавѣⷭ҇тадомеⷭ҇ти
лврамеданаӓ · ивѣ
рꙑⷫ҇ жевелисⷨꙑꙗ · аꙁⷣ
мⷪкⷭꙑкаменьꙑ йⷮтве
рⷣозапечатамо · то
гадⷳꙑꙋкнⷮⷶсноречⷷ
ӓсеꙁаⷶꙋтраⷳ҇ѿапойⷣе
лазорь · д҃ · роднⷥвъ
нꙑⷩ҇дрꙋⷯⷠъ · тⷮъѡнⷶ
кнѣмⷣдомеⷭ҇тивⷦ҇сⷷ
иѥслꙑшавъ̈адамъ
перⷡⷢоⷶнныⷩ҇ичлⷦ҇ь
инабⷮⷮрⷣꙋкама
полиⷷцⷮꙋⷨⷢсⷦꙑоⷷмⷣ

тⷶкⷪⷣⷪопⷶꙗгашⷷ · по
шⷣедаⷰꙋⷭꙑⷩ҇нⷡⷶацⷠ
ꙁⷣⷪ свⷮⷮⷮⷮⷮлꙑⷩ҇ⷣⷪдⷡⷶⷶⷷ
кꙗⷷлаꙁорⷷю · лⷷти
въпꙗⷮⷮⷮⷮⷮкоиⷮⷷ
рⷮꙋⷪⷢⷶнныйадамъ
пакⷷлимⷶꙇ̈ⷭⷣⷭ гⷩ҇со
ꙁалⷮ нⷶкрⷪⷪкꙑⷩ҇ⷡⷮ
кⷮⷮⷩ҇аꙁемлиⷭⷷⷩ҇бꙑ
ти · лⷷꙇ̈мⷶⷮⷮⷮⷡⷮ
адⷷмⷶⷩ҇огаⷮⷮⷮⷮⷮабꙑ
тиⷩ҇ꙇмⷪчиⷮⷮⷮⷮтⷪⷢⷪ
лирⷶⷩ҇аполнⷮⷮⷮⷮ
ѿⷮⷮлⷦⷪаⷭⷷпнⷮⷮⷮⷡⷮⷮ
въⷮⷮлⷮⷮⷷⷮⷮⷡⷨⷮⷮⷮⷮ
въⷮⷮⷮⷮⷮⷶⷶ · въдⷩ҇ⷷ
ӓдⷪⷮⷮмⷪⷮⷮмꙑ
ѿⷮⷮⷪⷮⷮⷮ · ꙁⷶⷮⷮⷮⷷⷢⷠⷷⷮ
иⷮⷮⷮгⷪⷮⷮⷮⷣⷮⷷⷮⷮⷶ
иⷮⷷⷮⷶⷨⷮⷮⷮⷮⷩ҇ⷩ҇
иꙋⷮⷮⷮⷮⷶ ѿⷮⷮⷮⷮⷮ
иⷮⷶⷮⷮⷮⷷⷮⷶⷮⷮⷩ҇ⷷ
вⷮⷷⷮⷩ҇ⷮⷮⷮⷷⷮⷷⷷ
сⷷⷮⷪⷮⷮⷮⷮⷷⷮⷷⷮⷮⷷ
лⷮⷮⷮⷮⷶ́ⷮⷮⷶⷮⷣⷮⷷ
дⷪⷮⷮⷶ · иⷮⷮⷮⷷⷮⷶⷮⷷ

се многогла бпаоть
ѿ вида есма . азъ
в мали тадрьвыхъ
всепскаребкии анип
в многа дпи праби
бы ада абею шего
полоианиюсть . в ма
ло времаси бѣтпкои
видѣ . ассоуже слица
ткое пресв бплаго
не вижю полаиога
лѣта . ни бдравѣ
трапы а неслышю .
гиаше азъ согрѣшии
па ви сечлкъ . толо
д бломоивбѣзами
есимдк̈сию . пежа
адюслтй носегода
тпалость ми ги . азъ
поит воем дѿбразд
створеиъ есмь .
а ни ида наволиьрога
сть ми са а пои во
емдѿбразд створе
па мо∥й мазлие, па
д ма ати . азъ впоро

д ∥ жи кал пкоюбѣ
ткендю∥пове пре
стѡм лесмиг̈ип
рѣы и патриархъ
авраимъ атвондрѿ
пжетеб граиота да
блатисп аебѣ̈ кака
въ злюва е на . и иыи
рѣемд то кою бпела
мѣ блаа тса валко
лѣ на земнаа . тоиы
чтосо грѣши въ лдѣ
сем мдчите в . и тако
бъ ыше . и нои пра
ведныи же тобюб лги
и збавлеи бы шию
тало топаи бои да а
апле можешии ба
вти . то аще водѣ
сии со грѣши а ниако
пазъ . ассе велии сыи
про к пӓ иӓ ба тъи
ги что со грѣши и ль бѣ
тои тъ̈ да се дпить
спами въ тли кадо
в ѣ . адида ги про сла

в҃еси на земли · и да
ꙗко на црквами
на многими лѣ[то]
славна · ꙗ трь и гос
мо что ти г҃и сгрѣшї
а то и сп͠амидꙗвкь
а дѣсемо · читаса · часо
сто мавьшаше · аще
бꙋдѣ тако сьгрѣвшї
ꙗко кнꙗзь · а севелїкы
вы трꙋцївшꙗ пртчь
кртаꙗгь · и ꙗкеⷬ са
ѡ блищии ꙗ а͠рхаглага
брнꙗ · въ пꙋстынивⷤ
стꙗ са ѡⷣ ночти ·
ꙗ дыни мⷣиныи · н͠о
ѡ нꙗꙅꙗ поргаⷩ вы
по что ти г҃и согрѣ
ши лꙗⷵ · а дѣсь нами
въ адꙋ ꙅемь мꙋⷱⷱⷱе
по него желаютъ
пꙋ рцитꙑкои · илꙗꙗꙁе
по ꙅꙋ ꙋгошатобⷫⷪⷵ
пꙋ все праведникь
на ꙁемлꙗ · то грⷤли
ра на шьши не хощеши

помилока пина · или
ско еврѣмен и жидшї
или самь хощешикⷣ
снити · посавсиедⷧ
помꙑчꙗцнⷷ сꙗ по
цꙗ ивꙑ · лꙗ пꙑг и до
лготрьпеликⷫ · по
прїидилопꙗ вꙋскорѣ
и избавинада · и свꙗ
жидꙗвола · и датꙗ
ꙋвѣда кꙑ бꙗ лꙗшꙗнⷦⷶкь
амꙑ вси ꙗци благокⷫ
рïи · поклонимⷭⷵ е
вⷯꙋⷮ · или кнꙗ т кое
стмь слававⷴ естⷣ ю
трꙗю · ѡцꙋ исꙑ н̄есто
дх҃а · н͠нꙗ и прⷭⷭⷩ о̄
въ нⷱꙋ вⷦꙑ по ꙃнⷭꙗ ли
въ ꙁ во вⷦꙑ вѣ рⷧⷵ пꙋꙗⷣⷬа
сꙗ кꙑ волнꙗю г҃рꙗ
шь ꙃⷱнⷦхⷪⷶ · пⷪ ꙋꙗⷱе
пⷩе стро шꙗꙃꙗ рⷧⷵстⷪ
Іꙗко по чꙋ на морⷶ
по стⷩ оⷷ врѣ мꙗ їⷷ
и доꙗꙁⷢⷵ · и бо ли на сⷣю
неꙗ ю поⷦ вⷩ г҃ⷫ коⷭⷶ пꙗⷬ

ва · нопрⷢ҇игаю ши ·съ цр꙯ѣ ви плачⷮ
мⸯ са грѣховⸯсвои · чаю ши ѿбⷢ҇а
прощенїа · иполучимⸯ жизнⸯю вѣ
чную · ѿхⷭ҇ і ꙋⷭ҇ нашемь · емⸯже
слава и вⸯвⷭ҇ кⸯы вⷯ ко мⸯ ⁖
+

СЛОВⷩ҇ ѿⷭ҇тⷢ҇ⷶ прⷪ҇рⷱ҇ гⷩ҇ ва вн ѿ е

Слыⷲ҇ни нбⷪ҇ и внⷤⷲ҇ уши зе мⷧ҇е · ꙗко
гⷩ҇ъ та съⷩ҇порⷪ҇дⷯихⷪ҇ ихⸯ и въ зⷩ҇есохⷯ
а · и тⷯ и ймене ѿвⷬ҇ргⷪ҇ша шасⷶ
лю еⷨ҇ой и непозна ша ме не дⷡ҇волⸯ
непознастеⷤⷤⷤⷤⷤⷤⷤⷤⷤⷤ жⷡ҇вⷲ҇шⷶгой · и ꙋⷭ҇е
кⸯыⷥ҇ сⷩ҇и гⷩ҇а свое го аⷭ҇ⷶ ⷶзⸯ ино
лю славⷯымо еⷶ҇ не да мⸯ но пⷹ꙼ⸯ шⷶ
сло по мо еⷶ҇ на зе млю ⷁаⷭ҇пⷮⷢ҇ люⷣи
иⷡⷲ҇льстⷮ сотонины еⷨ҇ⷹⷤ же глаⷲ҇е
а въⷣⷥ҇ сⷣⷶⷣ въ преи сподⷩ҇емⷩ҇ⷶ
дⷡ҇ · накла да тⸯ много ꙋ꙼꙯читаⷯ꙼
пер ты на жиⷡ꙼ыⷯи стрⷹⷫ҇пⷯы а въ
споⷣемⸯ пⷮⷣⷥ҇тихⷮⷶ и весельⷶⷯ꙼ · дрⷹⷹ
ми нⷧ҇мⷪ҇о дⷩ҇ь поло жимⸯ · пⷣⷶⷧ҇

въ скорбѣ оумьшимъ сѧ гѣмь ·
бгамъ нашимъ · оужебопаста
врема блго приатна · оужебо
слышимъ ропотъ волхвовъ пе
раскыхъ конь · не суть емоу дары ·
нѣномоу црю на земли родишоусѧ·
егоже ти пречтаи двца · повѣ
вающиплънами · прислана ющи
сѧ кнемоу · любовыю гаше · ѡ высо
кыи црю · начто ти сѧ восхотѣ
кнамъ нищимъ на землю съни
ти · пещеры восхотѣ · иливыи
слехъ скотийхъ восхотѣ полежа
ти · пеленами повива ємъ аты гй
слтѣнбй ѡблакы ѡдѣваи · тобѣ
богй суть нбса прстлъ а землапо
ножнѣ · егоже иродъ взоумныи сущи
жеты шѧ зубы своими · ви хотѣль
оубити · нопрейдитe прррци прѣ
йдѣти правѣници · исайꙗ єрѣ мъ
та ругающесѧ адꙋ ѡвѣща сила щи

ѡнемощныи дьӕволе · двд҃ гл҃и
на наны йже сеть вѣсть наживыи
свѣтъ ковлѧцѣ · се во двд҃ъ в замѣцѣ
камене авраꙗмъ дана авереꙗже
ꙋзна · ѡтвердо двд҃ъ заключенъ ·
двд҃ъ гл҃и стоѥма наны й же сеть
вѣсть · наживыи свѣтъ ꙑ ковлѧцѣ ·
тогда ре҃ двд҃ъ ꙗснымъ гласомъ ·
ꙇсаꙗ ꙇ ꙗремѣꙗ · ливанꙋмъ ароⷩ
ꙇезекиль · соломонъ · адамъ · авра
аме · ꙇсаче й ꙗковь · сомоиле · даниль ·
нвса з҃і пр҃ркъ послꙋшаите моѥго
гласа во адꙋ семъ · еже хоⷰ̃ ꙇзити
ѿ на на ꙗнь выи свѣтъ ꙑ ковлѧце · ла
зарь другъ гн҃ь да тотъ й же сеть вѣ
сть наживыи свѣтъ ꙑ ковлѧцѣ · то
гда оуслыша въ перво здⷶнныи й чл҃вⷦ̃
адамъ й вос · биса влице своѥ
рꙋками · гл҃а лазорю другꙋ гн҃ьню же
си нама вѣсть наживыи свѣтъ
ꙑ ковлѧцѣ на селима ѥ сꙇг҃и народⷣꙑ

коротко на свѣтѣ семъ жити
а многа лѣта въ адѣ мучинъ бы
ти . да сего дѣлаги чл҃кы на землю
на плодъ да ма в бо҃и жальнѣ
жаль а҃зъ бо҃и согрѣшши в двѣ лѣхъ
свои . но того ми г҃и жаль . о ш ми
твоего тварыю . адъ по смихаетъ
са и поругаетьса . аще г҃и азъ ада
мъ согрѣшши . а се твойизволници
а мои винуци . авраамъ с сномъ съ
исаакамъ . и со внукомъ іаковомъ
мъ . въ вратехъ сѣда въ преис
по днемъ адѣ . да сниди г҃и авра
ама дѣла . или ти г҃и авраамъ
согрѣшши . а се твои пррⷦъ мойсии
проведыйже злом черм ноемо
ре . и главыйстобою наси наистъ
и горѣ вскупинъ лицемъ к лицю
а то ти г҃и сна ми в адѣ . или
ти г҃и мойсѣй согрѣши . а исаиѩ
тебѣ г҃и что согрѣшши исчрева.

г҃

мтрна въ ꙅнесъ на нбⷭа · и тыисни
ди снимъ въ цр҃тво дв҃ч · а тотꙑ
г҃и снами воадъ · илитигийсана
что согрѣши · аситво й прⷬкы ве
ликыйданилъ · сн҃ъ е҃ст и ꙗꙗ цр҃а
й прⷬкⷹ породит вⷧ а златоё ꙗва
вилонъ · й ввержнъ к ольвомъ
в ровъ · а тотꙑ г҃и снами въ дⷣъ ·
или ти данилъ что согрѣши · аꙗр
м ꙗ г҃и что согрѣши · носꙗвый
древаныйкоꙁелъ на рамѣ · проⷪ
ѡ бразова спⷵныⷨ твоей стрⷵти ·
или ти г҃и тіи прⷪци что согрѣши
ша асесь дв҃дъ соломонъ · съ
дⷣавыйтистаа ст҃ыхъ въ і ер҃сали
мѣ · й сковⷣ вы дв҃ⷹ ѿ рⷧа ꙁлата ·
подобна херꙋвимꙑй серⷹмꙋ · й
гⷧаше ашⷹ буⷣетъ въ на ꙁемли то
снидетъ дх҃ъ ст҃ый во ѡⷬлⷶси · ѿ
рⷧаже в той чⷶ носивъ шⷹ ꙗ по
цр҃кви · въ ꙅне соста ꙗ на нбⷵⷶ ·

ноꙋжькогй невидимꙑ҃ твоєго ·
свѣта зарнаго слнца ниблг҃тна
го твоєго вѣтра · но тꙋгоѭжє є꙼
нꙗ҃на шего оꙋнꙑлиємꙑ · слꙑша
вьꙁⷨ гⷮ плⷱа҃ь ихъ въ адѣ · йприидѣ
к сестрѣ лазоревѣ мⷬб҃ є йма
рѣ꙼ ввиданию · йсмꙑшавшиꙗжє
мⷬꙑ҃ймарⷣа · сикоро тⷬ҃коста
инⷪдоста ноꙅи гⷩ҃ · глⷱꙋ а҃щебꙑ
тꙑбꙑлъ · небꙑоꙋмерлъбратъ
наюлазорь · йг҃лаⷮ кмⷬб҃ єйма
рѣ꙼ въ сⷦрснеть братъ ваю
лазорь · йг҃ла а҃дъ кодъꙗ҃волꙋ ·
силꙑ моꙗприскорбⷩꙗⷨꙗ҃миєⷮ꙼ꙑ
дꙈа ѿпꙋстити лазора · нꙋдⷨꙑ꙼
боємь ѿрꙑгнꙋти адама · тогаⷡв꙼
сⷦрⷤꙑ лазорь йꙁъ адоꙋ · йрⷧг҃й вопи
юⷮ йⷮпⷬ҃рцⷤ въбⷪадꙋ первоꙁⷣа пⷩꙑ
йчⷧкъ а҃дамъ потриархъ а҃врамь
со сном҃ъ йсакам҃ъ · йсовноꙋ҃ком꙼
йꙗ҃ковол꙼ъ дв҃дъ жⷤ вопіⷮ꙼ о

265

Ѿ снꙋ своемъ соломонѣ възведи
ги из адꙋ . и глаголꙗ к лазорю аще бы
не давда дѣла рабамоего возлюбле
наго . а соломона бых въ адꙋи
скоренилъ . предавыса гь воли
то на раⷰстьѣ . и снидѣхомъ надда
и вси полцинвныхъ . семiелъ расꙋ
илъ . и змаилъ манонилъ . та
ртаилъ михаилъ и гаврилъ . и вси
англи идоуть со крⷭтомъ . въ
мѣте врата вѣчныꙗ . да вни
дѣть црь славы . и глаⷣ адъ къди
ꙗволъ . хощеть оуна быти . црь
славы . и глаша англи съ пррⷪкꙑ
гь силенъ и страшенъ въ брани
хъ то боеть црь славы . тогда
рⷱ велик сынⷭ црь двдъ колибѣхъ
въ животе въ дахъ . ѿ же сокрꙋ
шит са врата мѣданаꙗ . и
вереꙗ желѣзны сотреⷮ са . то
га сокрꙋшиⷮ гь врата мѣднаа .

ѿ иꙁверга желѣꙁныꙗ соꙋре · ꙵꙗ
гла адамоу сита соꙁдалъ кꙋвъ
иꙗ · а сита рꙋкою иꙁводитъ исꙗ
а · того въ срⷭ҇ъ іс҃ · гла а҃плом
ѿши проповѣди те повсеи ꙁе
мли · крⷭ҇та ще воима ѿ ца и сн҃а
и ст҃го дх҃а · оучаще ꙗ соблюсти ·
а самъ въꙁнесесꙗ на нб҃а · исѣ де
ѿдеснꙋю ѿ ца · повсеи ꙁемли сꙗ
ва его · ꙗ ко тому по дбае всакосꙗ ⁖

СЛОВⷱ СА ДꙖⷮꙊⷭ ⷹ ⷿⷮ Ꙁ ѿ АПⷭ Ꙗ̈ КСꙖ Н Н ГꙊ

Помы слишꙿте братье · какꙋ ѿ чи
страⷨꙿ йⷨ аемъ йⷨ вти днⷪ сꙋ
днаго · станемъ оубо оумили
нны дѣлы своими ꙁлыми · иже
ꙗ сотворихомъ въ жи вотⷮ семъ
играюще пьюще весела ще сꙗ и поꙋ
сто ши дѣю щи · егоже не по до
баеть крⷭ҇тіаномъ твори ти ·
не рчемъ ни блаꙁнимъ сꙗ реⷦꙋ ще